DATE DUE

FEB 16 1995	
APR 1 1 1995	
NOV 3 0 1995	
FEB - 2 1998	
FEB 1 2 1998	
FEB 2 6 1998	
APR 13	
NOV 1 7 1998	

BRODART. | Cat. No. 23-221

INTERDISCIPLINARY CONTRIBUTIONS
TO ARCHAEOLOGY

Current Volumes in This Series:

THE AMERICAN SOUTHWEST AND MESOAMERICA
Systems of Prehistoric Exchange
Edited by Jonathon E. Erickson and Timothy G. Baugh

THE ARCHAEOLOGY OF GENDER
Separating the Spheres in Urban America
Diana diZerega Wall

EARLY HUNTER–GATHERERS OF THE CALIFORNIA COAST
Jon M. Erlandson

ETHNOHISTORY AND ARCHAEOLOGY
Approaches to Postcontact Change in the Americas
Edited by J. Daniel Rogers and Samuel M. Wilson

FROM KOSTENKI TO CLOVIS
Upper Paleolithic–Paleo-Indian Adaptations
Edited by Olga Soffer and N. D. Praslov

HOUSES AND HOUSEHOLDS
A Comparative Study
Richard E. Blanton

HUNTER–GATHERERS
Archaeological and Evolutionary Theory
Robert L. Bettinger

ORIGINS OF ANATOMICALLY MODERN HUMANS
Edited by Matthew H. Nitecki and Doris V. Nitecki

POTTERY FUNCTION
A Use-Alteration Perspective
James M. Skibo

RESOURCES, POWER, AND INTERREGIONAL INTERACTION
Edited by Edward M. Schortman and Patricia A. Urban

SPACE, TIME, AND ARCHAEOLOGICAL LANDSCAPES
Edited by Jacqueline Rossignol and LuAnn Wandsnider

The Archaeology of Gender

Separating the Spheres in
Urban America

The Archaeology
of Gender

Separating the Spheres in
Urban America

DIANA DIZEREGA WALL

*The City College of
the City University of New York
New York, New York*

PLENUM PRESS • NEW YORK AND LONDON

Library of Congress Cataloging-in-Publication Data

Wall, Diana diZerega.
    The archaeology of gender : separating the spheres in urban
America / Diana diZerega Wall.
        p.   cm. -- (Interdisciplinary contributions to archaeology)
    Includes bibliographical references and index.
    ISBN 0-306-44551-4
    1. Archaeology and history--New York (N.Y.) 2. Sex role--New York
(N.Y.)--History. 3. Women--New York (N.Y.)--History. 4. New York
(N.Y.)--Antiquities.   I. Title.   II. Series.
F128.39.W35   1994
305.3'09747'1--dc20   93-44321
                                                                      CIP

ISBN: 0-306-44551-4

© 1994 Plenum Press, New York
A Division of Plenum Publishing Corporation
233 Spring Street, New York, N.Y. 10013

Printed in the United States of America

For Brian and Bert
and my mother,
in memoriam

Foreword

Historical archaeologists often become so involved in their potsherd patterns they seldom have time or energy left to address the broader processes responsible for the material culture patterns they recognize. Some of us have urged our colleagues to use the historical record as a springboard from which to launch hypotheses with which to better understand the behavioral and cultural processes responsible for the archaeological record. Too often, this urging has resulted in reports designed like a sandwich, having a slice of "historical background," followed by a totally different "archaeological record," and closed with a weevil-ridden slice of "interpretation" of questionable nutritive value for understanding the past. The reader is often left to wonder what the archaeological meat had to do with either slice of bread, since the connection between the documented history and the material culture is left to the reader's imagination, and the connection between the interpretation and the other disparate parts is tenuous at best.

The plethora of stale archaeological sandwiches in the literature has resulted at the methodological level from a too-narrow focus on the specific history and archaeology of a site and the individuals involved on it, rather than a focus on the explanation of broader processes of culture to which the actors and events at the site-specific level responded. Addressing the broader evolutionary process is a far more difficult task than simply throwing together a sandwich without what archaeologists call "middle range theory" to connect the historical, the archaeological, and the interpretive data into an edifying and nourishing explanatory whole.

At the theoretical level, we sometimes see archaeological reports, written by those well versed in anthropological theory, presented in such an ethereal realm that, when the reader finally gets to the presentation of the material culture revealed by the excavation, reader shock hits suddenly, pushing one into a morass of endless descriptive minutiae, forcing the reader to break free of the quagmire by skipping that section and moving on to the interpretation, which usually bites heavily again into the earlier slice of theoretical bread. In such reports, one wonders why the archaeological data were even put into the sandwich in the first place, as they have contributed so little to the theoretical picnic repast.

Archaeological reports are notorious for being poorly written by those of us who are so captured by the specific challenge of describing what we have discovered that we write primarily for each other. As a writer, I sometimes find myself addressing one particular individual whom I know will share with me the joy of the particular discovery I am describing, and I am not very concerned about whether others will "enjoy" the process of reading about it or not. Those readers who are captured by the subject or the site involved, or by the time period, or for whom a report was commissioned, can perhaps enjoy it. All others beware. There are deadly boring stretches of desert road ahead, with no good-writing service stations for interminable miles of words strung along, like hypnotic center-line stripes endlessly flashing by as protesting eyes close in sleep.

It is with this background of expectation that I approached the reading of this book by Diana Wall. My surprise was great, therefore, when I found myself turning pages to see what I could learn about the archaeology of gender as her story unfolded through the use of some of the best professional writing I have enjoyed. She explains what she is going to do and the method she will use to accomplish her goal. She proceeds to take the city of New York as her "site," and using the legacy of documents about that complex subject, both historical and archaeological, she "explores whether middle-class and elite New York women, acting within the framework of contemporary American culture, contributed through their actions to the structural transformation that resulted in the division of this culture into man's and woman's spheres."

She examines the relationship between the actors and the cultural system, using a variety of data, and then she studies how the system influenced the actors. In exploring this interaction, she has a clarity of style that is enjoyable to read as her flow carries the reader along toward learning something important and basic about how New York City grew and evolved from the 18th, through the 19th, and into the 20th century and also about the process of urbanization applicable to cities elsewhere.

The reader is made aware of the post–Revolutionary War economic opportunities and the growth of corporate infrastructure and the specialization of trade toward a more impersonal market strategy, resulting in a separation of home and workplace. We are made aware of the changing social landscape in the city through the segregation by class resulting from the separation of commercial versus residential neighborhoods and how architectural styles followed. We learn how the elite came to move to the suburbs, by leapfrogging over the ring of residences of the poor, further separating the source of economic power in the inner-city workplace from the elite residential neighborhoods. This process separated the elite women and their families from the men, and the result was the division of the culture into man's and woman's spheres. The separation of home and workplace is seen as a hinge of this process, mirroring economic and social change.

Wall contrasts the continued development of strong family ties among the poor with the weakening of family ties among the elite. The resulting insecurity among the elite was countered, paradoxically, by the need to enforce the idea that blood is thicker than water, as family members saw less and less of each other when the woman's and man's spheres congealed as an expected way of life. This development is demonstrated by those areas of America where "old family" and "old money" are emphasized as values by the elite in order to keep control and exclusivity in the power center.

By carefully leading the reader by the hand through her flowing prose, Wall provides us with an understanding of the ritualization of family meals and, in turn, the influence this process had on the choice of ceramics, tableware, and other furnishings. Thus, we come naturally to the presentation of archaeological data relevant to this unfolding of the cultural processes responsible for the differences we see in the archaeological record. In other words, she manages to integrate enjoyably the elements of history and archaeology to allow an understanding of the process—a major goal of historical archaeology. She provides us with those ingredients I spelled out in my introductory paragraphs that are so often missing from archaeological reports. She has provided us with the theory and the middle-range theory–method–data link necessary for the understanding of urbanization. Along the way, she provides us with a better appreciation of the pivotal role women have played in this process.

STANLEY SOUTH
University of South Carolina
S.C. Institute of Archaeology and Anthropology
Columbia, South Carolina

Preface

Dissertations, like first novels, are often autobiographical: they are frequently the fruit of research that is related directly to a personal quest. This book, which is adapted from a dissertation and explores the development of some of the traditional values that structure the lives of middle-class women today, is no exception.

I grew up in a world of women. I was raised by my mother and, with my sister, attended girls' schools. It was only when I was almost grown that I appreciated the degree to which middle-class American culture is made up of two very different, often separate but complementary worlds: the worlds of men and women. I was fascinated by seeing them at work.

After I began to study anthropology, archaeology, and history, I learned that the peculiar set of gender relations that middle-class America looks on as traditional today are really quite modern: they developed only within the last 200 years. I also learned, however, that there was relatively little understanding of how these fundamental differences in the experience of middle-class men and women arose. A basic problem was that the women of the past tended to be mute: We know remarkably little about their day-to-day experience because very few of them kept diaries or wrote letters that have survived.

I thought that a way to encourage these women to "speak" might be through the use of a combination of traditional historical sources (those that have proved so fruitful to social historians: the data from federal census returns, tax records, and city directories) and a nontraditional new database derived from archaeological artifacts. These artifacts were the fruit of a new field of study: historical archaeology. I had been fortunate enough to have directed several of the large-scale archaeological projects that had taken place in New York City in the late 1970s and early 1980s. I knew that we had accumulated domestic materials from a number of late-18th-century and early-19th-century middle-class homes. I hoped that if we combined the information derived from historical and archaeological sources, we would be able to see some of the things these middle-class women were actually doing in their homes as the new vision of gender relations and domestic life developed. We could get a sense of the people who were living in their homes, discover the number of children they were raising, and even look at some of the goods they were purchasing to construct their changing vision of domestic life.

I wrote up this study as a dissertation for the Department of Anthropology at New York University. I owe an enormous debt to the members of my dissertation committee for their help and support despite the complete unfamiliarity of some of them with historical archaeology. Most of all, I thank the late Bert Salwen, without whom there would be no archaeology of New York City; he had the vision to see the modern city as an enormous archaeological site and to fight for its excavation. I also thank Thomas Bender of the New York University History Department for his perceptive critiques and encouragement throughout a project that, in many ways, was a new approach to the past he knew so well; Nan Rothschild of Barnard College, with whom I have been fortunate enough to work both in the field and at the computer throughout most of my professional career; Randall White, who graciously turned briefly away from his study of the Upper Paleolithic to offer insightful comments and encouragement about the study of the past of his adopted city; and to Howard D. Winters, whose teaching first inspired me to study archaeology many years ago.

I am also very grateful for the support I received in writing and revising this work. I thank New York University for awarding me a June Freier Esserman Dissertation Fellowship in Social Anthropology and a Claire G. Goodman Fellowship in Archaeology for dissertation research, as well as the National Endowment for the Humanities for a summer stipend to revise the dissertation for publication.

Gathering the historical data was a monumental task, one that I could not have completed without the graciousness of the archivists, librarians, and historians in charge of the collections in many of the city's repositories. I thank the staffs of the New York Public Library, The New-York Historical Society, the New York Municipal Archives (particularly Kenneth Cobb), and the Historical Documents Collection formerly housed at Queens College (particularly Leo Hershkowitz) for facilitating access to their document collections. I also thank Susan LaRosa, Michael Joseph, and Jane Pomeroy for their kind advice on picture research.

Many archaeologists and curators were extremely gracious in providing access to their archaeological collections; some of the archaeologists were so generous as to allow me to study their collections before their own site reports were finished. I thank Jean Howson and the late Bert Salwen of the Department of Anthropology, New York University, for access to the Sullivan Street collection; Terry Klein, then of Louis Berger and Associates, for access to the 75 Wall Street or Barclays Bank collection; Robert Bull of the Institute for Archaeological Research at Drew University for access to the Telco collection; Joel Grossman and Melba Myers, then of Greenhouse Associates, for access to the Broad Financial Center collection; Kate Gordon, then of the South Street Seaport Museum, for access to the 175 Water Street collection; and Nan Rothschild of the Department of Anthropology, Barnard College, Columbia University, for access to the 7 Hanover Square collection.

I also thank Jean Howson and Gabrielle Wall for their patient and perceptive assistance in compiling the historical data, Leonard Bianchi and Jerome Van Wert for their help in drafting some of the figures, and Arnold Pickman and the late Brian Douglas for their kind help in computerizing some of the data.

I thank my friends and colleagues who critically read parts of earlier versions of the study and brought relevant materials to my attention: Barbara Balliet, Nancy Dickinson, Roselle Henn, Jean Howson, Marjorie Ingle, Meta Janowitz, Jed Levin, Wendy Harris Palitz, and Arnold Pickman. Most particularly, I thank my friends Anne-Marie Cantwell and Nan Rothschild for their thoughtful critique of an early version of the manuscript and their encouragement to bring the project to conclusion. I also thank Sally Yerkovich, then of the South Street Seaport Museum, for showing me the ways to make the historical past more accessible to the public.

My association with Plenum Press has been a consistent pleasure. I particularly thank editors Eliot Werner, Herman Makler, and Margaret Ritchie for their help and support throughout the production of this book, and Stanley South for the kind generosity he expressed in his Foreword.

I cannot ignore my debt to my informants just because they lived so long ago. I particularly appreciate Margaret Hall, whose wonderful letters to her sister contained many penetrating (and amusing) insights into life in America from an Englishwoman's perspective, and Elizabeth Bleecker, who recorded the events of her life in her diary with a detail that, though often frustratingly vague to us today, was unusually rich for her time. I also thank the members of the Van Voorhis, Bowne, and Robson families and their anonymous contemporaries for leaving us the material evidence of their domestic life in the archaeological record; they have allowed us to explore aspects of the past in unprecedented ways.

Finally, but most important, I thank my own family, who instilled in me the curiosity to find out more about the family life of others of long ago.

DIANA DIZEREGA WALL

Contents

The Archaeology
of Gender

Separating the Spheres in
Urban America

Chapter 1

Introduction

But wives in those days were true *yoke-fellows*: they drew equal. Now, scores of them are worse than good for nothing.

GRANT THORBURN, nurseryman,
New York, 1845

When Grant Thorburn made this caustic comment in 1845, he was referring to some of the changes he had observed in the role of urban middle-class women in the half century that followed the American Revolution. During this period, American urban culture underwent a structural transformation that intimately affected the lives of its men, women, and children. This study examines some of the changes in women's roles that were associated with this transformation in middle-class families in New York City. These changes led to the development of what we today think of as the "traditional" middle-class American family, with women confining their activities to domestic life in the home (or "woman's sphere," as it was called in the 19th century) and men participating in the economic and political arenas of the larger society.

The goal of this study is to explore how the restructuring of gender occurred among the city's middle class and to examine the role that these urban women might have played in creating domesticity and in redefining their sphere. It looks on the spatial separation of the private home and the commercial workplace as a watershed and explores other, closely related phenomena as well: the development of separate residential and business areas in the city (the spatial expression of woman's sphere and man's sphere), changes in household composition, and changes in the quality of some of the goods that were used inside these homes.

We begin in this chapter with a brief overview of the history of the economic, demographic, and physical growth of New York during this period. Then, in the next section, we look at the structural transformation of family life that occurred at the same time. In the third section, we explore some of the

1

theories that have been used to explain the development of woman's sphere. Finally, I discuss the perspective used and the specific questions considered in this study.

OVERVIEW

Between the 18th and the mid-19th centuries, the transformation to the market economy was virtually completed in New York and the other American cities on the eastern seaboard. During the colonial period, New York City was never the primary port city of America; the largest port was first Boston and later Philadelphia. It was only in the 1790s, with the increase of trade during the European wars, that New York became the primary port in the nation, a position it has held basically ever since. The scale of both domestic and foreign trade increased dramatically between the 1790s and the mid-19th century, and particularly in the periods following the War of 1812 and the opening of the Erie Canal in 1825. The value of foreign and domestic exports alone rose from $2.5 million in 1792 to $52 million in 1850, and that of imports rose from $23 million in 1821 (the first year for which figures are available) to $111 million in 1850 (Albion, 1939:8, 12, 47, 390, 391).

New York had also become the foremost manufacturing center of America by the mid-19th century. The city had achieved this position without the widespread adoption of the factory system. The most important sectors of the manufacturing economy were the consumer finishing trades (which produced finished clothing, shoes, and furniture) and the building trades. Unfortunately, figures on the value of the goods produced in the city in the early 19th century are rare. In 1840, however, they were worth $23.4 million, an increase of 242% over the value of the goods produced only five years earlier (Wilentz, 1983:41; 1984:107, 112; D. Miller, 1967:113).

Before the Revolution, New York had been a relatively unpopular colonial destination for European immigrants. Throughout the 18th century, its population had grown relatively slowly, and its economy had depended in part on the labor of enslaved Africans. After the Revolution, the city's economic growth attracted an ever-increasing number of European migrants and immigrants. The population grew from 33,131 in 1790 to 312,710 in 1840, an almost tenfold increase. Before the 1830s, these newcomers were for the most part English-speaking Protestants. They included both migrants from the hinterlands and New England and immigrants from Great Britain. The later newcomers of the 1830s and 1840s, on the other hand, were mostly Irish Catholic and German immigrants.[1]

This growth in population was accompanied by a dramatic increase in the physical size of the city, which grew northward from the southern tip of

Manhattan Island. In the 1780s, the city extended north only to Chambers Street on the west side and to Hester Street on the east side (see Plate 1). The city's focus was on the East River port. The area west of Broadway (much of which was owned by Trinity Church) was relatively undeveloped, and much of the area north of Chambers Street to the east and west of Broadway consisted of unfilled marshes, ponds, and swamps. Only in the 1810s was this central area finally claimed by landfilling.

By 1840, the city had grown almost two miles farther to the north, to around 20th Street on the west side and 14th Street on the east side (see Plate 2). The city also grew farther to the east and west by claiming land from the East and Hudson Rivers. The easternmost block of landfill on the East River (between Front and South Streets) was added piecemeal during the three decades that followed the Revolution, and two blocks of landfill (from Greenwich to Washington to West Streets) were in place on the Hudson River by 1840. The phenomenal physical growth of the city had not been anticipated by the city's political elite: When the new (and current) City Hall was built in 1811 in what is now City Hall Park, just south of Chambers Street, its southern face and sides were made of marble, and its back was made of plain stone. At the time it was built, its location was so far uptown that it was felt that the back of the building "would be out of sight of all the world."[2]

These developments did not occur as a linear progression, however. They were marked by a counterpoint of depressions, panics, and yellow fever and cholera epidemics. Furthermore, and most important, the lives of most New Yorkers were completely transformed during this period.

THE TRANSFORMATION

Many classical social theorists have used dichotomous frameworks to explore changes in the forms of social integration involved in the transformation to modern society: Maine's status and contract (1906), Durkheim's mechanical and organic solidarity (1893/1933), and Tönnies's *Gemeinschaft* (or community) and *Gesellschaft* (or society) (1887/1957). These concepts continue to be useful today in studying certain kinds of social change. Thomas Bender (1978), for example, recently built on some of Tönnies's ideas.

According to Tönnies (1887/1957:33, 232, 249), *Gemeinschaft* is defined as the "intimate, private, and exclusive living together" characterized by the affective ties of friendship and kinship and exhibited in the arenas of the home, neighborhood, village, and town. Tönnies defined *Gesellschaft*, or public life, on the other hand, as "the artificial construction of an aggregate of human beings," characterized by the individualism and impersonality of the urban marketplace. Tönnies indicated, however, that *Gesellschaft* did not simply replace *Gemeinschaft*. Rather, "the force of Gemeinschaft persists, although with diminishing strength, even into the period of Gesellschaft and remains the reality of social life. . . . [T]he essence of both Gemeinschaft and Gesellschaft is found interwoven in all kinds of associations."

Following Tönnies, Bender (1978) pointed out that this dichotomy may be useful both to characterize "a whole society in a particular historical period, and to describe two patterns of human relationships [co-existing] within that society" (p. 34). Furthermore, he suggested that "[t]hese two kinds of interaction constitute . . . the social alternatives available in modern society" (p. 33).

For Bender (1978:77), colonial American towns and cities may be seen as being integrated primarily by *gemeinschaftlich*, or traditional kinds of associations, whereas the ties of the late-19th-century and modern cities might be seen as characterized by *gesellschaftlich*, or modern, associations. However, it should be remembered that modern forms of solidarity also existed in the colonial town, mainly among the elite, and that traditional associations continued to be important forms of social integration even after the "bifurcation" (to use Bender's term) of society in the 19th century and are still important today.

In this study, we use the spatial separation of the private home and the commercial workplace as the geographical expression of this bifurcation of modern society into the separate spheres of the "home" and the "world." The public arena of the market economy became characterized by modern forms of association (though not exclusively), and the home continued to be characterized predominantly (though, again, by no means exclusively) by traditional forms of association. The restructuring of the social landscape of the city expressed this bifurcation and resulted in the creation of commercial and industrial areas, where more modern forms of social relations predominated, and residential areas, segregated by class, where more traditional kinds of interaction prevailed.

Changes in the definition of the division of labor among men, women, and children were of primary importance in this transformation. The restructuring of society was accompanied both by the redefinition of the roles played by different family members and by changes in the family's economic strategies. For those who made up what was becoming the urban middle class, the artisans and shopkeepers of the period, this change involved a shift from the strategies of the family economy, where the family was a unit of production, to those of the family consumer economy, where the family became a unit of consumption.[3]

The colonial household, with its traditional forms of social integration, has been described as a "little commonwealth"—a microcosm of society (Demos, 1970; Ryan, 1981). Homes and workplaces were located in the same buildings, and there was relatively little differentiation by class in the locations of these structures within the city. Husbands and fathers were the titular heads of the household and mediated between it and the larger society. They were responsible for producing goods in the household to be sold at market and for buying goods at market to be used at home. Their employees, who were apprentices, journeymen, and clerks, often lived with them and formed part of the household. Male household heads were responsible for the moral and religious life of the members of their households, as well as all other aspects of their welfare. Prescriptive writings on raising children were addressed to fathers as well as to mothers during this time.

By the mid-19th century, the roles of husbands and fathers had changed. They were still the titular heads of the household, but their main responsibility was for the household's economic welfare. Their primary role was to represent the household's interests in the geographically separate, public arena of the market economy, where modern forms of interaction prevailed. Employees no longer lived with their masters, but in separate residential neighborhoods that were becoming segregated by class. Masters were usually not directly involved in production but had become managers supervising the work of their employees instead.

The ideology of the marketplace had changed. The principles of market exchange had replaced those of redistribution and reciprocity. Land, labor, and goods, which had traditionally been aspects primarily of social relations, had also become commodities to be bought and sold on the open market. Work, which had previously been regarded as a social and moral issue, was now isolated as simply an economic one, cut off from moral considerations. It was only after the American Revolution that the social value of an individual's work was no longer looked on as a measure of its legitimacy, and attitudes toward economic issues became more morally neutral (Crowley, 1974; Polanyi, 1944). The competitive capitalist arena of the market economy, and even the manufacturing and commercial districts of the city itself, had, for the middle class, effectively become man's sphere.

During the colonial period, wives and mothers had served as their husbands' "helpmates" or (as Grant Thorburn called them in the quotation at the beginning of this chapter) "yoke-fellows" in the home and were actively involved in the economic life of the household. Their primary responsibilities included producing items for household use (like food, candles, clothes, and even yarn and cloth) and sometimes for market, bearing children and caring for infants, and running the day-to-day operations of the household by performing those tasks that we look on today as housework. In her husband's absence, a wife was often able to take his place in running the family business or trade. The importance of a wife's contribution to the family's marketplace activities was openly accepted. Grant Thorburn (1834) decided to marry his sweetheart in the 1790s because the brother with whom he had run a store moved away to Philadelphia. As he put it, "So I resolved to push my courtship, calculating that if I got married, I would have a shopkeeper" (p. 47).

By the mid-19th century, the roles and responsibilities of middle-class mothers had changed. Most commercial and productive activities were no longer performed at home. Instead, women's activities were almost completely devoted to two separate aspects of social reproduction. One set encompassed domestic tasks and included keeping house, bearing and nurturing children, and ensuring the moral and emotional well-being of all family members. These wives no longer did the housework themselves, however. Instead, like their husbands', their role had become managerial: they supervised the domestic servants who actually did the work and who boarded in their homes.

Middle-class wives also negotiated their families' position in the class structure by building and maintaining social ties and promoting the image of the family's gentility, an image that was important in gaining entry for their children (particularly their daughters) into the ranks of the middle class. Wives participated in economic life primarily as consumers and shopped for the material goods they needed to shape both the social and the domestic aspects of their environment (Blumin, 1989:183–185).

The home had in many ways become a private haven or sanctuary for family members from the social interactions of the public arena of the market economy. Its ideology was different from, but complementary to, that of the public arena and stressed the importance of the traditional ties of kinship and friendship, as well as the values of loyalty and moral integrity, with an added emphasis on love and affection. By the 1830s, prescriptive writings on raising children, managing a household, and the moral responsibilities of women had become very popular. These were directed exclusively to women and enhanced the social value of their domestic role while stressing the importance of their self-sacrifice in its execution. Households and the newly forming residential neighborhoods where they were located had become the site of woman's sphere.

During the colonial period, childhood had been defined differently as well. Only infancy was looked on as a completely separate phase of life requiring special care. Older boys and girls were looked on as "little hands" and helped their fathers and mothers to the extent that they were able. Because the household was a microcosm of the larger society, children learned their adult roles at home. If boys were to learn a trade that was not practiced in their own home, they were apprenticed out to another household where they could learn the skills that they would need. Girls, too, might join other households where they could learn about woman's work, particularly if they came from households where there were many daughters and the contribution of their labor was not needed at home.

By the mid-19th century, the definition of childhood had changed. It was now looked on as encompassing a series of distinct phases of life. Throughout each phase, children were seen as requiring the physical and emotional nurturing that could best be supplied by their mothers at home. Home life was no longer viewed as a microcosm of society, however, and children could learn only the values and tasks that were integral to woman's sphere at home. Children, and particularly boys, had to learn the behavior, values, and ideology appropriate to man's sphere so that they could be prepared to deal with the impersonal world of the marketplace. Schools came to serve as the bridge between the two spheres (Bender, 1978:138; Ryan, 1981:234).

These changes, which have been outlined here for the middle class, in fact were experienced differently by the members of different social groups and classes. Some of these differences, particularly in household economic strategies, are outlined briefly below.

Merchants made up the economic elite in New York from early colonial times until after the mid-19th century. Their families, too, lived and worked under the same roof in the 18th century, but the merchants had separate homes and countinghouses by the mid-19th century. Their wives and young children had not usually been involved directly in their economic activities during the period when the businesses and residences were housed in a single structure. Rather, merchants' wives, like their middle-class sisters of the next century, shored up the class standing of the family by "maintaining extensive social ties, [and] organizing lavish entertainments" (Ryan, 1983:86). Such social ties were important for ensuring that their children would gain entry into the ranks of the elite both through marriage and, for their sons, through clerkships in the mercantile businesses of family friends and relations. These elite households evidently followed the strategy of the family consumer economy well before the period that concerns us here. By the mid-19th century, however, these wives and mothers of the elite had also been affected by the domestic ideology of woman's sphere.[4]

The composition of the poor and the attitudes toward them changed as well during this period. Under the traditional economy, the majority of those who needed assistance were looked on as an inherently limited group of "deserving poor," consisting of the infirm, widows, and orphans, as well as the "working poor," who were seasonally or temporarily unemployed because of economic depression or illness. Later in the 19th century, the poor, who as a group had grown dramatically in numbers, were looked on as a threat to the social order.[5]

Most of the journeymen who would have been able to look forward to becoming mastercraftsmen in their own right in the 18th century became, along with the semiskilled, part of a permanent wage-earning working class by the mid-19th century. Many children who would earlier have been apprentices now made up a pool of child labor. These wage earners lived in working-class neighborhoods and either worked in their employers' shops or at home as part of the outwork system. The wages of poor family members were often pooled into a single fund to pay for the support of the household and its members. This strategy has been referred to as the *family wage economy.* In these households, wives and mothers stretched these wages and often scavenged goods to help make ends meet. Except for periods when many of these women worked in domestic service in middle-class and wealthy homes (as many did; more women worked "in service" than in any other job in the 19th century), they were affected only indirectly by the ideology of woman's sphere. This ideology was limited to middle-class and elite women in New York (Boydston, 1986; Dudden, 1983; Rock, 1979; Stansell, 1980, 1983, 1986; Tilly and Scott, 1978; Wilentz, 1984).

Several foreign travelers to America in the 1820s and 1830s noticed the bifurcation of middle-class America into man's and woman's spheres. Basil Hall, an Englishman, visited America with his wife Margaret in the late 1820s. He later wrote (1829/1964, Vol. 2) that he was "struck in every part of the country through which [he] had passed, with this strong line of demarcation between the sexes" (p. 152). The men "are almost exclusively engaged abroad by occupations which the women cannot possibly comprehend; while the women, for their part, are quite as exclusively engaged at home, with business equally essential and engrossing, but with which the men do not meddle in any way" (p. 156). "[T]he men and women of America [have] such different classes of occupations, that they seldom act together; and this naturally prevents the growth of that intimate companionship, which nothing can establish but the habitual interchange of opinions and sentiments upon topics of common enjoyment" (p. 157). He compared the situation in America with that of England, where "[t]he virtual control which women in England exercise over the conduct of the men, extends to every thing public as well as domestic" (p. 159).

Alexis de Tocqueville (1835/1945, Vol. 2), who visited America in 1830–1831, also remarked on the differences between the spheres:

> The Americans have applied to the sexes the great principle of political economy which governs the manufacturers of our age, by carefully dividing the duties of man from those of woman in order that the great work of society may be the better carried on. . . . In no country has such constant care been taken as in America to trace two clearly distinct lines of action for the two sexes and to make them keep pace with the other, but in two pathways that are always different. American women never manage the outward concerns of the family or conduct a business or take a part in political life. (pp. 211–212)

Several writers also noted that women's retirement from the world occurred only at marriage, and that an unmarried American girl enjoyed much greater freedom than her European counterpart (Child, 1838; Grund, 1837/ 1968; Tocqueville, 1835/1945, II, 198).

THEORETICAL PERSPECTIVES

Much of the debate around the development of woman's sphere has focused on the question of whether this change in women's roles constituted an enhancement or a decline of women's power when compared to their position during the colonial period. Although the extent of women's power in the colonial era is by no means completely clear, most of the studies agree that the answer to this question depends on the larger context in which we look at women's power. If the context is that of society as a whole or the political and economic arenas (man's sphere), most writers agree that women suffered a loss of power. If the context is that of the home and family (woman's sphere), most writers agree that their power was enhanced.[6]

The goal of this study is somewhat different. Here, we explore the processes that led to the restructuring of gender relationships in late-18th- and early-19th-century American urban culture. Theoretical approaches used to explain this aspect of the transformation fall roughly into two groups: those that view women as relatively passive in the transformation and those that look on women as taking a more active role in redefining the spheres.

Passive Women

Many feminist and Marxist-feminist works view women as victims who were thrust passively into woman's sphere. Some studies draw on the premise that the inequality between the sexes is based on the "male 'need' to dominate the female" (Scott, 1986:1058). Although this approach has been applied to the study of gender relationships in the 19th century, it cannot be used to explore the changes in these relationships because, as the historian Joan Scott (1986) pointed out, they are ahistorical: By not showing how this relationship is used to structure the rest of society, these scholars minimize the issue of how this power relationship can change.[7]

Marxist-feminist approaches, on the other hand, are deeply concerned with the origins of and changes in gender relationships during this transformation. Some see the explanation of these changes as lying outside the sexual division of labor, and in changes in the modes of production integral to the rise of capitalism. Women are often portrayed as victims reacting to the forces of capitalism and the dominance of men.[8]

Maxine Margolis (1985), a cultural materialist, provided an example of this kind of approach:

Over time changes in a society's material base will lead to functionally compatible changes in its social and political structure along with changes in its secular and religious ideology, changes that enhance the continuity and stability of the system as a whole. (p. 3)

Although Margolis cautioned that she does "not postulate a simplistic, mechanistic correspondence between material conditions and structural and ideological phenomena" (p. 3), she did not describe the actual mechanisms through which changes in the modes of production affect changes in the roles women play. In fact, time lag is the only factor that Margolis used to explain any lack of correspondence or tension between material conditions and structural and ideological phenomena.

As Scott (1986) pointed out, the Marxist-feminist approach is invaluable in stressing the asymmetrical nature of gender relationships and the importance of the rise of capitalism in shaping modern life. Perhaps it is not the most fruitful perspective for examining gender relationships, however, as these relationships are affected only indirectly by changes in the modes of production (p. 1059). This approach may, in fact, be particularly inappropriate for studying the emergence of woman's sphere during the period examined in this study, because the ideology of woman's sphere is looked on as complementing that of the capitalist marketplace. In looking on women as merely reacting or adapting to the restraints of capitalism, the Marxist-feminist approach tends to ignore the vital ways in which women may have actively contributed to the creation of the relationships that make up the modern American cultural experience.

The Marxist-feminist approach also fails to explain the differences in the impact of the rise of capitalism (a world economic system) on different aspects of different cultures in various parts of the world. If the development of capitalism in itself provides an adequate explanatory framework for this structural bifurcation of American culture, how was it possible for the traveler from England, the hegemonic power at the time in the capitalist world system, to note with wonder the "strange, and to European eyes, most unwonted separation of the sexes" in the United States?[9] There would presumably have been an equally strong line (if not a stronger one) between men's and women's occupations in England as well.

Women as Agents

Other scholars, such as Nancy Cott (1977), Kathryn Kish Sklar (1973), and Mary Ryan (1981), have portrayed women as agents who were more active in the creation of woman's sphere. Although these studies recognize the constraints that enveloped women in their exercise of power in the 18th and 19th centuries (as well as today), they also credit women's active participation in and contribution to the reformulation or reinvention of American culture during this period.

Ryan (1981) was most explicit in pointing out the importance of the actions of women themselves in reshaping their lives. She examined changes in society and family life and the emergence of the middle class in Oneida County, New York. She concluded that, as the conditions of commercial capitalism "opened up both the family and the community to the possibility of change, . . . men and women took advantage of these opportunities and in their collective action exerted a degree of control over the course of family and social history" (p. 240). She stressed that her study suggests that "acting within the substantial sphere of human experience designed by the concept of social reproduction, women have exerted a degree of leadership, power, and creativity quite disproportionate to the humble role granted to them by historians" (p. 240).

THE PRESENT STUDY

This study builds on the work of Cott, Sklar, and Ryan and explores the role of women (and men) as agents in this reformulation of American culture. I see the Revolution, in marking the end of America's role as a colony, as an event opening American culture to congeries of new possibilities and accelerating the transformation to modern life. Men and women acted on these new possibilities differently, each within the framework of their relationship within traditional colonial culture: Men continued with and enhanced their role of mediating between the household and the larger society, and women continued with and enhanced their role in social reproduction, maintaining the household, and caring for small children. However, the new content and values that their different actions picked up in their practice vis-à-vis these new possibilities resulted in cultural tensions and disjunctures. These tensions were resolved, but their resolution changed the relationship between men and women and the relationship of each of these groups to other cultural categories as well.[10]

This study focuses on some changes in social practice among middle-class and elite women in New York before these practices coalesced into the new ideology of woman's sphere. It looks on the separation of the home and the workplace as a watershed in early-19th-century life in the city: This separation marks the point when we know that marketplace activities were removed from the home, and it serves as the spatial expression of the bifurcation of society into man's and woman's spheres.

If we can see evidence of changes in the social practices that we associate with the development of woman's sphere *before* this separation occurred, it would indicate that women (as well as men) actively contributed to the development of woman's sphere and to the enactment of the transformation itself. If we see evidence that woman's sphere emerged only *after* the home was separated from the commercial workplace, it would suggest that women passively reacted, or adapted, to economic changes that were initiated in the larger society. In this case, we might interpret that women either created woman's sphere in the vacuum of the home after marketplace activities and the men who performed them had left during the day, or that women simply accepted the role in woman's sphere that was handed to them by the larger society.

The period I focus on here is the half century bounded by the end of the Revolution and the 1830s. As mentioned above, I see the Revolution as accelerating the beginnings of the cultural transformation. I use the 1830s as a terminal cutoff date because a clearly articulated prescriptive literature defining woman's sphere became extremely popular during that decade. I do not look on this literature as initiating this change in women's lives. Rather, I see the literature as addressing women who had already been converted to this new ideology, thereby indicating that the transformation of women's roles was well under way.[11]

This study of the changes in social practice associated with the transformation of home life in New York City is divided into four sections. First, in Chapter 2, I examine when the separation of the home and the workplace took place among the middle class and the elite of the city. Changing social practices in the marketplace, or man's sphere, are used as a backdrop for this discussion.

Second, I explore (in Chapter 3) the changing social landscape of New York that resulted from the separation of private homes from commercial workplaces during this period. This exploration plots the bifurcation of the city into spatially distinct men's and women's worlds—the city's commercial and residential neighborhoods, respectively—which created the social geography of the city that we know today.

Then, I change the focus of the study and (in Chapters 4, 5, and 6) look inside the homes of the middle class and the elite to examine some of the changes relevant to the development of woman's sphere that were taking place there.

In Chapter 4, I look at the composition of the household and consider three different ways in which it changed. First, I examine changes in the birthrate. By the 1830s, childhood had been redefined as a phase of life requiring the intensive maternal nurturing of children as well as the money to educate them. The role of mothering was correspondingly redefined and enhanced as part of woman's sphere, and it became much more labor-intensive as greater amounts of time and energy were deemed necessary for raising each child. The redefinitions of childhood and motherhood were associated with a lowering of the birthrate, which resulted in the presence, on average, of fewer children in each of the city's middle-class households.

Second, the development of woman's sphere was also associated with the enhancement of the quality of domestic life. This phenomenon was accompanied by an increase in the numbers of domestic servants who lived in the homes of the city's middle class and elite. These servants did the housework that was necessary to maintain the quality of an elaborated home life.

Finally, I look at the privatization of family life: the removal from the home of the men and boys who were not related to the family by blood or marriage (such as boarders and the journeymen and apprentices who worked in the family business). In exploring these aspects of changing household composition, I consider whether each of these changes can be seen beginning in the combined homes and workplaces of the city's middle class.

In Chapters 5 and 6, I examine changes during the period of study in a more quotidian aspect of domestic life: family meals. In the late 18th century, these meals were not especially important in daily life, because most family members were together for much of the day anyway. By the mid-19th century, however, with men going out to work and older children going off to school, family meals had become elaborated as secular rituals and served as daily reunions for family members. In Chapter 5, I outline some of the changes that took place in the structure of these meals. Then, in Chapter 6, I use the elaboration of the ceramic dishes that were used to present these meals as a marker to determine whether the ritualization process began in the combined homes and workplaces of the city's middle class, or whether the process began only later, after the establishment of separate, private homes. Changes in style, relative cost, and use of different and contrasting sets of tablewares are all examined in exploring this question.

One of the great challenges of this study was to tease out what women were actually doing inside their homes during this period. Given women's position in American culture in the 18th and 19th centuries, we cannot look to the written sources that we traditionally use to write their story. Jane Austen was well aware of this fact over 175 years ago: Anne Elliot, the heroine of *Persuasion* (1818/1898), will not allow Captain Harville to cite examples from books in their discussion of the nature of women. As Elliot puts it, "Men have had every advantage of us in telling their own story. Education has been theirs in so much higher a degree; the pen has been in their hands. I will not allow books to prove anything" (p. 242).

Instead, I looked at two different kinds of sources to derive the raw data from which I make inferences about women's actions in the urban context. The first set includes the public records, such as city directories, city tax records, and federal manuscript census returns that have proved so fruitful to social historians studying the "people without history" (Wolf, 1982). Although these records list only household heads, business proprietors, and property owners explicitly by name for the period of study—categories of New Yorkers who were predominantly men—they can be used to reconstruct the households and neighborhoods of which woman formed a part. To construct this data set, I drew six 2% samples from the city directories at decade intervals from 1790 to 1840. I then looked up each of the directory entries in the city's tax assessment records for the same individual for the appropriate year, so that I could take economic level, or class, into account. I divided each of the samples into three groups based on the assessed wealth of the sampled individuals. These groups are designated, in ascending order of wealth, as the working class, the middle class, and the wealthy. I also plotted the location of the homes and workplaces of the people in three of the samples on maps of the city, so that I could show the changing social landscape of the city through time. Finally, I looked up each of the individuals in the directory samples in the United States manuscript census returns for the appropriate year to allow an analysis of the changes in household composition through time.

The samples range in size from 86 to 1790 to 720 for 1840 and include a combined total of 2,396 for all of the years. This method and its advantages and limitations are discussed at length in Appendix A. Aspects of this data set are used in discussing the separation of the home and the workplace (Chapter 2), the changing social landscape of the city (Chapter 3), and changes in the composition of the household (Chapter 4).

The other data set is derived from archaeological sources. One of the oft-stated goals of historical archaeology has been to use the material culture generated from excavations as a window through which to view the experiences of women and other groups who are not well represented in the political and economic documents that make up the bulk of our historical records. Nevertheless, historical archaeologists, with a few notable exceptions,[12] have for the most part neglected the study of women. This is particularly ironic because the field is so well suited to examining the construction and reconstruction of "womanhood." So many of the artifacts we excavate are women's goods—the bits and pieces of crockery and glass that make up the rich fabric of domesticity and woman's sphere.

The data set I use here is derived from the ceramic dishes found at six different archaeological sites in New York. The ceramics were used in middle-class and wealthy households dating from the 1780s to the 1830s. Some of these households were combined with, and others were separated from, their associated workplaces. I discuss the nature of this sample and the households in which the ceramics were used in Appendix E. I use the ceramics to construct a data set to supply information for the analysis of the ritualization of family meals, the subject of Chapters 5 and 6.

I also develop narratives around three of the households that have been explored archaeologically so that these homes become illustrations showing how the city's middle class was transformed during the period of study. The household of Catherine Richards and her husband, Daniel Van Voorhis, who established a silversmith shop on Hanover Square in the 1780s, provides a good example of artisan life in the city during the early Federal period. Penelope Hull and her husband, Richard Bowne, had a combined home and drug shop on Pearl Street during the first two decades of the 19th century; they show how some of the city's more successful shopkeepers lived during the later Federal period. Finally, Eliza Bool and her husband, Benjamin Robson, a physician, demonstrate some of the strategies of a professional household during the later antebellum period. Narratives about aspects of life in these households introduce Chapters 2 through 6 and are used to contextualize the issues discussed in these chapters.

This study explores the relationship between the development of the cult of domesticity in woman's sphere and the development of capitalism in man's sphere in middle-class and wealthy families of late-18th- and early-19th-century New York City. Using an interdisciplinary approach and new sets of data, I hope to show that models that view changes in domestic life as being automatic reactions to changes in economic life are simplistic and ignore the active role that women played in the re-creation of culture in the new nation. Rather, the process of modernization that resulted in the division of society into men's and women's worlds in America might best be seen as the result of a mosaic of changes in social practice, with both men and women viewed as actively participating in redefining their spheres. The study should help us understand both the complex processes that led to the development of the form of the family that has dominated middle-class American life for approximately 150 years and the modernization of New York and other American cities.[13]

NOTES

1. The city's population grew from 4,375 in 1703 to 21,863 in 1771, a fivefold increase. In 1746, 2,444 (21%) of its 11,717 inhabitants were either African or of African descent, and most of them were enslaved. The population figures are from Rosenwaike (1972); Wilentz described the immigrants (1984:109).
2. Blackmar (1989) provided the most comprehensive explication of the dynamics of the physical growth of the city; the quotation is from Haswell (1896:86).
3. Mills (1951) discussed the composition of the middle class in the early 19th century. Family strategies are discussed in Medick (1976) and Tilly and Scott (1978); the following discussion draws heavily on the work of Cott (1977), Degler (1980), Margolis (1985), Matthai (1982), and Ryan (1981, 1983).

4. Pessen (1973) is still the best source on the city's elite.
5. Gilje (1987), Hodges (1986), Rock (1979), Rosenberg (1971), Stansell (1986), Walkowitz (1982), and Wilentz (1983, 1984) have all added to our understanding of the formation of the working class in New York.
6. Such writers include Cott (1977), Degler (1980), Lebsock (1985), D. S. Smith (1979); but see also Epstein (1981:158).
7. This discussion is adapted from J. W. Scott (1986). Welter (1968) provided an example of such a feminist approach.
8. Adapted from J. W. Scott (1986). Examples of such studies are those of Hayden (1982), Margolis (1985), Matthai (1982), Strasser (1982), and Zaretsky (1976).
9. Wallerstein (1980) described Great Britain as a hegemonic power in the 19th century; Hall (1964, II:152) is quoted more extensively above.
10. This approach is adapted from the one that Sahlins (1981, 1985) used in examining the impact on the Hawaiians of the arrival of the first Europeans (Captain Cook and his fleet). He showed how the actions or practices of particular social groups (in this case, Hawaiian men, women, and chiefs) acting within the traditional framework of their culture in regard to a new event or phenomenon (in this case, the arrival of the Europeans) can effect a structural transformation. Many historians (including Foner, 1976, and Kerber, 1980) have taken the position that the Revolution opened America to numerous possibilities and opportunities and hastened the transformation to modernity.
11. This is the position taken by Cott (1977:2).
12. The exceptions referred to include Burley (1989), Deagan (1973, 1983), and Yentsch (1990, 1991a,b).
13. Antebellum New York City has received a great deal of attention from political, labor, social, and intellectual historians, especially in the last decade or two; see, for example, Bender (1988), Blackmar (1979, 1989), Bridges (1984), Gilje (1987), Hartog (1983), Hodges (1986), Pessen (1973), Rock (1979), Rosenberg (1971), Stansell (1983, 1986), Walkowitz (1982), Wilentz (1983, 1984), and Wilkenfeld (1978), as well as the earlier works of Ernst (1949), Gilchrist (1967), Pomerantz (1965), and Willis (1967).

Chapter 2

The Separation of the Home and the Workplace

The Van Voorhis Household, 1780s

Daniel Van Voorhis, a silversmith, and his wife, Catherine Richards, were married in New York just before the Revolution. Like many patriots, they left the city during its occupation by the British army. Van Voorhis fought at the Battle of Princeton, where he was promoted to the command of his company by General Washington. He later became silversmith to the Continental Congress. After the war, when the British army had left the city, the couple returned to New York. There, they opened a gold, silver, and jewelry shop on Hanover Square in the East Ward in lower Manhattan (see Plate 1), and they lived above the store with their children, journeymen, and apprentices.

As a mastercraftsman in the post-Revolutionary city, Van Voorhis often worked in partnership with other jewelers and silversmiths. Some of his partners were relatives, such as his son, John Richards, and his third cousin, Garret Schanck.

Van Voorhis was involved in a wide variety of economic activities. He made silver pieces to order for wealthy customers. Because gold and silver were scarce in the new nation, he made most of these objects from metal that his customers supplied. He also advertised himself as a jeweler and performed more mundane tasks such as making glass faux gems to replace the stones in his customers' rings.

In addition to being a craftsman, however, Van Voorhis acted as merchant and shopkeeper, selling both wholesale and retail. Some of his trade was in sundry items, like the buttons, combs, and brass buckles he sold to casual

17

shoppers. He also supplied goods wholesale for country shopkeepers and other silversmiths in the city. In 1792, he and his partner, Garret Schanck, consigned a quantity of goods to a ship's captain, William Howel, to sell in India and China.

In 1803, Van Voorhis left his craft and became a weighmaster at the customs house. We do not know why he left the business; he may have suffered from the heightened competition in the trade at this time. Two decades later, after he moved to Brooklyn, Van Voorhis returned to his trade and, like many contemporary goldsmiths, also worked as a dentist, making gold teeth.[1]

The Bowne Household, circa 1805

Before the turn of the 19th century, Oliver Hull and his son John had a drug shop on Pearl Street in the East Ward in lower Manhattan (Plate 1). In 1800, John moved to upstate New York, and his father took Richard M. Bowne in to help with the business. Bowne lived with the Hull family above the store. Three years later, Oliver Hull died, and Bowne became a junior partner in the business. The next year, he married Penelope Hull, his late boss's daughter, and thus cemented his business ties to the Hulls with the those of kinship. The family continued to live above the shop until after Bowne's death in 1818.

Like their contemporaries in the drug business, the Hulls and the Bownes were quite diversified in their economic affairs, acting as merchants, shop-keepers, and providers of health care. In a 1790s newspaper advertisement, Oliver Hull & Son, Druggists, offered medicine chests and "DRUGS and MEDICINES, Patent Medicines, Perfumery, Surgeons Instruments, etc., etc." for sale and attested that the store was "replenished with fresh supplies from Europe, as occasion requires." They presumably resold these goods to other druggists and country shopkeepers, prescribed and mixed up medicines for their customers, and handled a retail drug trade.[2]

The Robson Household, 1820s

While Van Voorhis and Bowne were active in their businesses at the turn of the 19th century, Benjamin Robson was in his teens and studying medicine in a doctor's office. After a brief stint as ship's doctor on the *Samson*, which plied between New York and India, he returned to New York and set up his own practice. For more than three decades, he continued to run his practice out of his home, which was located, first, on Roosevelt Street in the Fourth Ward and, later, on Harman Street or East Broadway in the Seventh Ward. Robson was also affiliated with some of the hospitals and dispensaries that served the city's poor.

Throughout much of the 19th century, before the professionalization of medicine and the standardization of medical treatment, the relationship between a physician and his middle-class and wealthy patients—his source of income—was based on the doctor's position in his patients' community. Patients would call the physicians they knew, respected, and trusted. Physicians presided over the most important events in their patients' lives—birth, childbearing, and death—as well as various nonterminal illnesses. A doctor had to be available around the clock for health emergencies. It was therefore essential that he live in the same neighborhood as his patients.

Robson was typical of his peers for most of his career in that he ran his practice out of his home. He was unusual, however, in that he moved out of the neighborhood where he had originally started his practice; he had to start up again in a new locale when he moved to East Broadway. He may have had some help in establishing himself in the new neighborhood because his father-in-law, Henry Bool, lived there and may well have helped him become known and trusted in the community.[3]

*   *   *   *   *

The separation of the private home from the commercial workplace is a fundamental watershed in the development of modern urban life. It marked the end of the integrated family economy and the beginning of the family consumer economy for middle-class urban dwellers, the development of the family wage economy for the incipient working class, and the beginning of the complete restructuring of the urban real estate market. It was also the spatial expression of a redefined set of oppositions in American urban culture: man's sphere and woman's sphere.

Considering its importance, we know surprisingly little about how this change actually occurred at particular times and in particular places. Even for such a well-studied city as New York, we have conflicting interpretations. Scholars tend to agree that, in the last decades of the 18th century, combined homes and workplaces predominated among those working in both the commercial and the manufacturing sectors of the economy in New York and the other large eastern seaboard cities. Furthermore, most scholars also agree that this pattern of integration had broken down by the later 19th century (Blackmar, 1989; Tilly and Scott, 1978).[4]

Scholars disagree, however, on exactly when this change took place. Elizabeth Blackmar (1979:136; 1989:114), for example, tells us that craftsmen

moved away from their shops at the end of the 18th century and that successful merchants and professionals had done so by the second decade of the 19th
century. Allan Pred (1966:209–211), on the other hand, indicates that this
shift took place somewhat later, with only 23% of New York's industrial workers working outside their homes by 1840. David Gordon (1978:34–35), in
contrast, says that, for the most part, shops and residences remained spatially
integrated until the rise of industrial capitalism in the later 19th century.

This chapter examines the timing of the separation of the private home
from the market-oriented workplace among the elite and the middle class of
New York. It also explores some of the developments in the economic life of
the city during the late 18th and early 19th centuries, changes that help
explain the timing of this change.

The Revolution opened up a myriad of possibilities for both the politiciza-
tion of the populace and the economic expansion of trade and manufacturing
in America. Such eastern seaboard cities as Philadelphia and New York "stood
poised between tradition and modernity; and the Revolution . . . greatly accel-
erate[d] the transition between older and more modern forms of economic and
political life" (Foner, 1976:68). The impact of the Revolution was felt particularly in New York, as the city jumped from fourth place in port activity among
the colonial cities in 1770 (after Philadelphia, Boston, and Charleston) to first
place 27 years later. In the intervening years, the city had been occupied by the
British, ravaged by fires, and repopulated after the evacuation of 30,000 British
loyalists in 1783. The evacuation of the city by the British loyalists at the end of
the war and the confiscation of their property soon thereafter opened up
unprecedented opportunities in the city. Many of those who left came from the
ranks of the city's wealthiest and most influential citizens, and their departure
created openings near the top of the city's political and economic power structure. These openings were rightly seen as opportunities and attracted many
different kinds of people from many places outside the city (Albion, 1939:5–8;
Wilkenfeld, 1978).

The Revolution, in effecting the transition of the colonies from colonial to
independent status, removed all of Britain's mercantile restrictions on trade
and manufacturing in America. The northern and Middle Atlantic states,
which had been dominant in the colonial trade, now had the potential for
developing into core economic areas within the capitalist world system. In
addition, the timing of the Revolution was significant. Adam Smith's *The
Wealth of Nations,* the first systematic articulation of the *laissez-faire* philoso-
phy that developed in the 18th century, was published in England in 1776. In
Smith's view, the self-interested pursuit of gain, free of legislative regulations
for the common good and the tenets of the "moral economy," provided the
greatest benefits for society.[5]

The men of the middle and elite classes acted on the political and economic opportunities unleashed by the Revolution within the framework of their position in the structure of colonial society. But in so doing, their actions affected their relationships with the men, women, and children of both their own and different classes and culminated in an ideological change. With the commodification of labor and goods, people no longer measured the legitimacy of work by its value for the community and the common good; rather, work became morally neutral. These changes in economic life were expressed in other aspects of urban society as well. People began to separate their private homes from their commercial workplaces and, in so doing, removed their morally charged home life away from the morally neutral marketplace. Thus, they began to create separate geographical spheres for men and women.

The entries in the New York City directories allow us to explore whether those listed maintained homes and workplaces that were separate or combined: The directories give for each entry either a single address referring to an integrated home and workplace or two addresses referring to a separate home and workplace. We can see the increase through time in the number of middle-class and elite New Yorkers who made the decision to establish separate homes by comparing the number of listings for those in the six 2% random samples drawn from the directories.[6]

Figure 2–1 shows the percentages of the members of the middle class and the elite who listed themselves with separate homes and workplaces in the city directories at 10-year intervals during the half century after the Revolution. The graph shows an overall gradual increase among the city's proprietors who maintained separate homes during the period, from 2% in 1790 to 70% in 1840, with slightly sharper rises in the first decade of the 19th century and in the 1830s. The graph also indicates that, by 1840, a large majority of the members of the city's middle-class and wealthy families—the proprietors of its countinghouses, workshops, and stores—had in fact moved their homes away from their commercial workplaces.

The graph is deceptive, however, in that it implies that the change was a gradual, ongoing process among both groups during this period. In fact, changes in the economic life of the city affected differently those working in the various sectors of the economy. The periods when the majority of the city's merchants, shopkeepers, and artisans chose to move their homes away from their workplaces therefore varied as well. In order to understand this change, we have to consider the experience of each of these groups separately.

THE MERCHANT ELITE

The merchants continued to form New York's economic elite from the 17th through the mid-19th centuries. Before the Revolution, however, their

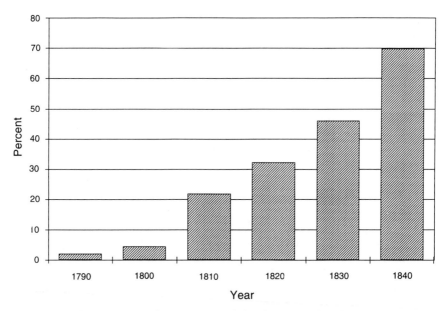

Figure 2–1. The percentages of the members of the elite and middle class in the directory samples who maintained separate homes and workplaces, by year.

commercial activities were tightly controlled by Great Britain. There was a shortage of capital in North America, and many merchants there were merely the agents of their British counterparts. The British Navigation Acts also restricted the merchants to trading within the British Empire. These acts, ironically, encouraged economic development in manufacturing and commerce in the northern colonies in two important ways. First, although the acts prohibited the use of foreign vessels in the British colonial trade, British shipping simply did not have the capability to carry the trade. The acts therefore granted colonial shipbuilders the right to build vessels for this trade. Shipbuilding became one of the few important industries in the colonies. Second, the acts also permitted the export of fish, meat, livestock, and lumber, the major products of the northern colonies, although the export of meat and cereal to Britain itself was banned. The colonists therefore turned to the British colonies in the West Indies for trade. There, they developed a complex trade network that has been referred to as the triangular trade, whereby lumber, provisions, and slaves were shipped to the West Indies; rum and trinkets were shipped to Africa; and molasses from the West Indies, slaves from Africa, and manufactured goods from England were all shipped to the northern colonies in return. Some northern colonial merchants were extremely successful in this trade (Danforth, 1974; Nettels, 1952; Pessen, 1973; Wallerstein, 1980).

In spite of the success of the colonial trade, however, commercial life in the colonies was more similar to that of the Middle Ages than to that of the modern world. Most commercial transactions were face-to-face, between people who knew each other personally and were often related to each other as well. Most important, the market did not dominate economic life as it would in the nineteenth century (e.g., see Foner, 1976:26; Wilkenfeld, 1978:219).

With independence, American trade was no longer subject to British mercantile policy. In New York, the Revolution "unleashed a whole new set of business conditions to which merchants responded creatively by moving into new ventures, with new forms of organization and new credit mechanisms."[7] As their old trading ties with Britain and the British West Indies were broken, the merchants created new ones in areas where they had not traded before. These areas included the Baltic; China; India; the Dutch, French, and Spanish East and West Indies; the Middle East; and Latin America; as well as, later, the developing U.S. West. After the War of 1812, the United States also became a major source of raw materials (such as cotton and other agricultural products) for industrializing Britain and an important market for British manufactured goods (Albion, 1939; Bjork, 1967; Wilkenfeld, 1978:154–155).

The European wars of the 1790s and the early 19th century also helped the economy of the new nation: American ships became the primary neutral carriers during these wars, and New York itself became the commercial center of the nation in the 1790s. The scale of both domestic and foreign trade continued to increase dramatically in the 19th century, particularly during the European wars and after the War of 1812, with the implementation of the regularly scheduled packet service in 1818 and the opening of the Erie Canal in 1825. During this period, the value of the foreign and domestic exports that passed through the Port of New York rose from $2.5 million in 1792 to $34 million in 1840. The merchants fulfilled the potential for increasing the volume of trade by becoming more specialized in their business activities and by creating separate entities to handle different aspects of their operations (Bjork, 1967; Chandler, 1977:15; Cochran, 1988:15, 17–19; the figures are from Albion, 1939:8, 390).

The general merchant of the colonial period bought and sold all kinds of products and carried out a variety of commercial roles, such as exporting, importing, wholesaling, retailing, shipping, banking, and insuring sea voyages. Beginning in the 1790s and continuing throughout the early 19th century, many of the roles that had been performed by the general merchant were broken down and handled instead by new, separate, specialized entities, such as insurance companies, banks, and, later, the transportation corporations that built the turnpikes and canals. The organizational innovation that allowed this specialization was the business corporation (Chandler, 1977:15; Davison, 1967). As Thomas Cochran (1972:76) pointed out, "[t]he ability to create by charter an abstract, indestructible, immortal, and to some degree irresponsible entity that could gather the savings of a community or nation and pour them into immense works did, in truth, alter the character of the business system more than any other change of this period."

Throughout this time of economic expansion, the merchants also began to specialize in one or two lines of goods (such as textiles, drugs, provisions, or hardware) and in one particular kind of trade, such as retailing or wholesaling and importing or exporting (Chandler 1977:15, 19–20; Cochran 1971:18). New occupational titles expressing these more specialized commercial roles were introduced: commission merchants, brokers, jobbers, factors, importers, and auctioneers. The merchants began specializing in the 1790s, but the rate of specialization increased strikingly just before the enactment of Jefferson's 1808 embargo (Cochran, 1977:15) and again after the War of 1812 (Chandler 1977:25). Cochran (1977) described this specialization as "probably as important as the division of labor was in manufacturing plants for raising levels of efficiency" (p. 18).

The world of the merchant became less personal, as a great number of specialists could be involved in transferring raw materials from their original producers to manufacturers and finished goods back to consumers. Merchants began to advertise on a larger scale, and newspapers began to carry a great deal of commercial news in response to the merchants' growing need to manipulate this larger, more impersonal market.[8]

The development of the impersonal, specialized market was associated with a change in ideology among the merchants. With the volatile and increasingly competitive nature of the expanding economy, financial failure became more and more common. In order to compete successfully, merchants began to redefine their world as one where the marketplace was increasingly cut off from moral considerations. In fact, it has been noted that, as early as the 1770s, most merchants no longer supported the fixing of "just" prices of the moral economy; the *laissez-faire* maxim that "'trade can best regulate itself' had won virtually universal approval in the mercantile community" (Foner, 1976:152–153). By the mid-19th century, older merchants looked back at the "golden age" of their youth, before the ideal image of the "merchant prince," with its connotations of statesmanship, philanthropy, and charity, had been replaced by the parvenu businessman motivated by the desire for profits (Horlick, 1975:181).

It has been noted and stressed in the literature, however, that this expansion in the scale of trade and increase in specialization did little to alter the internal organization of mercantile businesses until well into the 1840s. It was only in that decade that merchants introduced economies of scale requiring extensive bureaucratization. The size of these enterprises did not grow beyond their traditional 18th-century limits before that period because the volume of trade handled by an individual enterprise was not great enough to warrant an increase in the division of labor within an individual mercantile firm (Chandler, 1977:16, 49; Cochran, 1977:53).

Countinghouse personnel continued to consist of the merchant proprietor(s) —who (like the Hulls and Richard Bowne introduced at the beginning of this chapter) might be joined in a partnership—a confidential chief clerk, a cash keeper, a bookkeeper, several copiers, and errand boys. The proprietor's partners and agents in other cities continued to be looked on as holding positions of extreme trust. This need for trust continued to be expressed by the appointment to these positions of sons and sons-in-law and other male kin and, again like the Hulls and Richard Bowne, the sealing of business ties with those of kinship (Albion, 1939:261; Chandler, 1977:37–38).

Clerkships continued to be structured similarly to apprenticeships throughout the early 19th century. Bookkeepers or chief clerks controlled the process of recording the transactions of the business. They supervised the clerks and copying clerks, who were similar to journeymen, and the office boys, who can be likened to apprentices (Braverman, 1974:298–299; Horlick, 1975:70, 73, 106).

In addition, as under the apprenticeship system, there was a limited mobility built into the clerkship system:

> [A] clerk took his regular degrees. He was first set to delivering goods from the store. . . . He was also obliged to receive goods and to keep correct accounts of such as he received in store or delivered to purchasers. In doors [sic] he was obliged to copy letters; when the clerk could do that correctly and neatly without making an error or a blot, then he was promoted to making duplicates of letters to go by the packet ships. Then he was promoted to copying accounts. Next, he was trusted with the responsible duty of making these accounts. (Scoville, 1885:110–111).

For the most part, senior clerks were only semimanagerial in the early-19th-century mercantile establishment. Proprietors continued to manage their firms themselves, with little delegation of authority, until the 1840s (Braverman, 1974:293; Chandler, 1977:3).

Through the mid-19th century, the clerkship system also provided training for merchants. Most merchants used their families' social networks and influence to get their training. Fathers found clerkships for their sons and carefully made the necessary arrangements with their sons' future employers, who were usually friends or relatives: "Friends and relatives were expected to provide clerkships for one anothers' sons" (Horlick, 1975:73). The clerkship usually lasted approximately four years for sons of the elite. After his training, a young man with capital either established a business on his own or with partners, or he was taken on as a junior partner in an established house (Horlick, 1975:73–74).

In contrast to our myths about the prevalence of self-made men in this period, it has been estimated that around 95% of the elite in antebellum New York came from wealthy and/or eminent families. Occasionally, however, a young man of obscure social origins found a clerkship and, after working his way up by degrees and perhaps (like Richard Bowne) marrying the boss's daughter, managed to be taken on as a junior partner in an established firm. Apparently, however, this form of recruitment to the ranks of the merchant elite became harder to achieve as the century progressed (Horlick, 1975; Pessen, 1973).

The clerkship system began to break down only in the 1840s, after the period of interest here, when merchants instituted economies of scale that required proportionately more workers in low-level positions as white-collar employees. In the 1840s, for example, it became common practice for the merchants to require newly hired clerks to post security to guarantee their honesty. The elite merchants and their middle-class clerks were becoming distinct social groups with separate class interests (Horlick, 1975:166).

In late-18th-century New York, a merchant typically housed his business and residence in the same building, which was usually located in the general area of the eastside port, while his warehouse, used for storing goods, was located near the docks. Typically, the merchant had "his sitting room or dining room directly in back of [his] store on the first floor [of this integrated structure], his drawing room and bedrooms upstairs, and children's and servants' bedrooms on the third floor" (from Scoville, quoted in Rosebrock, 1975:13). Later, however, he reorganized his commercial space by removing his workplace from his home and relocating it closer to the docks, where only his warehouse had been before. He adopted a new form of workplace, the countinghouse, which incorporated both office and storage facilities into the same building. In this new kind of building, the merchant used the front of the ground floor for moving and displaying goods, the rear of this floor for the countinghouse or office, and the upper floors for storage (Blackmar, 1989:48).

We should remember, however, that throughout the colonial period, merchants had traditionally carried out some of their business away from their integrated homes and workplaces. They had particular taverns and coffeehouses where they met to transact business with each other at certain hours of the day. After the Revolution, they continued this practice, meeting daily at the Tontine Coffee House (see Plate 4) from the time of its erection in 1792 until the 1820s, when the Merchants' Exchange (see Plate 9) was built for this purpose (Albion, 1939:265; Robert Venables, personal communication, 1985).

The question that concerns us here is when most of New York's merchants

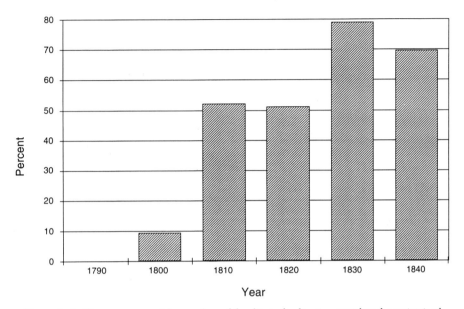

Figure 2–2. The percentages of the members of the elite in the directory samples who maintained separate homes and workplaces, by year.

decided to reorganize their use of space and separated their homes from their workplaces. Figure 2–2 shows the percentages of the members of New York's elite in our samples who were listed with separate homes and workplaces. The percentages ranged from 0% to almost 80% during the period. However, this increase was by no means steady or gradual; the figure shows definite leaps and plateaus. There was a large leap, for example, in the first decade of the century. Then, between 1810 and 1820, the percentages remained relatively constant. Next, in the 1820s, there was another, though smaller, leap. Finally,there was a slight decrease in the 1830s.

The leaps in these percentages can be correlated with the boom periods in the commercial sector. The marked rise in the first decade of the century followed the expansion of trade that began in the 1790s and extended throughout the Napoleonic Wars. The other rise, evident in the 1820s, also correlated with the increase in the volume of trade and the associated growing impersonalization of the market that occurred after the opening of the Erie Canal in 1825. The plateau between 1810 and 1820 may have expressed the effects of the depression of 1819, and the decrease for 1840 was probably related to the depression of 1837, which resulted in the collapse of many mercantile houses and the effects of which were still being felt early in the next decade. When times got hard, members of the elite may have chosen to resort to combined homes and workplaces again.

This study suggests, then, that the separation of the home and the workplace among New York's commercial elite in fact followed the expansion of trade on the part of the merchants in the late 18th and early 19th centuries. This expansion, in turn, was marked by trade specialization in an increasingly impersonal and morally neutral marketplace, where the legitimacy of economic activities was no longer measured by their social value.

THE MIDDLE CLASS

In looking at the members of the middle class who chose to maintain residences separate from their workplaces, we find a picture emerging that is quite different from that of the merchant elite. Figure 2–3 shows that there was a gradual but steady increase in the percentages between 1800 and 1830, with a somewhat larger leap between 1830 and 1840. In order to understand the social meaning of this graph, we should look inside the middle class at the artisans and the shopkeepers who made up almost three-quarters of it and examine the changes that were taking place particularly among the artisans during this period.

The Artisans

Like the merchants, New York's artisans were deeply affected by the Revolution, and its effects were manifested politically as well as economically. A primary legacy to the artisans was their new identity as a political entity. Before the war, the artisans in the mercantile trades (the most successful trades in the colonies) saw their economic interests as closely allied with those of the merchants, for whom they produced most of their goods. They emerged from the war with an egalitarian ideology, with the interests of masters and journeymen alike being seen as distinct from those of the merchant elite. It was only after the War of 1812 that the journeymen and masters in the trades began to interpret the republican ideal quite differently.[9]

Britain's mercantile policy was successful in suppressing the development of most American industries (with the important exception, noted above, of shipbuilding). However, even after the Revolution, there was no large-scale move toward industrial production. Such a move was inhibited primarily because merchant-investors were disinclined to invest heavily in American manufactures that would probably not be able to compete favorably with British goods (Cochran and Miller, 1961:8–10).

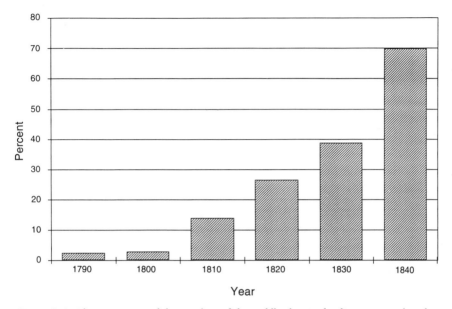

Figure 2–3. The percentages of the members of the middle class in the directory samples who maintained separate homes and workplaces, by year.

The ideology of the moral economy, with its notion of "just" prices, persisted much longer among the artisans as a group than among the merchants. Most of the manufacturing sector of New York's economy was organized by the artisan system of production well into the 19th century. In the early small shops, mastercraftsmen, helped by their journeymen and apprentices, produced goods to order for the merchants who marketed them. The journeymen in most trades were paid by the piece, according to a list of "just" prices. If the apprentices were not the master's own children, an arrangement was made whereby the master agreed to supply them with room and board and to instruct them in the skills of the trade. In exchange, the master had the use of the apprentices' labor for the period of the apprenticeship and was often paid a fee. When Daniel Van Voorhis, the silversmith, undertook the apprenticeship of Garret Schanck in 1784, for example, Schanck's father, John, paid Van Voorhis £32. Apprenticeships traditionally lasted for seven years but in fact were often shorter and usually terminated on the apprentice's 21st birthday. Schanck's apprenticeship, for example, lasted only four and a half years (Laidlaw, 1986, Note 3; Wilentz, 1984:28).

Family ties were very important in sealing business ties among the artisans as well as among the merchants. As mentioned above, Garret Schanck was Van Voorhis's third cousin. After Schanck served his apprenticeship with Van

Voorhis, the cousins were partners for several years. Later on, Van Voorhis went into partnership with his own son, John Richards. Another one of Van Voorhis's partners, William Coley, was transformed into a relative by becoming the godfather of two of the Van Voorhis children when Coley sponsored them at their baptism at Trinity Church.[10]

Although a mastercraftsman was in fact a capitalist, in the formal sense that he owned the tools, the materials, and the results of the productive process, he was, as Karl Marx (1867–1894/1976, Vol. 1) noted,

> an artisan in the first instance and . . . master of his craft. Within the process of production he appear[ed] as an artisan, like his journeyman, and it [was] he who initiate[d] his apprentices into the mysteries of his craft. He [had] precisely the same relationship to his apprentices as a professor to his students. Hence his approach to his apprentices [was] not that of a capitalist but of a *master* of his craft. (p. 1029)

As master, he was responsible not only for the vocational training but also for the moral welfare of his apprentices. Artisan republican values of independence, egalitarianism, and cooperation were shared for the most part by the masters and their journeymen alike (Wilentz, 1984:141).

By the middle of the 19th century, New York had become the primary manufacturing city in the country. Earlier in the century, many of the masters severed their clientage ties with the merchants and began, like Daniel Van Voorhis, to market their own goods. After 1800, their organization, the General Society of Mechanics and Tradesmen, which had first been used as a "friendly society," began to support domestic manufactures against foreign competition and the merchants' interests. With the founding of the Mechanics' Bank in 1810, it became possible for more of these artisan entrepreneurs to enter the world of credit and capital and to produce directly for the growing market (Wilentz, 1984:38–39, 107).

In competing with the merchant capitalists for a share of the market, these entrepreneurs developed a uniquely metropolitan form of industrialization. The factory system was not a viable option for most of New York's manufacturers, because the lack of available waterpower and the high cost of the city's real estate precluded both a high degree of mechanization in production and the centralization of work (Wilentz, 1983, 1984).

Instead, metropolitan industrialization was achieved primarily through the reorganization of the productive process. Many of the masters working in many of the crafts resorted to an intensification in the division of labor, and they simplified and routinized the work process. To increase production and cut costs, they began to use the labor of the growing ranks of semiskilled immigrants who were flooding the city. The apprenticeship system was gradually abandoned, and apprentices were no longer trained in a craft; rather, they were used as child labor to perform simple tasks. This change began in the 1790s and increased dramatically in the 1820s, as competition intensified in producing for the expanding local and national markets (Wilentz, 1984:33, 113).

Metropolitan industrialization took highly diverse forms, and its effects were felt unevenly in the various trades. The crafts that rapidly expanded for the growing market tended to experience these effects the most. These crafts have been identified as the consumer finishing trades (such as shoemaking, tailoring, and cabinetmaking) and the printing and building trades. They have been referred to as the *conflict trades* because so much of the labor unrest that occurred in the early 19th century took place within them. These trades employed from one-half to three-quarters of the journeymen in New York (Rock, 1979; Wilentz, 1984:31–32, 120–132).

In other trades, however, the artisan system tended to predominate until the mid-19th century. This was the case in some of the maritime crafts, such as the ship carpenters' and coopers' trades, where tasks could not be easily subdivided; the trades that catered to a local, neighborhood market, such as the food provision trades like butchering and baking; and those that specialized in the production of luxury and custom goods, including, for example, watches, and custom-made clothes. We should remember, however, that some shops in even the most rapidly expanding crafts continued to be organized by the artisan system of production. In addition, some shops in the trades that, for the most part, continued to be traditionally organized also expanded production and underwent an intensification in the division of labor during this period. The effects of the industrialization process were therefore extremely diverse (Rock, 1979; Wilentz, 1984:32–43, 112, 137–140).

In the late 18th century, the masters controlled the labor process. By the mid-19th century, however, they could fill many different roles in manufacturing. Masters could work as entrepreneurs completely divorced from the productive process, as foremen-supervisors of work either in garret shops manned by unskilled labor or performed at home under the outwork system, or as traditional masters in shops that were still organized by the artisan system.

Needless to say, the social relations of production in those trades that rapidly expanded during this period were transformed. Under the earlier artisan system, journeymen and apprentices could, somewhat realistically, look forward to becoming masters in their own right. With the debasement of skilled work, the commodification of labor, and the increasing size of the capital investment needed to open a competitive shop associated with metropolitan industrialization, however, journeymen became part of a permanent wage-earning working class and could no longer expect to become masters. Successful entrepreneurs and their journeymen redefined the Revolution's legacy of artisan solidarity. Although this was a gradual process that began in the later 18th century and was not completed until well after the period under study, evidence of this new ideology began to appear in the first decade of the 19th century, when the masters began to try to reshape the work ethic of the city's labor force to suit the new needs of the more competitive economy. In addition, Sean Wilentz (1983, 1984) has pinpointed the early 1830s as a time when artisan ideology had graphically changed.

The early trade unions in New York had been organized by craft, and their members consisted of both masters and journeymen in the various trades. This unity within the crafts was expressed in the processions that marked many of the holidays, such as the Fourth of July and Evacuation Day (commemorating the British evacuation of New York in 1783), in the late 18th and early 19th centuries. Both the journeymen and the masters marched together, by trade, carrying the emblems of their trade that symbolized the unity of their craft. This tradition persisted until the 1830s (Wilentz, 1983).

In 1833, the General Trades' Union was established. This confederation of unions was the first in New York to consist solely of wage-earning journeymen from a cross section of various trades. As Wilentz (1983) pointed out, both in its inaugural procession and in those commemorating subsequent holidays, the journeymen members of this union marched together, by trade, expressing a new class solidarity of wage earners as opposed to the earlier solidarity of the vertically integrated crafts.

This overview of changes in the artisans' world shows that, during the period of study, many mastercraftsmen acted on the possibilities of the ex-panding market by reorganizing both the marketing of goods and the produc-tive process by intensifying the division of labor. This reorganization was associated with the adoption of a *laissez-faire* ideology by the masters in many of the city's shops. It involved the commodification of labor and of the goods produced in the shops. In addition, although evidence of this ideological shift can be seen beginning in the early decades of the century, it was clearly manifested in the 1830s. We can examine the separation of the home and the workplace among the masters in the artisan trades against this background.

Figure 2–4 shows the percentages of the middle-class masters in the artisan trades in the samples who chose to maintain homes that were separate from their workplaces. The percentages show an overall increase from 0% in 1790 to 65% in 1840, and the curve is roughly similar to that for the middle class as a whole (shown in Figure 2–3), although there are some differences between them. First, there was a large jump in the percentages between 1800 and 1810. Then, there was a slight increase between 1810 and 1830. Finally, there was another jump in the 1830s, when the percentages almost doubled.

The periods that show sharp rises in the percentages of those maintaining separate homes and shops (the decade before 1810 and the 1830s) are the same periods that we documented above as being marked by an intensification in the commodification of goods and labor. It was during the first decade of the

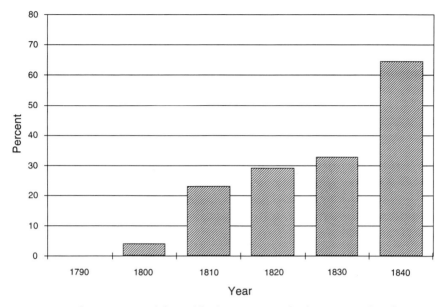

Figure 2–4. The percentages of the middle-class artisans in the directory samples who maintained separate homes and workplaces, by year.

century that some mastercraftsmen began to increase production and compete with the merchants for a share of the expanding market. By the 1830s, the commodification of labor had resulted in a major shift in class alignments among those working in the city's trades. We should also note that the period with the sharpest increase in the percentages of those who maintained separate homes and workplaces—the 1830s—was the same for these mastercraftsmen and the middle class as a whole (compare Figures 2–3 and 2–4).

The Shopkeepers

Shopkeepers were the other large group that, along with the artisans, made up the middle class in the early 19th century. Unfortunately, New York's shopkeepers have not been subjected to the same intensive study that has been aimed at the city's merchants and artisans. Presumably, "shopkeepers" included both relatively small-scale retailers, some of whom may have expanded their operations to supply the consumer needs of the ever-growing local market, and those who were aspiring to become part of the merchant elite.

Figure 2–5 shows the percentages of the middle-class shopkeepers who maintained separate homes and shops. Unlike those for the artisans and the middle class as a whole, the percentages for the shopkeepers show a gradual

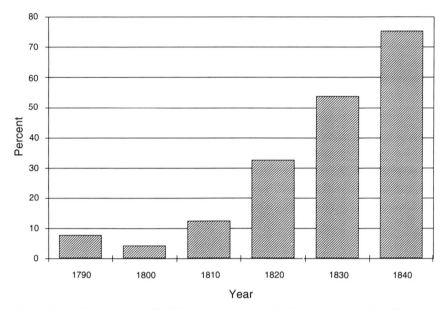

Figure 2–5. The percentages of middle-class shopkeepers in the directory samples who maintained separate homes and workplaces, by year.

and even increase throughout the early 19th century, from 4% in 1800 to 75% in 1840.[11] There are none of the sharp leaps or plateaus that we saw in the percentages for the artisans and the middle class as a whole. This finding suggests that, among the shopkeepers, this was a gradual process, presumably associated with a growth in the scale of trade in a marketplace that was becoming increasingly impersonal. The sharper jumps in the percentages of those listed with two addresses in the samples of the middle class as a whole are clearly expressions of the economic and social changes that occurred within the artisan sector.

CONCLUSION

The data from the directory samples provide a clear picture of the period when most of New York's proprietors chose to establish residences that were spatially separate from their countinghouses and shops. Whereas in 1790 only a few of these proprietors had made this change, by 1840 almost three-quarters of them had done so. The data from the samples show that this change was made at different times by those who belonged to different socioeconomic classes and who worked in different sectors of the economy. Members of the city's elite, who worked mostly as merchants in the city's commercial sector, were the first to make this change, most of them doing so in the first decade of the century. The majority of middle-class proprietors followed suit only later, in the 1830s.

The directory data also suggest that the decision to establish a separate residence may have been closely associated with developments in the economic life of the city. Among the merchant elite, the separation of the home and the workplace closely followed the unprecedented expansion of trade and the growth of the impersonal market in the 1790s. For the artisans, the decade that saw the greatest increase in the adoption of this residence pattern—the 1830s —closely followed the period when the commodification of labor had resulted in a new alignment in the class structure of the workers in many of the city's shops. The decision on the part of the city's proprietors to adopt separate residential and commercial properties had a profound impact on the social geography of the city.

NOTES

1. This reconstruction of Daniel Van Voorhis's career is derived from a number of sources. I am very grateful to Christine Wallace Laidlaw (1986, 1988), who generously gave me access to the results of her extensive research on the silversmiths of Monmouth County, New Jersey. Some of these silversmiths worked with Daniel Van Voorhis. Information on Van Voorhis's experiences in the Revolutionary War is from his obituary in *The Star,* Brooklyn, 17 June 1824. Mallory Gordon found this obituary, and Meta Janowitz kindly brought it to my attention. The obituary never mentioned that Van Voorhis was a silversmith; rather, the newspaper's interest was confined to his wartime activities.

   Gottesman (1954:75–77) reproduced several newspaper advertisements for Van Voorhis and his partners in the 1780s. Both C. M. Williams (1949:117–122) and the Van Voorhees [*sic*] Association (1935:95–96) provided brief (and occasionally inaccurate) overviews of Van Voorhis's career.

   Laidlaw provided insight into the silversmith craft in general (1986:3, 6, 16) and into Van Voorhis's own career (1986:16, 34). Some of the products and goods mentioned were found in an archaeological excavation on the basement floor of Van Voorhis's shop at 27 Hanover Square at the 75 Wall Street Site. These goods include buttons, buckles, and heavily worn faux gems, as well as a green glass rod that may have been used as a source of glass for making green faux gems (75 Wall Street Collection, South Street Seaport Museum; Olive Jones, personal communication, 1988). In her diary (1799–1806), Elizabeth Bleecker, a broker's daughter, mentions going to Van Voorhis's shop several times at the turn of the 19th century; once she bought a fan there for a friend (entries for 15 June, 29 July, and 1 and 3 August 1799, and 13 May 1800).

   Van Voorhis's career in Brooklyn was tracked through the Brooklyn city directories (Spooner, 1822–1825). The Van Voorhees Association handbook says that Van Voorhis left the trade after the death of his son and partner, John Richards Van Voorhis, in the yellow fever epidemic in 1805. This is unlikely, however, as Van Voorhis petitioned the city's Common Council to become a weighmaster in 1801; he was finally appointed at the end of January 1803 (City of New York, Minutes of the Common Council, 1917–1930, III: 52, 198).

2. The information on the Hulls and the Bownes is from Hull (1863:32–33) and Wilson (1987:36) and the city directories for the appropriate years. The advertisement for Oliver Hull & Son, Druggists, is from *The Diary, or Evening Register,* 1 January 1794; Meta Janowitz kindly brought the ad to my attention. Gill (1972) described the diversified activities performed by druggists in colonial Virginia.

3. Much of this background information on Robson's career is from his obituary in *The New York Times* (19 August 1878). All of the locational information on Bool and the Robsons is from the city directories for various years in the 19th century. Rosner (1982:13–16, 30–34) stressed the importance of a physician's place in his community in building and maintaining his practice before the professionalization of medicine in the later 19th century. Jean Howson kindly referred me to this reference and interpretation.

4. Blackmar (1979, 1989), Cochran (1972), Gordon (1978), Harrington (1935), Nash (1979), Pred (1966), Warner (1962, 1968), and Wilkenfeld (1976) all also mention this phenomenon.

5. Wallerstein (1980), Foner (1976:153); Gilje (1987:10–11) has applied E. P. Thompson's "moral economy" model (1971) to 18th-century New York.

6. I discuss the advantages and disadvantages of this methodology at length in the essay in Appendix A; the data used to construct the bar graphs in this chapter are presented in Appendix B.

7. The quotation is from Foner (1976:27) and refers to Philadelphia, although it is even more appropriate to New York. (Albion, 1939; Bjork, 1967; Wilkenfeld, 1978:154–155)

8. The 1794 advertisement for the druggists Oliver Hull & Son mentioned above (Note 2) provides an articulation of the more restrained attitude toward advertising in the late 18th century and implies that advertising at that time was not regarded as in the best of taste: The advertisement mentions that the firm has "not been in the practice of soliciting attention by pompous advertisements in the public papers."

9. The following discussion draws heavily on Wilentz (1984), whose study has quickly become the classic work on the formation of the working class in New York City.

10. Laidlaw (1986) provided extensive information on the career of Garret Schanck. Coley's partnership with Van Voorhis is discussed in Gottesman (1941); his sponsorship of the Van Voorhis children is mentioned in the records of Trinity Church as published by the New York Genealogical and Biographical Society (1959, 1960).

11. The inflated figure for 1790 is caused by the small size of the sample for that year: There was one person who maintained a separate home and workplace in the sample.

Chapter 3

The Changing Social Landscape
of the City

The Van Voorhis Household, 1780s

When the Van Voorhis family returned to New York after the Revolution, they opened their silversmith shop on fashionable Hanover Square in the East Ward of the city (see Plate 1), the ward where most of the city's wealthy families lived. In 1788, they moved to Queen Street, a block to the north in the same neighborhood, where they stayed until the mid-1790s. From then until 1803, when Van Voorhis left the trade, the family moved almost every year. Most years, they lived above the store, but some years, they lived away from it, in less expensive neighborhoods to the west or north of the East Ward. Each year, however, they kept their shop in or near the East Ward so that it would be accessible to their wealthy customers. Perhaps they lived away from the store when they could not find a house they could afford in the East Ward that was large enough to accommodate both their domestic and their work space.

Archaeological excavations at the site of the Van Voorhis shop at 27 Hanover Square suggest that the family lived in one of the old Dutch houses built with its stepped gable facing the street (see Plate 3). Demolition debris from the building included materials typical of Dutch architectural detail, such as terra-cotta pantiles for the roof, green- and orange-glazed ceramic tiles for the floor, and delft tiles for flanking the fireplaces and lining the baseboards.

In spite of their Dutch name and the Dutch style of their house, however, the Van Voorhis family belonged to an Episcopal church and not a Dutch

37

Reformed one; they had their children baptized at Trinity Church, on Broadway at the head of Wall Street.[1]

The Bowne Household, circa 1805

Richard Bowne joined the partnership of Hull and Bowne in their Pearl Street drug shop in 1803. Pearl Street near Hanover Square was then the site of the homes and businesses of general merchants active in both the retail and the wholesale trades. By the time of Bowne's death in 1818, however, the neighborhood had changed. A contemporary observer noted that "Pearl Street contains all the large houses. Here everything is sold wholesale. The shops are well supplied with goods and this street is considered the richest, though its appearance is less brilliant than Broadway" (Stokes, 1915–1928, Vol. 5, p. 1597).

In addition to Pearl Street's conversion to the wholesale trade during this period, there was an even greater change in that very few of the proprietors of these commercial establishments continued to live on that street. They had moved their homes over to the west or north of what was now becoming a business district. The Bownes, in their Federal-style house with its pitched roof (see Plate 8), were one of the few families still living there. After Bowne's death, the firm was taken over by his in-laws, the Hulls, and Oliver Hull lived there for only two more years before he too moved his home away from the shop.[2]

The Robson Household, 1820s

In moving first from Roosevelt Street to East Broadway in 1829 and then up to Washington Square 12 years later, Dr. Benjamin Robson and his family may have been following his wealthier, paying patients as they moved farther and farther away from the bustle of the commercial heart of the city. Robson had lived on Roosevelt Street in the Fourth Ward since 1810, three years before his marriage. At that time, this was a "good street" in a mixed neighborhood. Some of the city's wealthier residents made their homes here after they moved them away from their downtown workplaces.

The Robsons were moving up in the world as well as uptown when they moved to East Broadway: The tax assessment for their new home was more than twice as much as that for their old one. East Broadway in the Seventh Ward was a prominent street, near the Rutgers estate. Perhaps with the help of his father-in-law, who lived in the area, Robson built up his practice among the local wealthy residents as well as presumably among the ship-builders who lived nearby and worked at the local shipyards.

In 1841, after their children were grown, the Robsons moved again, but this time they left the practice behind them on East Broadway. They moved their home up to the newly developed wealthy residential suburb around Washington Square (see Plates 2 and 13), where they lived in a residential-style late Federal house, with an iron-railed stoop and a front areaway, next door to their daughter, Mary. Mary was married to Francis P. Sage, a flour merchant who commuted down Broadway in the omnibus every day to his countinghouse on South Street (see Plates 7 and 16).[3]

*   *   *   *   *

The decision on the part of 19th-century middle-class and wealthy New York-ers to establish homes that were separate from their commercial workplaces had a profound effect on the social landscape of the city. The city's built environment is a social product and provides a tangible expression of the social processes at work. As the way of life of the people in the city was transformed, the social geography of the city was transformed, too. This geo-graphical transformation created new social environments that served as arenas that, in turn, affected the restructured social relations of the people who lived and worked in them.[4]

This chapter explores the spatial expression of the transformation of the city from one where, in the late 18th century, workplaces and homes were relatively integrated, to one where, in the mid-19th century, they were separate for a large part of the population. This change resulted in a city with its workplaces clustered together in a commercial center by the East River port, the site of man's sphere, where social relations were structured primarily by the impersonal ties of the marketplace. The commercial center was sur-rounded by residential neighborhoods, where social relations were structured more by the affective ties of home life, or woman's sphere. As class relations became increasingly structured by the capitalist social relations of the mar-ketplace, it became harder and harder to maintain the illusion of egalitarianism in these mixed residential neighborhoods. The neighborhoods began to be-come segregated by class.

Two different kinds of information are useful in exploring the transforma-tion of the social landscape of the city in the early 19th century. The first consists of changes in the distributions of the locations of homes and work-places across the city. Here, we look at evidence for the beginnings of two different phenomena: the creation of commercial and residential neighbor-hoods and the segregation of the residential neighborhoods by class. The other variable examined is architectural style. New Yorkers first used architectural style as an integrating device to mask differences in wealth and function in the egalitarian post-Revolutionary city. Later, in Jacksonian New York, they used it as a marker to define, on the one hand, the social boundaries between the commercial center and the residential neighborhoods (or man's and woman's spheres) and, on the other, the socioeconomic affiliation of the residential neighborhoods that were becoming segregated by class.

Two models are helpful in exploring the changing social landscape of New York. Sjoberg's model (1960) of the preindustrial city helps us to see the structure of the colonial and early Federal city, and Burgess's model (1925) of the early-20th-century city is useful for discussing the city's structure in the later 19th century. Both models are based on the image of concentric circles.

Sjoberg's model (1960) applies to late-18th-century New York, with its combined homes and workplaces, before the bifurcation of the spheres began. Although Sjoberg noted that there is little functional differentiation in the use of most types of land in the preindustrial city, he stressed the preeminence of an inner central or core area over an outer periphery (pp. 95–98). This preeminence is expressed in the distribution of social classes: The elite tend to concentrate in the central area, alongside the middle class and the poor. The peripheral area is inhabited primarily by the middle class and the poor, and the poorest, most marginal people are confined to the city's outskirts.

The importance of the central area is also expressed in its choice as the site of the most prominent governmental and religious buildings in the city. Because religious and political activities have more legitimacy in preindustrial cities than economic activities, most of the prominent structures are related to these functions. Sjoberg noted that zones within the city are also differentiated on a much finer scale, by ties of occupation, ethnicity, and kinship.

Sjoberg's rationale (1960:99) for this model was that members of the elite, in striving to maintain their dominance in society, must be centrally located, near the resources that are the source of their power, in order to ensure ready access to their resources. Conversely, most of the poor are separated spatially from these resources, to which they are denied access.

Burgess's model (1925:50–56), designed for understanding Chicago's structure in the early 20th century, divides the city into a series of five concentric zones: an innermost downtown business district; an encircling transitional zone, characterized by business, light manufacturing, and slums; a working-class residential area; a middle-class residential area; and, finally, an outermost elite residential area, where the homes of the rich are located.

Burgess did not provide an explanatory framework or rationale for his form of urban structure. In a comparison of his model to Sjoberg's, however, the obvious difference is the physical separation of the different worlds of the commercial workplace and the home for the middle class, elite, and some of the working class, and the firm segregation of the residential communities by class. In addition, the spatial relationships among the residential communities are reversed. The very poor, who in Sjoberg's model are confined to the outer periphery, are in Burgess's model, located in the inner city, just outside the commercial district, so they can walk to work. The rich, instead of living at the core, now reside in suburbs on the outer periphery of the city, and the men in these neighborhoods ride to work.

Following Burgess's model, space has different meanings that are structured by class and gender. For the men of the elite and the middle class who can afford to commute, space is traversed by arteries passing between their workplaces in the core business district and their homes near the periphery of the city. Their wives' arenas are their relatively class-consistent residential communities. For the men and women of the poor, who by economic necessity continue to live within walking distance of their work, space is a barrier dividing their communities from the residential neighborhoods of the elite and the middle class.

Although we should remember that both of these models are only ideal constructs, they provide an approach to looking at changes in the use of space within the city. Sjoberg's model is most relevant to the beginning of the period under study, the late 18th century, whereas Burgess's model becomes relevant only toward the end of the period, in the 1830s.

Archaeologists and folklorists have traditionally used architectural style to examine cognitive systems or "mind sets," and to examine "changes in attitudes, values, and world views" (Deetz, 1977:93). More recently, they have also begun to look on architectural style from a somewhat different approach. H. Martin Wobst (1977), an archaeologist, suggested that "the outer surfaces of living structures" are among the few items of material culture that are "broadly visible and that enter a multitude of social contexts" (p. 329). Wobst looked on architectural style, as well as other kinds of style, as "that part of formal variability that can be related to . . . information exchange" (p. 321). It can be used both as an integrating device within social groups and to mark and maintain social boundaries between them (p. 321).[6]

William Askins (1985), also an archaeologist, used a similar approach to examine the use of architectural style in marking ethnic and class identity in Sandy Ground, a multiethnic 19th-century working-class community on Staten Island in New York. He found that Sandy Grounders used house styles in two different ways: to mark the boundaries between occupational or relative class positions and to mask ethnic diversity. In this study, I use an approach that is similar to those of Wobst and Askins to explore how architectural styles were used by early New Yorkers at various times, first to mask and then to mark the changing boundaries of function, class, and gender in the city.

Three years provide examples that illustrate the changes that took place in the structure and architecture of New York during the period under study. The year 1790 is a base year, showing the city before the separate spheres were created. The year 1810 illustrates the city after the separation of the home and the workplace had occurred among most of the city's wealthy merchants, the first group that made this change. Finally, the year 1840 shows both the changes in the city after the majority of middle-class proprietors had moved their homes away from their shops and the beginnings of the new social landscape of residential neighborhoods that were becoming segregated by class—presaging changes that became more fully developed in the later 19th century.

The first step in this part of the study involved using the data from the directory samples for 1790, 1810, and 1840 to map changes in the city's structure. For each of these years, the approximate locations of the city's separated workplaces and the residences of the working-class, middle-class, and wealthy New Yorkers in the samples were plotted on maps of the city. Then each of the maps was divided into quadrats, or squares, approximately $1/16$ of a square mile in size. The quadrats were then grouped into larger zones characterized by similar distributions of workplaces and kinds of residences. The quadrats and the zones are shown on the maps in Figures 3–1, 3–2, and 3–3.[7]

Contemporary prints, paintings, and drawings provide information on changes in the city's architectural styles. An overview of the changing face of the city is presented in the images reproduced in Plates 3 through 17.[8]

THE CITY, CIRCA 1790

In 1790, New York was just recovering from the effects of the British occupation. Its population of 33,000 extended north from the tip of the island for only about a mile on the western side of the island, to Chambers Street, and for a mile and a half on the east side, to Hester Street (see Plate 1 and Figure 3–1). New York was still a "walking city": It could be easily crossed on foot in half an hour.[9]

Scholars agree that, on the whole, the 1790 city showed relatively little functional differentiation in the use of land, particularly in comparison to the late-19th-century city. In fact, late-18th-century U.S. cities have been described as a "jumble" of occupations, classes, shops, and homes (see Plates 3 and 4). There was, however, a clear cluster of buildings whose occupants worked in commerce in the vicinity of the East River port, the hub of the city's economy. These structures housed the merchants' warehouses and combined residences and offices, as well as the integrated homes and shops of artisans working in the mercantile trades or in crafts that relied on the patronage of wealthy customers (such as that of Van Voorhis, the silversmith). This area corresponds to Sjoberg's core.[10]

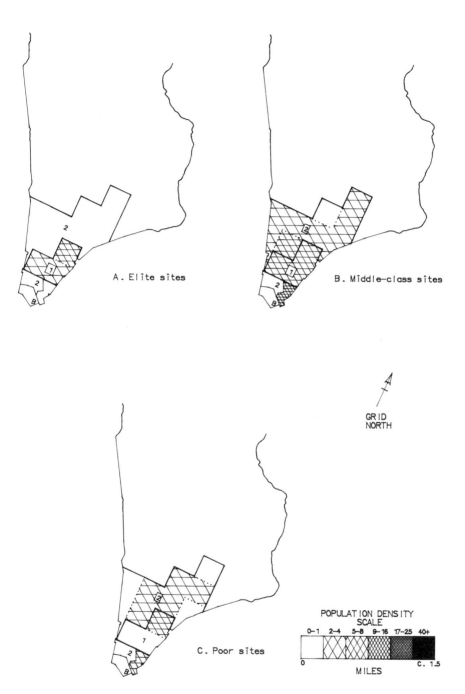

A. Elite sites

B. Middle-class sites

GRID
NORTH

C. Poor sites

POPULATION DENSITY
SCALE

0-1 2-4 5-8 9-16 17-25 40+

0   C. 1.5
MILES

Figure 3–1. The distributions of the homes and workplaces of the New Yorkers in the directory samples in the core (1) and periphery (2) of the 1790 city. *B* shows the location of the Battery.

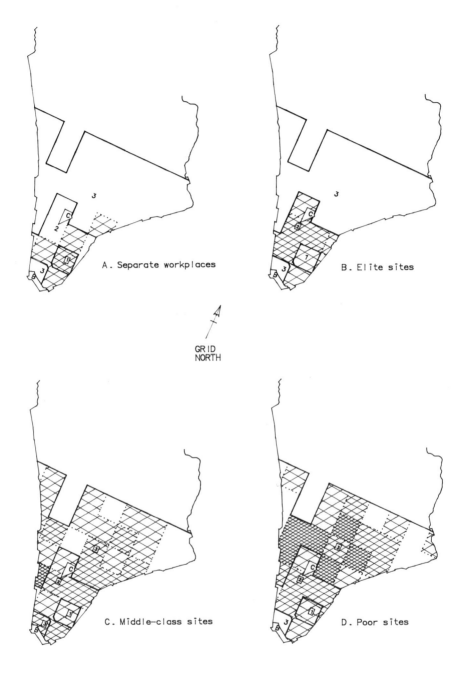

A. Separate workplaces

B. Elite sites

GRID
NORTH

C. Middle-class sites

D. Poor sites

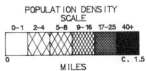

POPULATION DENSITY
SCALE

| 0–1 | 2–4 | 5–8 | 9–16 | 17–25 | 40+ |

0   C. 1.5

MILES

People working in trades and occupations that were not closely tied to the port or that did not depend on the patronage of the wealthy lived and worked to the west or north of the city's center, where property could be leased more cheaply (Blackmar, 1979:133). This area corresponded to Sjoberg's periphery.

Within both the core and the periphery, neighborhoods could be defined more finely on the basis of occupation and class. These neighborhoods were confined to streets or segments of streets. Boarding was important in providing living accommodation for many of the poor, thus tending to integrate spatially the city's poor and middle class. This does not mean that the people appeared homogeneous, however. Social distinctions were extremely clear-cut in the 18th-century integrated city because workers often wore distinctive clothing: No one could confuse the artisan in his leather apron for the cartman in his white frock, or either worker for the finely dressed merchant (see Plates 4 and 6; Abbott, 1974:41–43; Blackmar, 1979:134, 143).[11]

Figure 3–1 shows the distributions of the members of each of the three classes in the 1790 sample on maps of the city. The merchant elite were concentrated in the quadrats immediately adjacent to the East River port. Following Sjoberg, this area is identified as the core of the city, and the rest of the city is identified as the periphery. We cannot by any means characterize the core as an exclusive enclave of the rich, however. They made up only about a third of those living in the central area; most of those who lived there were members of the middle class, although some of the poor lived there, too (see Figure 3–1 and Appendix C). It is this mixture of classes in the core that contributes to the image of the city as a "jumble" of classes. The periphery was remarkable for the absence of the elite: They constituted fewer than 5% of those living here. The 1790 city thus conformed quite closely to Sjoberg's core–periphery model.

In 1790, the spatial integration of the three classes was expressed in the architectural styles used for the private buildings of the period: Structures that provided housing and workspace for most of the social groups in the city were of a similar size and scale. In addition, the prevalent simple Federal style used in building most of the structures, for rich and poor alike, expressed the egalitarian republican values of the time and, in effect, somewhat veiled the differences in wealth among the classes. This use of a common Federal style stressed the social integration of late-18th-century New York. The fabric of these similarly styled buildings did vary, however: Most of those built in the core tended to be of brick, whereas most of those at the periphery were made of wood (see Plates 3 and 4) (Bender, 1982a:22; Blackmar, 1989:48; Wright, 1981:26).

←_____

Figure 3–2. The distributions of the homes and separate workplaces of the New Yorkers in the directory samples in the business district (1), the residential core (2), and the periphery (3) of the 1810 city. B shows the location of the Battery and C indicates City Hall Park.

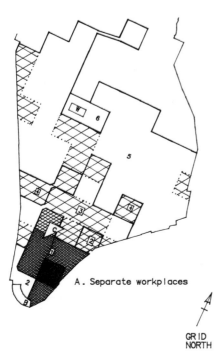

A. Separate workplaces

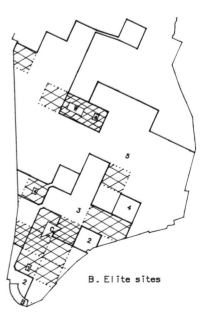

B. Elite sites

GRID
NORTH

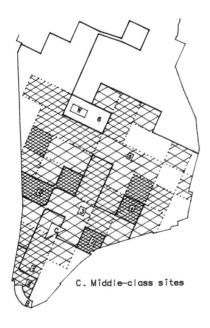

C. Middle—class sites

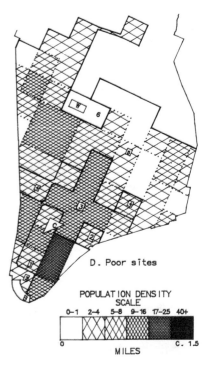

D. Poor sites

POPULATION DENSITY
SCALE

| 0–1 | 2–4 | 5–8 | 9–16 | 17–25 | 40+ |

0   C. 1.5

MILES

John Joseph Holland's 1797 watercolor drawing of Broad Street in the city's central area provides a striking view of the Federal city (reproduced here as Plate 3). In this picture, the only exceptions to the two- and three-and-a-half story, relatively uniform Federal houses on either side of Broad Street are the older structures built in the Dutch style, with their stepped gables facing the street. Only a few of these old houses survived the fires that ravaged the city in 1776 and 1778 during the British occupation. The Van Voorhis household apparently lived in a similar Dutch-style house when they were on Hanover Square in the 1780s.

The larger buildings that stood out against the background of the relatively uniform Federal houses of the 1790 city also concretized the values of the new republic and the community rather than those of the economy. They were built in a grander Federal style. These buildings, like those of Sjoberg's preindustrial city, consisted of governmental and religious structures (like Federal Hall and the churches shown in Holland's view of Broad Street in Plate 3), and they tended to be located in the central part of the city. Prominent buildings devoted to commerce only began to appear in the 1790s (like the Tontine Coffee House, shown in Plate 4). In fact, the importance of the city's commerce was further understated by the lack of large shop windows: Merchants' and shopkeepers' wares were revealed only when one entered their premises.[12]

The spires and cupolas of the 1790 city's skyline belonged to its approximately 20 churches and synagogues (representing 10 denominations) and to Federal Hall. Both Federal Hall and 11 of the 20 religious structures serving the whole city were located in the three quadrats identified as the core of the city.[13]

The religious and governmental functions of these grander buildings emphasized the importance of the values associated with the church and the state (the sources of the legitimacy of the elite) and deemphasized the importance of wealth (the actual source of their power). Economic activities were not yet regarded as fully legitimate in the 1790 city.

THE CITY CIRCA 1810

By 1810, the structure of settlement in New York had begun to change. The city, whose population had almost tripled, to 96,000, in 20 years,[14] had grown farther to the north, to what is now Broome Street in the eastern and

---

Figure 3–3. The distributions of the homes and separate workplaces of the New Yorkers in the directory samples in the 1840 city: (1) the business district; (2) and (4), the middle-class zones; (3) the working-class zone; (5) the periphery; and (6) the suburb. *B* shows the location of the Battery, *C* indicates City Hall Park, and *W,* Washington Square Park.

central parts of the island, and to Leonard Street on its west side (Figure 3–2). As discussed in Chapter 2, by this time most of the city's wealthy inhabitants who had formerly lived in homes and workplaces in the core or central area of the city had moved their offices out of their homes and into a new form of commercial structure, the countinghouse, where their goods were also stored.

Figure 3–2 shows the locations of the new, separate workplaces and the residences of the people in the samples across the 1810 city. Although the wealthy continued to cluster their homes in the southern part of the city, the structure of this area had changed: The separation of the home and workplace was expressed spatially, and Sjoberg's core–periphery model no longer described the city. It was now necessary to add an innermost third zone, similar to Burgess's business district, where most of the buildings were separate workplaces (see Appendix C). The single quadrat that made up this zone was located in the Wall Street area, adjacent to the East River port (see Figure 3–2A).

Most of the homes of the city's wealthy families were located in the quadrats that made up what was for them a residential neighborhood arranged around the business district (see Figure 3–2B). Their homes were concentrated to the south (on the Battery, on Whitehall, and Pearl and Beaver Streets), to the west (on Broadway [see Plate 6] and some of the streets that entered Broadway from the west, like Park Place), and to the north of the business district (on Cherry, Roosevelt [where Dr. Robson started his practice in this year], Oak, Madison, Oliver, and Harman Streets). The men of this group were still able to walk to their work in the business district and to come home for their dinners at midday.[15]

Like the 1790 core, this area that served as a residential neighborhood for the wealthy was not an exclusive enclave for the rich; their homes made up only a quarter of those there (see Figure 3–2 and Appendix C). The image of the "jumble" of classes and occupations still applied to this neighborhood. The proportions of the poor and middle class in this area were changing, however; whereas in 1790 there were more middle-class than poor people living in the core, in 1810 the middle class and the poor were equally represented there. The poor were increasing and the middle class were decreasing in the area.

The city's periphery in 1810 was similar to that of the 1790 city and was still remarkable for the absence of the elite (see Figure 3–2B). However, the proportions of the poor and middle class in this outer area were changing, too; whereas in 1790 there were more middle-class householders in this area, by 1810 these proportions had reversed, and the poor were beginning to predominate on the periphery as well as in the core of the city.

The area with the heaviest concentration of middle-class residents was located to the southwest of City Hall Park, particularly in the vicinity of Greenwich Street (see Figure 3–2C and Plate 5). The area with the heaviest density of poorer residents was located farther out on the periphery, to the north of the core and middle-class neighborhoods (see Figure 3–2D). Many of the homes of the poor were adjacent to the low and swampy areas of the Collect Pond, but well within walking distance of their workplaces in the core of the city. For all three classes, New York was still a "walking city."

These changes were not yet clearly expressed in the architecture of the city, however. Both domestic and commercial private structures were still small in scale and in a uniform Federal style. The new countinghouses in the commercial core of the city had usually simply been converted from older homes and workplaces (see Plate 9). These similarities in style veiled the developing structural opposition between the worlds of the marketplace and the home, and the relative uniformity of the buildings continued to obscure the growing differences of wealth in the city (Lockwood, 1976:16).

Monumental buildings continued to be set off from the Federal architectural background. The new City Hall, completed in 1812, was built in City Hall Park in the elite residential area of the city (see Plate 6). In addition to the religious and governmental structures that continued to dominate the skyline, the city's first monumental building devoted to commerce—the Tontine Coffee House—was built in the early 1790s in the heart of what was becoming the business district, at the corner of Wall and Water Streets (see Plate 4). It housed the Stock Exchange and several insurance offices as well. The monumental scale of this structure shows that economic activities were achieving a certain legitimacy in their own right.

Another change in the city's skyline resulted from a new way of docking ships in the harbor. Until the 1790s, ships were anchored out in the East River away from shore, and smaller boats, called *lighters*, were used to load and unload them. In the 1790s, this practice changed, and the ships began to be docked along the shore, with their bowsprits extended over South Street (see Plate 7). The effect of the proximity of the ships to each other was repeatedly referred to as the "forest of masts" that greeted visitors arriving in New York until the middle of the century. A visitor to the city in 1807 noted that these "tall masts mingled with the buildings, and together with the spires and cupolas of the churches, gave the city an appearance of magnificence" (Still, 1956:69, quoting John Lambert). The "forest of masts" also, coincidentally, emphasized the growing importance of commercial life in the city.[16]

The number of churches and synagogues in the city had doubled to 40 since 1790. Their locations show the changing character of the commercial and residential areas in the city as well as the city's growth. The business district was not chosen as the site for the construction of any new churches during this period; 22 churches were located in the central residential area, while 18 were situated in the outer area of the city (including 14 on the periphery, 2 in Greenwich Village, and 1 in Bouwerie Village).[17] In addition to being the site of most of the separate workplaces, the business district was also remarkable for its relative dearth of churches, those landmarks expressing the moral values of home life.

THE CITY CIRCA 1840

By 1840, the city had dramatically changed. In the 30 years since 1810, its population had more than tripled, from 96,000 to over 312,000 (Rosenwaike, 1972). In addition, as discussed in Chapter 2, most of the city's middle-class proprietors, who had formerly lived in combined homes and workplaces throughout the city, had moved their homes away from their shops. Employers also no longer regularly provided living accommodation for their employees. All of these factors dramatically increased the demand for space in the city and consequently the value of the city's real estate. The value of land in one of the city's wards had increased by more than 700% between 1789 and as early as 1815 (Willis, 1967:113). By 1840, the city's perimeter had moved north to 14th Street, engulfing what had been the separate village of Greenwich in the late 1820s (see Plates 2 and 17 and Figure 3–3; Lockwood, 1976:6).

The city's growth was facilitated by the Commissioners' Plan of 1811, which laid out most of Manhattan Island in the grid pattern of rectangular blocks that could be easily divided into the individual building lots that we know today. These lots, and even whole blocks, became abstract units that were bought and sold. Speculators bought parcels of land on the outskirts of the city and later either resold them for development, when the growing city had engulfed them and their value had greatly increased, or developed them themselves. In addition, much of the oldest part of the city had to be rebuilt: In 1835, approximately 700 buildings in the commercial heart of the city were destroyed in the Great Fire (see Plate 9; Lockwood, 1976:27; Mumford, 1961).

Figure 3–3 shows the 1840 locations of the homes of the city's residents in the samples and their separate workplaces. Several of the areas that were just beginning to be visible in the 1810 city had become much more developed by 1840, and there were some new areas as well. The zones of the 1840 city were unique because of their relative exclusiveness: More than half of the properties in the business district were devoted exclusively to business, and more than half of the residents of each of the five other zones belonged to one particular class (see Figure 3–3 and Appendix C).

The business district (Zone 1 on Figure 3–3) had grown since 1810, and there were now seven quadrats with heavy concentrations of separate workplaces (see Figure 3–3A). Most of the buildings here were devoted solely to work (see Appendix C). The composition of the people who lived in the area had changed, too; most of those who lived there now were poor. Their homes clustered in the eastern part of the area, near the river, whereas those of the middle class and the elite that still remained here were along its western edge. Except for the high concentration of poor living there, the area was similar to Burgess's business district.

The image of the "jumble" of different kinds of people no longer applied to the central part of the city. For the most part, only the men and women of the poor still both lived and worked in the area, and they were almost its sole occupants at night. Most middle-class and wealthy men were there only in the daytime and went home to their residential neighborhoods at night. Middle-class and wealthy women went to the shops on lower Broadway but rarely went into the heart of the business district at all; they did not feel comfortable there. In fact, as early as 1819, Lewis Pintard (quoted in Bender, 1982b:34), who lived with his family on Wall Street above the insurance company where he worked, described his womenfolk as "nearly prisoners during the hours of business." By the early 1830s, the author of a series of views of the city had to explain the lack of women on the city's commercial streets to "distant readers" by noting that women rarely went there (see Plate 8; Fay 1832:46; also quoted in Kouwenhoven, 1972:138). On 31 August 1839, *The Mirror* asked:

> Did you ever see a female in Wall-street, dear reader? . . . The sight of a female in that isolated quarter is so extraordinary, that, the moment a petticoat appears, the groups of brokers, intent on calculating the value of stocks, break suddenly off, and gaze at the phenomenon.

For most members of the middle class and the elite, the business district had become man's sphere (see Plate 15).

The homes of the middle class predominated in two areas in the city (Zones 2 and 4 in Figure 3–3C; see Appendix C). The first consisted of three discontinuous areas encircling the business district (Zone 2), and the second (Zone 4) was in two areas to the northwest and the northeast of the working-class zone. This latter zone corresponded to Burgess's middle-class residential area, located beyond his working-class zone. Only about a quarter of the middle class lived in these relatively class-exclusive zones, however (see Appendix C). These middle-class residential neighborhoods were relatively secluded: Most of them were located near the water's edge, and for the most part, they were out of the way of the members of the working class, who were still walking to and from work.

The old working-class area near the filled Collect Pond was now known as the Five Points district, the most notorious slum in the city (part of Zone 3; see Figure 3–3D and Plate 14). In addition, the working-class zone had grown much farther to the south. It now extended down into the business district and along the Hudson River. There was still an elite presence in this zone, to the southwest and the east of City Hall Park (see Figure 3–3B). However, these areas were being flooded by the poor (see Figure 3–3D). This district roughly corresponded to Burgess's transitional area (characterized by slum housing and light industry) and working-class residential zone.

The proportions of the homes of the members of the three classes on the periphery (Zone 5; see Plate 10) remained much as they had been in 1810. Most of those who lived there were poor and middle class (see Figure 3–3). Again, few of these homes were occupied by the elite.

The new "suburban" area (Zone 6), located near the northern edge of the city, was unique in that it was the first neighborhood that could be described as an elite residential enclave. This zone included Washington Square (where the Robsons moved) and the streets to its east that ran perpendicular to Broadway: Bond Street, Fourth Street, Bleecker Street, and Great Jones Street (see Plates 2, 11, 12, and 13 and Figure 3–3B).

Philip Hone, former mayor of the city, remarked on his move to the new suburb in an 1837 entry in his diary. His old elite neighborhood on lower Broadway opposite City Hall Park (see Plate 6) was becoming enveloped by the business district:

> [A]ll the dwelling houses are to be converted into stores. We are tempted with prices so exorbitantly high that none can resist, and the old down-town burgomasters, who have fixed to one spot all their lives, will be seen during the next summer in flocks, marching reluctantly north to pitch their tents in places which, in their time, were orchards, cornfields, or morasses a pretty smart distance from town, and a journey to which was formerly an affair of some moment, and required preparation before hand, but which constitute at this time the most fashionable quarter of New York. (Quoted in Nevins, 1927:202)

Most of the middle-class and elite men who lived too far away to walk conveniently to work (like the Robsons' son-in-law, Francis P. Sage) commut-ed on the omnibuses, which became the common form of transportation within the city in the early 1830s. The movement of the commuters and the omnibuses and stages that carried them to and from work added greatly to the "bustle" of traffic along the city's avenues (compare Plates 6 and 16, which show the same stretch of Broadway c. 1820 and in the 1840s). The omnibuses supplemented the stages that had serviced several routes on the island, con-necting lower Manhattan to Greenwich, Manhattanville, and the shipyards in the Dry Dock area on the Lower East Side, as well as points in between. In the early 1830s, the term *omnibus* came into general use; the form of these vehicles became standardized and differentiated from that of the stages, which were designed to cover longer distances. These new vehicles could carry 12 seated passengers and had standing room as well. The number of buses had been increased to 80 by 1833 and to 108 by 1837 in order to serve the increasing numbers of commuters in the city. Their fares, however, remained relatively high at 12½ cents for a one-way local trip within the city, with a reduction to 8 cents if 12 or 16 tickets were purchased at once. The stage fares to the outlying communities of Manhattanville, Harlem, and Yorkville were higher. The high fares precluded the possibility of public transportation for the poor; daily wages for a common laborer of the period were only a dollar, and even those for a skilled craftsman were rarely more than two. The poor *had* to live close to their workplaces.[18]

Some members of the middle class and the elite commuted to and from the city of Brooklyn. They traveled by ferry from the foot of Fulton Street in lower Manhattan to Fulton Street in Brooklyn.

A definite change had occurred in the architecture of the city by 1840. The Federal style of the earlier buildings that underscored the city's republican values had begun to give way to the Greek Revival style in the late 1820s. New Yorkers used different forms of the Greek Revival style to make clear statements about a building's residential or commercial function and, in residential structures, about the class of the occupants.

Greek Revival commercial structures were often built with a granite-pillared lower façade surmounted by brick upper stories (see Plates 8 and 16). Countinghouses and shops built in this style, though still small in scale, looked quite grand, the whole front of the building's first floor consisting of a series of widely spaced columns separated by the doorway and large windows displaying the array of goods available inside. The shop signs adorning these structures, advertising the name of the business and the nature of the goods sold, had become much larger and more obtrusive by this time. These structures were a far cry from the plain façades of the earlier Federal buildings; they were unequivocally commercial (Rosebrock, 1975:25, 35–36).

Most of the city's Greek Revival residential structures looked quite different from their commercial counterparts (compare Plate 11 with Plates 15 and 16). Their façades included short staircases or stoops that led up to the front door, which was framed by white columns and topped by a pediment. The doorway and window trim on Federal residential buildings had been relatively modest, whether the trim was executed in cheaper brownstone or more expensive marble or granite (see Plates 3, 4, 6, and 9). On the Greek Revival house, however, both the proportions of the structure and the fabric and elaboration of the decoration used in the windows and doorways, in the railings lining the stoops, and in the fences setting off the small yard or areaway in front of the house allowed for the display of a range of wealth and elegance that had not been common in Federal houses. The variety in the degree of detail used in these elements made statements about class (as opposed to egalitarian values) more obvious than they had been before. This style was first adopted by the rich in New York and was particularly prominent in the Washington Square area, the isolated elite enclave that was developed at the time when this style was first introduced (see Plates 11, 12, and 13).[19]

This innovation and its implications for egalitarianism did not go unnoticed by travelers to New York and other American cities. Chevalier (1836/1967:290) noted it in the 1830s: "The style of the new houses in Chestnut Street, Philadelphia, with their first story of white marble, is a blow at equality. The same innovation is creeping in in New York."

In addition, these houses were often built in "rows," making up a street front of uniform structures designed as a visual whole (see Plates 11 and 12). The uniformity of these row houses reinforced the idea of class-segregated residential areas. Their single line of flat roofs (some of which actually sloped down toward the back of the buildings) changed the city's skyline and replaced the earlier erratic line of pitched roofs with dormer windows of the Federal city. They were in direct visual contrast to the older street fronts made up of Federal houses of varying heights (see Plates 3 and 4; Lockwood, 1972:60, 62, 79).

Homes built for the poor were quite different from those of the middle class and the elite (see Plate 14). Landlords converted old Federal single-family homes for multiple occupancy by installing interior walls to divide the space into apartments. They also introduced wooden and brick tenements in the 1830s. These were the first buildings in New York designed specifically for multifamily occupancy (Ernst, 1949:48).

The monumental structures devoted to government and commerce were built in a contrasting stone-fronted, templelike version of the Greek Revival style. The banks and insurance companies formerly housed in adapted Federal houses on Wall Street in the business district were rebuilt in this style after the Great Fire in 1835 (compare Plates 9 and 15). Three unusually large structures were built in this style before 1840: the new Customs House; the Merchants' Exchange, which housed the Stock Exchange and was first built in the 1820s (see Plate 9) and rebuilt after the fire; and Astor House on Broadway (see Plate 16), which was the city's largest and most fashionable hotel from the time it was built in the mid-1830s until mid-century. Only one residential complex was built in this style, however: Colonnade Row, on Lafayette Place near Washington Square (see Plate 12). This row contained the mansions of some of the city's wealthiest families, including the Astors, the Vanderbilts, and the Delanos (Lockwood, 1976:28, 149–150).

By 1840, the city's churches were closely associated with the morality of home life and woman's sphere. Earlier, around 1830, when the English traveler Frances Trollope (1839/1984) visited the city, she remarked on the sexual composition of its congregations during the Second Great Awakening. The congregations appeared, she said, "during the time of service, like beds of tulips, so gay, so bright, so beautiful . . . the long rows of French bonnets and pretty faces; rows but rarely broken by the unribboned heads of the male population; the proportion [in New York] is about the same as I have remarked elsewhere" in America (p. 302). The middle-class men of the city, it seems, spent the day of rest differently and went instead to a pleasure ground in Hoboken, New Jersey, which could be reached easily by ferry.

This redefinition of religion as part of woman's sphere was soon expressed in the architectural style of the city's churches. By the 1840s, they were no longer being built in the same style as the governmental and commercial buildings of man's sphere. Rather, they were built in their own distinctive Gothic Revival style (see Plates 10 and 15).[20]

There were now almost 120 churches and synagogues in the city, approximately three times as many as there had been in 1810. Their spatial distribution had changed as well. In 1810, more than 20 of the city's churches were located in what became in 1840 the city's business district. In 1840, only 11 of them were still located downtown. Almost all of the churches that appeared in the intervening 30 years were built in the city's new residential areas. Furthermore, approximately 18 churches had moved north from their downtown sites, following their congregations as they moved uptown.[21]

Thus, architectural style was used in new ways to define the social boundaries of the 1840 city. There was a clear difference in the styles used for commercial and residential neighborhoods—man's and woman's spheres— and distinctions began to appear that served to segregate the residential areas by class as well. Monumental buildings were now built specifically to serve commercial functions in a style that was strikingly similar to that used for government buildings, suggesting that economic activities had achieved a new legitimacy in the city. In addition, governmental and religious structures were now executed in different styles, indicating a new dichotomy between the government and religion. These patterns were expressed spatially as well. Whether built on a monumental or a small scale, most of the government and commercial structures were confined to the business district: man's sphere. The new Greek Revival homes expressed class identity in the elaboration of their detail as the city was becoming segregated by class. They and the Gothic Revival churches were confined to the city's residential neighborhoods: woman's sphere for the elite and the middle class.

CONCLUSION

Between the 1790s and the 1840s, then, the social landscape of New York City dramatically changed. For middle-class and wealthy families, the landscape served first to veil and then to mark some of the cultural differences that were arising with the structural transformation in gender and class relations that occurred during this half century.

The 1790 city was relatively integrated, with its arenas of the workplace and home spatially coterminous for most of the city's population. Although the wealthy confined themselves to the core of the city, they lived and worked alongside the middle class and the poor.

By the 1840s, much of this had changed. Middle-class and wealthy families had moved their homes away from the old core, which was now a commercial district and, for the middle class and the wealthy, man's sphere. The new homes were in residential neighborhoods, which were becoming woman's sphere. Except for the presence of domestic servants, these neighborhoods were becoming relatively class-exclusive.

The wealthy and the middle class were removing their family life from what they perceived as threatening developments in the lower city. During this period, as the city became swamped with the poor, street riots became much more frequent than they had been before. At the turn of the century, Elizabeth Bleecker, a broker's daughter, recorded in her diary the occurrence of several gatherings of "the mob."[22] But the situation got worse. In a four-year period in the 1820s, the number of street riots increased almost threefold over the number that had occurred over a four-year period a decade earlier (Gilje, 1987:238–241).

There was also the serious problem of health. The epidemics of yellow fever that scourged the city during the warmer months at the turn of the 19th century were reported first in the low-lying, land-filled areas of the East River port. In moving their families away from the core, the wealthy and the middle class were moving them to higher, well-drained, and therefore more healthy ground to the north and the west. The last yellow fever epidemic, in 1822, was unusual in that it first appeared in the middle-class and wealthy neighborhoods on the west side of the island, rather than in the poorer areas on the east side. This occurrence may well have influenced the middle class and the wealthy in deciding to move their homes permanently to the healthy areas of Greenwich and Bouwerie villages, where many had earlier fled during the epidemic months to escape the fever.[23]

Most of the poor and the working class, however, had to stay close to the lower city. For many of them, home and work life remained relatively integrated. Some of them—both men and women—worked at home as part of the outwork system. Their children also often continued to work, forming a pool of unskilled child labor.

Patterns of motion within the city had changed as well. In the early 19th century, after most of the wealthy merchants had moved their homes away from their countinghouses, they continued to walk to work in the business district. By 1840, many of them and some of the middle class had moved their homes farther away to the edge of the city. As in Friederich Engels's Manchester (1845/1958), these men commuted to and from work on omnibuses that passed through working-class neighborhoods on shop-lined arteries like Broadway and the Bowery so that they never saw the hearts of these slums at all. Middle-class and wealthy wives spent most of their lives in residential neighborhoods that, with the exception of their household help, were becoming segregated by class. Confining their activities to their homes and much of their shopping to their neighborhood retail stores, for them their neighborhood had replaced the "walking city."

Some of the middle class and most of the poor lived in different areas close to the city's business district and walked to work. However, in the course of the day, the members of neither of these groups had occasion to see either each other's residential neighborhood or the new enclave of the rich, with its elegant structures on the edge of the city. And they had little idea of the changes that were going on inside each other's homes.

NOTES

1. The information on the Van Voorhis family's residence pattern is drawn from the city directories (Duncan, 1791–1795; Franks, 1787, 1851/1786; Hodge, Allen, and Campbell, 1789–1790; Longworth, 1797–1799; D. Longworth, 1800–1803; Low, 1796) and contemporary maps of the city; the archaeological information is from the 75 Wall Street Collection at the South Street Seaport Museum.

2. The locational information on the Bownes is from the city directories for the appropriate years.

3. The locational information on the Robsons is from the city directories for the appropriate years; the tax assessment information is from the City of New York, Tax Assessment Records, 1828—Fourth Ward, and 1829—Seventh Ward; Blackmar (1989:102) mentioned the prominence of East Broadway.

4. This approach is adapted from Harvey (1973), Berry (1982), and Blackmar (1979, 1989).

5. Ottensmann (1975:9–13) also used Sjoberg's model for examining American cities before 1820.

6. Glassie (1975) and Deetz (1977) have provided good examples of cognitive studies. Conkey (1978) used a similar approach.

7. The sampling method is described in Appendix A. I used base maps adapted from Hodge, Allen, and Campbell (1789) for the 1790 sample, from David Longworth (1808) for the 1810 sample, and from J. C. Smith (1839) for the 1840 sample. Except in those cases where a specific block location for a house address was listed in the directories or tax records, the locations were plotted in the order of house number by street and ward for the 1790 and 1810 samples. For the 1840 sample, I used a directory feature, the "Runner's Vade Mecum," which lists the block locations of the house numbers on each of the city's streets.

The size of the quadrat, or square, is a compromise; it encompasses the smallest area that can be meaningfully characterized, given the small size of the sample. The use of quadrats and the small sample size also precluded the possibility of identifying smaller neighborhoods, which were often confined to relatively short segments of streets that might be only a block or two in length. The distributions of the homes and workplaces in the samples are presented by zone and year in tabular form in Appendix C. Chi-square tests (Siegel, 1956) were run on the data presented in these tables. Their values, which are listed in Appendix C, show that the distributions of the residences of the members of the three classes and of the city's workplaces by zone were significantly different from each other at the .01 level for each of the years.

8. Lockwood (1972, 1976) provided a particularly good discussion of New York's architecture; many of the graphic sources are reproduced in Kouwenhoven (1972) and Stokes (1915–1928).
9. Rosenwaike (1972) provided information on New York City's population.
10. Warner (1968:50) wrote about the "jumble" of people in the late-18th-century city; Abbott (1974), Bender (1982a:22), and Blackmar (1979:133; 1989) have all written about the concentration of commercial activities at the city's core. I should point out that one historian, Abbott (1974), took issue with the application of Sjoberg's model to early American cities. His primary objection was that the model was initially designed for the study of early cities that were dominated by a closed religious or political elite, whereas the power of the elite in the early U.S. city was based on merchant capitalism. Abbott (1974:37–38) suggested that any resemblance between the structure of Sjoberg's cities (which Sjoberg described as "premodern" or "precommercial" rather than preindustrial) and the early U.S. cities is merely coincidental. This seems to be an extreme position, especially as trade has been an important factor in the development of most cities.
11. Lofland (1973) noted the importance of ordered personal appearance in the preindustrial city, as opposed to the importance of ordered space in the modern city.
12. Noted by Wansey (1796/1969:74), who visited the city in 1794.
13. The numbers and the locations of the city's churches and synagogues are derived from Stokes (1915–1928, III:928–937).
14. Rosenwaike (1972) provided the information on the city's population.
15. Blumin (1976:115) noted this pattern of "moderate" separation of the domestic and economic spheres in early-19th-century Kingston, New York.
16. Both Strickland (1971:43), who visited New York in the 1790s, and Dickens (1842/1957:79), who visited it a half century later, used this image.
17. The data on the churches and synagogues are derived from Stokes (1915–1928, III: 928–937).
18. Both Haswell (1896:231) and Greene (1837:260) provided accounts of transportation in the early 19th century; Taylor (1966) provided the classic modern discussion of public transportation in America's cities.
19. Lockwood (1972:8) described the detail on Greek Revival houses; Wright (1981:36) noted the class ramifications of these differences in architectural detail in the 1830s house.
20. Landau (1982:13) noted the preference for the Gothic Revival style for the city's churches in the 1840s.

21. The information on the churches is derived from Stokes (1915–1928, III: 928–937) and Mayer (1844).
22. Entries for 28 February, 16–18 July, 14 September, and 28 October 1799, and 30 October 1802 in Bleecker's diary provide examples.
23. Duffy (1968) provided the classic work on issues of public health in New York; Griscom (1858) discussed the city's yellow fever epidemics in particular.

Plates: The Changing Face of the City

Plate 1. Map of New York, as surveyed in 1782 and drawn in 1785 by John Hills; lithograph by G. Hayward for *Valentine's Manual* (1857). The city extended northward to Hester Street on the east side of the island; the west side had not yet been developed farther north than Chambers Street. (Map Division, The New York Public Library, Astor, Lenox, and Tilden Foundations.)

Plate 2. Map of New York, c. 1840, published by the Society for the Diffusion of Useful Knowledge (1840). The city had grown north to around 23rd Street on the west side and 12th Street on the east side. (Map Division, The New York Public Library, Astor, Lenox, and Tilden Foundations.)

Plate 3. Broad Street, looking north to Wall Street and City Hall, 1797; watercolor by John Joseph Holland. Note the jumble of two-and-a-half- and three-and-a-half-story Federal buildings, as well as the two old Dutch houses on the right, built with their stepped gables facing the street. The Van Voorhis family lived and worked in a similar old Dutch house on Hanover Square in the 1780s. On the left side of Broad Street, a coachmaker, a cooper, a schoolmistress, and a tavern keeper lived and worked alongside a broker, a merchant, and a "gentleman" on this main street in the core of the 1790 city (Stokes, 1915, I: 446–447). The large building at the head of Broad Street is the old Federal Building, which in 1790 housed the City Hall. (I. N. Phelps Stokes Collection, Miriam and Ira D. Wallach Division of Art, Prints and Photographs, The New York Public Library, Astor, Lenox, and Tilden Foundations.)

Plate 4. The intersection of Wall and Water Streets in the core of the city, looking northeast, c. 1797; oil painting by Francis Guy. The large building to the left is the Tontine Coffee House, a meeting place for merchants, which also housed the Stock Exchange. This structure was built in 1792–1793 and was one of the city's first monumental buildings devoted to commerce. The building on the far right is the Merchants' Coffee House, and the wooden building in the center of the picture housed a shop where furniture and trunks were sold (Stokes, 1915, I: 453). Note the physical proximity of the houses in different architectural styles and of the members of the city's various classes, with the black and white laborers in the foreground packing casks and barrels for the ships whose masts are visible in the Coffee House Slip at the foot of Wall Street, a block to the east, and the men and women of the middle and merchant classes on the sidewalks and the balcony of the Tontine Coffee House. (Courtesy of The New-York Historical Society, New York, NY.)

Plate 5. Corner of Greenwich Street, near the Hudson River, c. 1810; watercolor and pencil drawing by the Baroness Hyde de Neuville. These wooden houses were typical of respectable middle-class neighborhoods on the city's periphery during the first decades of the 19th century. (I. N. Phelps Stokes Collection, Miriam and Ira D. Wallach Division of Art, Prints and Photographs, The New York Public Library, Astor, Lenox, and Tilden Foundations.)

Plate 6. The intersection of Broadway and Chatham Street (now Park Row) with the recently completed City Hall on the right, c. 1819; watercolor by the Swedish Baron Axel Leonhard Klinckowstrom. The column to the left belongs to Episcopal St. Paul's Chapel. Many of the city's wealthiest merchants (including John Jacob Astor and, later, the diarist Philip Hone) lived on these Broadway blocks facing City Hall Park. Klinckowstrom set out to show "all the vehicles" common in the city, from the pushcart used by the porter to move small loads, and the horse and cart led by the cartman in his white frock, to the elegant coach. Note the absence of any form of public transportation like stages or omnibuses. For most of its residents, New York was definitely a "walking city." (Museum of the City of New York, bequest of J. Insley Blain.)

Plate 7. South Street, looking south from Maiden Lane, 1828; watercolor by William Bennett. South Street on the East River was at the heart of the city's commercial district for much of the 19th century. The ships moored perpendicularly to South Street with their bowsprits extending over the street; their masts formed the image of the "forest of masts" that greeted travelers arriving in New York harbor through the middle of the century. (Museum of the City of New York.)

Plate 8. Pearl Street House & Ohio Hotel, near Hanover Square, c. 1831; engraving by M. Osborne. Theodore Fay (1832), who wrote the commentary for the series of views of New York that included this image, felt the need to explain the absence of women in this picture: "It will be observed, that the specimens of humanity given in this plate are . . . entirely of the masculine gender. This must be explained to distant readers as resulting from the fact that amid the business sections of this once quiet town . . . the fairer part of creation rarely, if ever, venture. We should as soon expect to see a Liverpool packet steering her course under . . . sail up through Broadway, as to detect a woman in this part of Pearl-Street, or in Wall-Street, or south [sic], or thereabouts" (p. 46). It was not always so, however: Until around 1820, the Bownes were among the families that lived and worked on Pearl Street, in one of the late Federal houses shown here in the distance on the far left of the block. (Courtesy of The New-York Historical Society, New York, NY.)

Plate 9. The Great Fire of the City of New-York, 16 December 1835; lithograph drawn by Alfred Hoffy, printed by J. T. Bowen, and published by H. R. Robinson in 1836. The Great Fire destroyed more than 700 buildings in lower Manhattan's commercial district. When this part of the city was rebuilt after the fire, it had a very different look (compare with Plate 15). This view shows the first Merchants' Exchange on Wall Street, which had been built in 1825–1827; the businesses on either side of it (the offices of insurance companies like the Fulton Fire Insurance Company and newspapers like the New York American) were housed in buildings that had been converted from the combined homes and workplaces of an earlier era. (Museum of the City of New York, J. Clarence Davies Collection.)

Plate 10. Night-Fall, St. Thomas Church, c. 1835; watercolor by George Harvey. This Episcopal church was located at the corner of Houston Street and Broadway, to the south of the exclusive residential enclave that was developing in the Washington Square area. Note the mixture of different kinds of people and the wood-frame houses that give the general feeling of a country town that persisted on this part of the city's periphery. St. Thomas's, consecrated in 1826, was a good example of an early Gothic Revival church. (Museum of the City of New York, bequest of Mrs. J. Inslay Blair.)

Plate 11. Leroy Place, located on Bleecker Street between Mercer and Greene Streets, c. 1831; engraving by Alexander L. Dick from a drawing by Alexander J. Davis, from Fay's Views in New-York and Its Environs (1831–1834). This street front of residences two blocks south of Washington

Square was designed as a visual whole for the city's elite in 1827. (Courtesy of The New-York Historical Society, New York, NY.)

Plate 12. La Grange Terrace–Lafayette Place, c. 1831; engraved by Alexander L. Dick, from a drawing by J. H. Davis, in Fay's *Views in New-York and Its Environs* (1831–1834). This row of nine townhouses in the city's elite suburb included the most massive and monumental residential structures of the early-19th-century city; they were the only residential buildings that resembled the templelike Greek Revival commercial structures of Wall Street (see Plate 15). Some of the city's wealthiest families lived here, including the John Jacob Astors, who had earlier lived on lower Broadway (see Plate 6). The row was named after La Grange, the French home of the Marquis de Lafayette, who was extremely popular when he revisited New York in 1824. Part of the row, now called Colonnade Row, still stands today. (Courtesy of The New-York Historical Society, New York, NY.)

Plate 13. The Mount Washington Collegiate Institute, showing the southwest corner of Washington Square, looking toward the southeast, c. 1849; engraving by James Smillie. The old Potter's Field (where the poor who died during the city's yellow fever epidemics were buried) was converted first to a parade ground and later to Washington Square Park. It became the focus for the development of expensive homes for the city's wealthy residents in the second quarter of the 19th century. In 1841, the Robsons moved into one of the late Federal houses with only their roofs, chimneys, and dormer windows visible above the trees to the right of the park. (Courtesy of The New-York Historical Society, New York, NY.)

Plate 14. The Five Points, c. 1827; lithograph from *Valentine's Manual* (1855). This neighborhood (named after the intersection of Orange, Cross, and Anthony Streets in the Sixth Ward, shown here) was the city's most notorious slum in the 19th century. The image shows how the poor were beginning to be viewed by some members of the city's middle class in the early 19th century. (Courtesy of The New-York Historical Society, New York, NY.)

Plate 15. Wall Street, 1850; watercolor by August Köllner. This view shows Wall Street looking west from William Street toward Trinity Church at Broadway. The imposing templelike Greek Revival buildings on the right side of the street are those that replaced the converted Federal residences that housed the city's banks and insurance companies before the Great Fire in 1835 (compare with Plate 9). Note that most of the people shown in this image (which was drawn "from nature"—see the note at the lower left-hand corner) are men. This view was later redrafted for a lithograph that was published by Goupil and Co.; the lithograph is quite different from the watercolor shown here in that the figures of about a dozen women have been added to the view. The Gothic Revival Trinity Church shown here is the present one; it was rebuilt after it was destroyed in a fire and was completed in 1846. (Courtesy of The New-York Historical Society, New York, NY.)

Plate 16. Broadway, c. 1850; watercolor by August Köllner. This view shows Broadway looking south from its intersection with Chatham Street (now Park Row) toward Trinity Church. City Hall Park was to the back of the artist. Although oriented in the opposite direction, this view is of the same intersection shown in Plate 6; St. Paul's Chapel here is the church with the columns on the right. Note the increase in the density of the traffic in the intervening 30 years, particularly in the number of omnibuses carrying middle-class and wealthy commuters to and from their work in the commercial heart of the city. For these residents, New York was no longer a walking city. The Broadway townhouses of the city's rich merchants had been replaced by the massive Astor House hotel, on the right next to St. Paul's. The merchants had moved their homes uptown. (Courtesy of The New-York Historical Society, New York, NY.)

Plate 17. New York City, looking south from Union Square at 14th Street, c. 1849; lithograph by C. Bachman. This view documents how the city had grown and changed since the Revolution. Note the uniformity of the architectural style and scale of the buildings that made up this new elite suburban residential neighborhood, particularly in comparison to the early views of Broad, Wall, and Water Streets a half-century earlier (shown in Plates 3 and 4). Washington Square Park is the rectangle of foliage at the middle of the right side of the view; it was no longer at the city's northern edge. (Courtesy of The New-York Historical Society, New York, NY.)

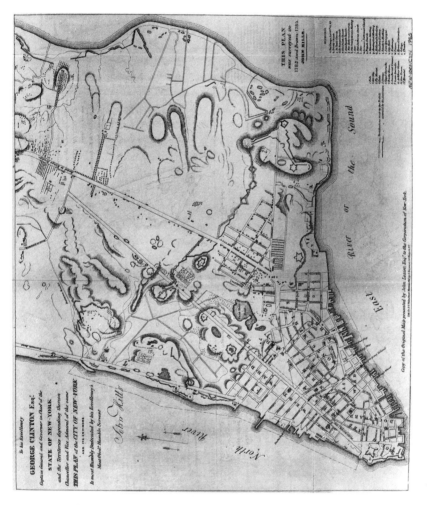

Plate 1. Map of New York, as surveyed in 1782 and drawn in 1785 by John Hills; lithograph by G. Hayward for *Valentine's Manual* (1857).

67

Plate 2. Map of New York, c. 1840, published by the Society for the Diffusion of Useful Knowledge (1840).

Plate 3. Broad Street, looking north to Wall Street and City Hall, 1797; watercolor by John Joseph Holland.

Plate 4. The intersection of Wall and Water Streets in the core of the city, looking northeast, c. 1797; oil painting by Francis Guy.

70

Plate 5. Corner of Greenwich Street, near the Hudson River, c. 1810; watercolor and pencil drawing by the Baroness Hyde de Neuville.

71

Original watercolor drawing by   *Broadway - gatan och Rådhuset i New York.*   Baron Klinckowström.

Plate 6. The intersection of Broadway and Chatham Street (now Park Row) with the recently completed City Hall on the right, c. 1819; watercolor by the Swedish Baron Axel Leonhard Klinckowstrom.

Plate 7. South Street, looking south from Maiden Lane, 1828; watercolor by William Bennett.

Plate 8. Pearl Street House & Ohio Hotel, near Hanover Square, c. 1831; engraving by M. Osborne.

Plate 9. The Great Fire of the City of New-York, 16 December 1835; lithograph drawn by Alfred Hoffy, printed by J. T. Bowen, and published by H. R. Robinson in 1836.

Plate 10. *Night-Fall, St. Thomas Church*, c. 1835; watercolor by George Harvey.

Plate 11. Leroy Place, located on Bleecker Street between Mercer and Greene Streets, c. 1831; engraving by Alexander L. Dick from a drawing by Alexander J. Davis, from Fay's *Views in New-York and Its Environs* (1831–1834).

Plate 12. La Grange Terrace–Lafayette Place, c. 1831; engraved by Alexander L. Dick, from a drawing by J. H. Davis, in Fay's *Views of New-York and Environs* (1831–1834).

Plate 13. The Mount Washington Collegiate Institute, showing the southwest corner of Washington Square, looking toward the southeast, c. 1849; engraving by James Smillie.

Plate 14. The Five Points, c. 1827; lithograph from *Valentine's Manual* (1855).

Plate 15. Wall Street, 1850; watercolor by August Köllner.

Plate 16. Broadway, c. 1850; watercolor by August Köllner.

Plate 17. New York City, looking south from Union Square at 14th Street, c. 1849; lithograph by C. Bachman.

83

Chapter 4

Changing Household Composition

The Van Voorhis Household, 1780s

Daniel Van Voorhis, the silversmith, and Catherine Richards were married in 1775, just before the Revolution. Over the next quarter of a century, the couple maintained a very large household by today's standards. They had a total of nine children—six boys and three girls (one of whom died in infancy)—over the 20-year period between 1776 and 1796. Six of them had been born by 1790, the year of the first Federal census. The household then consisted of sixteen individuals: six men 16 years of age or older, five boys younger than 16, and five women and girls.

The five women and girls in the household presumably included Catherine Van Voorhis herself (who was probably in her thirties) and two of her daughters, Susanna (who was 10) and Elizabeth (who was 1). The other two females were probably "help": young women or girls who helped with the housework and looked after the small children. The help lived and probably ate with the family and may even have been related to them, too.

The adult men in the household presumably included Daniel himself (who was 39 in 1790), Garret Schanck (Daniel's third cousin, who was now his junior partner; he had earlier been apprenticed to Van Voorhis and had worked as his journeyman), and four additional men who were probably apprentices or journeymen who boarded with the family. The five boys in the household included the four Van Voorhis sons—John Richards (who was 14 and who later became his father's partner), Daniel Cornelius (who was 8), Richards (who was 5), and William (who was 4). The fifth boy may have been John Schanck, Garret's younger brother, who apparently was apprenticed to Garret at this time and who turned 16 in 1790.[1]

The Robson Household, 1820

In 1813, Dr. Benjamin R. Robson married Eliza M. Bool, the daughter of a ship captain. Compared to the 1790 Van Voorhis household, the Robsons' in 1830 was quite small; just seven individuals were listed as composing it in the 1830 census. The Robsons had only three children: two sons (Benjamin R., Jr., and William H.) and a daughter, Mary. In 1830, Benjamin, Sr., was 45, his wife Eliza was 37, and all of the children were in their teens.

Unlike the Van Voorhis household, where most of the nonfamily living with the household were men who presumably worked in the family business, the two people who lived with the Robsons in 1830 whom we cannot identify as family members were women. These women were probably domestics.[2]

*   *   *   *   *

In this and the following chapters, we shift the focus of study to look inside the city's middle-class and wealthy homes and see when the changes that we associate with the creation of woman's sphere actually began. Did they begin in the combined homes and workplaces of the city's middle class, or did they start only later, in the isolated homes that we associate with domesticity today? This chapter looks at changes in the size and composition of the household. The variables considered are those that we see in comparing the Van Voorhis household of 1790 with the Robson household 40 years later: declines in the overall size of the household, in the number of children in each family, and in the number of men who were not family members who boarded with the family, and an increase in the number of live-in female domestic servants who helped with the housework in these homes.

To explore these questions, this chapter draws on information from the Federal manuscript census returns for the household heads in the six directory samples. The actual phrasing of the questions that we can ask of the census returns is limited by the nature of the records. The census returns for these early years consist of a single line of information for each household, which is listed under the name of the household head. Neither the names of the other household members nor their relationship (if any) to the household head is included. In addition, the age, sex, and racial categories into which the population was broken down for recording in the census returns are not consistent for the various years. Unfortunately, the data for blacks and whites in the returns are so incomparable that African-American New Yorkers cannot be included for most parts of the study.[3]

Here, the census data on the white population are divided into the age and sex categories that are comparable for most of the years and that can be used to look at the questions under analysis in this study. These data make up three categories: children under 10 years of age, females 10 years of age or older, and males 10 years of age or older. I chose the age of 10 as a cutoff both because it was commonly used in structuring the census returns and also because middle-class children tended to live with their natal families until they were at least 10 years old during the early part of our period. Boys were usually apprenticed out at around the age of 12, although later, when apprenticeships had become debased, this age became somewhat younger. While they were apprenticed, boys lived either with their employers or in their workrooms. Girls also tended to live at home until they were at least 9 or 10, when they might go into domestic service and live with their employers (Stansell, 1980:37–38).

We should remember, however, that given the nature of the Federal census returns for this early period, we cannot identify the actual roles of most of the individual adults in the households; we can only infer them. A woman living in a household could be the wife and mother of the family, an older daughter or relative, a boarder, or a domestic servant, and a man could be the husband and father of the family, an older son or relative, or a boarder or a journeyman working in the family's business. However, in spite of these limitations, the census returns do yield a wealth of information about changing household composition that is not available from any other source.

Finally, as discussed in Appendix A, only approximately one-half to three-quarters of the individuals listed in each of the directory samples for each of the sample years were also listed in the census records for the appropriate year. When the census data are further subdivided for comparative purposes, the samples in some cases become extremely small (all of the figures from which the bar graphs were derived are shown in Appendix D). Both for this reason and because of the inferential nature of the census data, the interpretations made in this chapter can be regarded only as suggestive.

HOUSEHOLD SIZE

Historians have long looked on changes in the average number of individuals living in the household as an important interpretive issue in exploring the relationship between the rise of industrialization and changes in family life. The traditional assumption has been that the household was a large and complex entity in preindustrial times in the Western world, and that the nuclear family became the common household unit only with the rise of industrialization. This belief led to the further assumption that the mean number of people living in each household decreased considerably through time, particularly in the 18th and 19th centuries. However, more recent work done on English and Continental households shows that this assumption simply is not true. The mean household size in England, for example, remained relatively constant throughout the period of industrialization, at approximate.y 4.75 from the 16th century (the earliest period for which records are available) until 1901.[4]

Peter Laslett (1972b:154–156), in his study of household size in England during this period, included a breakdown by the occupations of the household heads that gives an idea of the relationship between household size and wealth or class. He found that those of high status ("gentlemen") tended to have larger households than those of lower status ("laborers" and "paupers"), and that the households of those of middling status ("yeomen," "husbandmen," and "tradesmen and craftsmen") tended to fall in between. In addition. those listed with traditionally urban occupations ("tradesmen and craftsmen") tended to have a smaller number of people living in their homes than those in traditionally rural occupations ("yeomen" and "husbandmen").

The data for North America, on the other hand, tell a different story. Unfortunately, no census was taken for all of the colonies that were later to become the United States: the decennial Federal census began only in 1790. However, there are data for some of the individual colonies. They suggest that the mean size of the household in predominately rural America was considerably larger than in Europe at the same time and that it may have decreased in the 18th century. In Massachusetts, for example, the mean household size in 1764 was 7.2, and by 1790 it had decreased to 6.9. The figures are somewhat different for the cities. In New York City in 1703, the mean household size was 5.48. By 1790, this figure had actually grown, to 6.2.[5]

For the United States as a whole in the late 18th to mid-19th centuries, the mean size of the household showed a slight decrease, from 5.79 in 1790 to 5.55 in 1850 (no slaves are included in these figures). This trend toward a smaller size of household became increasingly marked in the late 19th and early 20th centuries, with the average number of individuals in the American household decreasing from 4.76 in 1900 to 3.37 in 1950 (U.S. Bureau of the Census, 1975:41).

Figure 4–1 shows the mean size of the middle-class and wealthy households in the samples from New York City during the period of study. The figures are similar to Laslett's (1972b) in that there were considerably more individuals in the wealthy households than in those of the middle class. However, the shapes of the curves for the two groups are quite similar: They both show an increase and then a decline in the number of household members during the period of study. The curve for the elite shows a relatively steady increase from 1790 to 1820 and then a steady decline from 1820 to 1840. That for the middle class shows a decline in household size from 1790 to 1800, an increase from 1800 to 1830, and, finally, another decline from 1830 to 1840. In order to understand these trends, we have to look inside these households and

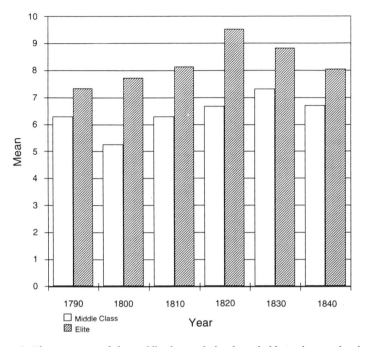

Figure 4–1. The mean size of the middle-class and elite households in the samples, by year.

examine the changes in the proportions of the men, women, and children who made up their members.

THE CHILDREN

Penelope Hull and Richard M. Bowne, the Pearl Street druggist, were married in 1804 in Stanford, New York. Both the bride and the groom came from relatively large families. Richard was the third child in a family of eight children. Penelope was also the third-born, but in a much larger family. Her father had 11 children by his first wife, Mary (who died in childbirth at the age of 40 in 1802), and seven by his second wife, Amy. Penelope and Richard Bowne had five children, considerably fewer than their parents had had. Of their four children who survived to adulthood, each also had fewer offspring than their grandparents: Ann and Samuel each had six, Mary had seven, and Eliza had only four.[6]

Scholars have long seen the decline of the average number of children in the early American household as an important issue in the history of the family. This change has been documented in the United States as a whole from at least as early as 1810, and there are indications that it may have begun considerably earlier, in the 18th century (Degler, 1980:179–180). Table 4–1 shows some of the figures that are commonly cited for the birthrate in the United States for the period of study. The table shows that, as in Laslett's England, the birthrate was considerably lower in urban areas than it was nationally. There was also a consistent and definite reduction in the rate after at least as early as 1810.

Although scholars have traditionally associated this decline with the beginnings of industrialization and urbanization, in fact it started years before either of these processes was fully under way. Some studies have correlated the decrease in the birthrate with modernization and have stressed the fact that the birthrate went down as it became harder and harder for parents to gain entry for their children into their own socioeconomic class. In rural agrarian areas, for example, the decline in the availability of arable land meant not only that a couple needed fewer children to help farm the land but that they had less land to bequeath to their sons to help them get established as adults. In cities, the growth of commercial capitalism created a parallel situation as more and more men lost control of the means of production and not only could not ensure a living for their children in a family business but had to pay for their children's training or education so that the children could make their own way. Other studies have stressed the fact that, as parents lost the means of guaranteeing access to a living for their children, they also lost their bargaining power in reaping the benefits of their children's earnings as adults, that is, their return on their investment in their children (Degler, 1980:181; Folbre, 1983; Forster and Turner, 1972; Grabill, Kiser, and Whelpton, 1958:15; Ryan, 1981; Sanderson, 1979; Yasuba, 1962).

Additionally, some historians attribute the decline in the birthrate at least partially to the increasing autonomy of women within the home as part of the development of woman's sphere, which involved a change in the values relating to women's roles and the position of children in society. With changes in the organization of labor and growing concern about preparing children to become the future citizens of the republic, adults redefined the meaning of childhood from the 18th-century definition of a pair of "little hands" helping their parents to the modern definition of a special phase of life requiring extensive nurturing and education. With this new interpretation of childhood, parents expected to spend considerably more time, energy, and even money in preparing each child for adulthood. It was therefore in the interest of both mothers (who were beginning to spend more time and energy on nurturing each child as well as enduring the perils of childbirth) and fathers (who were responsible for the increasing financial costs of their children's support and education) to curtail the number of children they had.

This downward trend in the birthrate, which was probably related to most

Table 4–1. Commonly Cited Fertility Rates for the
Period under Study and Their Derivation

Year	Rate 1[a] National	Rate 1[a] Middle Atlantic	Rate 2[b] National
	Urban areas		
1800	1,281	852	7.04
1810	1,290	924	6.92
1820	1,236	842	6.73
1830	1,134	722	6.55
1840	1,070	711	6.14

[a]Rate 1: Based on the number of white children under 5 years old per 1,000 white women aged 20–44 (Grabil, Kiser, and Whelpton, 1958, p. 17).
[b]Rate 2: Total fertility rate for the white population, based on the average number of children per woman that would have been born to a hypothetical subject at the childbearing rate experienced in the observed population (Coale and Zelnik, 1963, pp. 36–37).

of the above-discussed phenomena, was begun without the introduction of new methods of birth control. Abstinence, coitus interruptus, and abortion (which, if carried out before "quickening," or the third month or so of pregnancy, when the first movements of the fetus can be felt, was not criminalized until later in the century) continued to be the most common methods of birth control throughout the period of study (Degler, 1980; Ryan, 1981, 1983; D. C. Smith, 1979; Wells, 1975).

The data on the changes in the birthrate of the New Yorkers studied here were derived from the census information on the household heads in the samples. (Unfortunately, the data from the 1790 census returns could not be used in this study because they are not comparable with those for the rest of the period.) Figure 4–2 shows the changes in the average number of children in the households of the population of the city as a whole. The figure shows an anomalously low mean number of children in each household for 1800, which was followed by a marked increase in their mean number by 1810. This increase also appears, though to a lesser degree, in the published national rates that were most directly derived from the census records and was somewhat higher in urban areas (see Table 4–1). The explanation for this increase, which appears in the data from Delaware and Indiana as well as from New York State, is unclear. Anomalous reductions in fertility are often associated with crises. It is possible that the low birthrate exhibited for the city in 1800 was related to the recovery, repopulation, and rebuilding of the city after its occupation by the British during the Revolution. If "crisis" conditions persisted for 10 years after the British evacuation in 1783, their associated effect on the birthrate as measured here would still be expressed in the 1800 birthrates.[7]

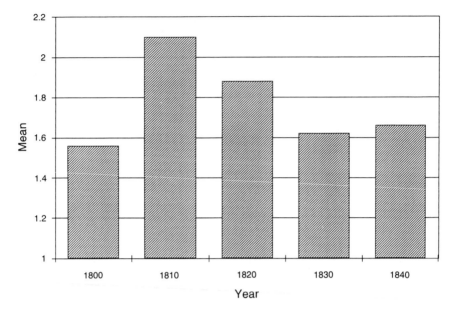

Figure 4–2. The mean number of children in all of the households in the samples, by year.

The decline in the birthrate shown nationally after 1810 is also evident in the data from New York, with a steady decrease between 1810 and 1830. Between 1830 and 1840, the rate remained relatively constant.

Next, we look at changes in the birthrates in middle-class and wealthy families. We would expect a decline in the birthrate in both groups with the development of commercial capitalism and the adoption of the social practices associated with woman's sphere. It also seems likely, however, that wealthy couples continued to have, on average, more children than their middle-class counterparts simply because they had more money to educate them and to hire servants to do much of the time- and energy-consuming housework that was involved in running an early-19th-century household. The infant mortality rate among the children of the rich was also presumably lower than that among the poor or even among the middle class.

Figure 4–3 shows the average number of children in the households of each of these groups. Like the figures for the city's population as a whole, the 1800 figures were anomalously low for the middle class and the elite. As expected, too, the households in the elite group showed a higher mean number of children than those of the middle class for all but one of the years after 1810; the small mean number of children for the elite in 1830 may simply have been due to the small size of the sample for that year. In addition, the figure

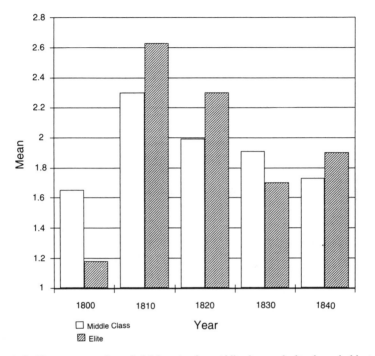

Figure 4–3. The mean number of children in the middle-class and elite households in the samples, by year.

shows an overall decrease in the average number of children in the wealthy households from 1810 to 1830, with a slight increase in 1840.

In the middle class, the mean number of children in each household was lower than that for the elite for most of the years. After 1800, these figures decreased fairly steadily, from a high in 1810 to a low in 1840, a decrease suggesting that attitudes toward children among this group were changing during this period.

The data show, then, that the decline in the birthrate, which is interpreted here as expressing, at least in part, new definitions of both motherhood and childhood and the development of the ideology of woman's sphere, began at least as early as the 1810s among middle-class and wealthy families. As we saw in Chapter 2, however, whereas most members of the elite chose to move their homes away from their workplaces a decade earlier (in the first decade of the 19th century), most members of the middle class made that decision only much later, in the 1830s. This difference implies that the decision to have fewer children was not a direct result of the separation of the home and the workplace and the isolation of these women in the home.

THE ADULTS

Scholars have long interpreted the cultural transformation of the late 18th and early 19th centuries as affecting the composition of the adults in wealthy and middle-class households as well. There was a decline in the number of grown men in these homes as families no longer supplied accommodation for the apprentices and journeymen who worked in their shops. There was an increase in the number of women in these households, however, as the elaboration of domestic life required an increasing number of domestic servants to maintain the home.

The changing relationship between employers and employees in the city's workplaces, discussed in Chapter 2, drastically changed the living arrangements of the male labor force. In the 18th century, apprentices and even journeymen often boarded with their employers' families. Daniel Van Voorhis, the silversmith, for example, had five men over the age of 16 who were not members of his immediate family living in his household in 1790. They presumably worked with him at his craft as apprentices, journeymen, and partners. With the hardening of the lines between the classes associated with the development of capitalism and the commodification of labor in the 19th century, these men and boys were no longer treated like family members in their employers' homes.

This detachment of employees from the home life of their employers was apparently a long and gradual process, however, and did not happen overnight. Stephen Allen (quoted in Travis, 1927, passim), who later became mayor of New York, described in his memoirs a state of "semidetachment" from his master's home as an apprentice during the British occupation of New York. In 1779, he joined his older brother as apprentice to a Loyalist sailmaker, James Leonard. Leonard had three apprentices living in the garret of his house, where each had a hammock and a pair of blankets for bedding. Later, as he became more successful, Leonard moved his home away from his sail loft to Beekman Street, and the family decided "that there was no room for the boys" in the new house. The boys continued to live in the sail loft but had their meals at the home of their master. They apparently ate two of their meals—breakfast and midday dinner—with the family in what Allen described as the cellar of the house, which is where most families cooked and ate their meals at that time. The boys ate their supper (which invariably consisted of two slices of baker's bread and butter and which they were served in the backyard or on the street) on their own.

As the war progressed and Leonard's business of supplying the British with sails increased, he took on more apprentices (they now totaled five). He also arranged for his journeymen to lodge with the apprentices at the sail loft.

Allen's mother (who had been widowed) objected to this situation, however. Allen reported that after she had remarried, she remonstrated with Leonard that no good would come to her sons from this kind of living arrangement, and she persuaded Leonard to provide her oldest son with accommodation at his home. She also arranged for Stephen to board and lodge with her while he finished his apprenticeship.

As early as the late 18th century, then, there were already apparently two different, contradictory interpretations of the appropriate way to treat apprentices and journeymen. One, strongly held by Allen's mother, stressed that they should be treated as part of the family, whereas the other, held by Leonard the sailmaker, indicated that apprentices should be treated like employees.

The relationship between the family and its domestic help also changed dramatically during the period of study, although the nature of the relationship was determined in part by whether the help were black or white and, if they were white, whether they were native- or foreign-born.[8] In the 18th century, most white household help in the middle-class United States tended to be relatively casual and transitory. Young girls who were old enough to work but not yet married might go out to work temporarily with another family. They were usually hired for a specific task (such as spinning, or spring cleaning, or helping with an illness or a new baby), and when the task or episode was over, they would go back to their own homes. Employers tended to hire these girls at certain points in the family cycle: when the children were small (as in the Van Voorhis family in 1790, when five of the six children were under 11) or after the children had grown up and left home. When the daughters of the house were in their teens, most families had little need of additional household labor from outside the family. These hired girls who worked as "help" alongside their middle-class employers were usually members of the same class and were treated for the most part as members of the family.

In the 19th century, this casual and almost familial relationship between employers and their white domestic help began to change. Like their husbands in the city's workplaces, middle-class mistresses began to routinize and rationalize housework. The social relations between a female employer and her domestics became somewhat like those that prevailed between male employers and employees in the city's workplaces. The mistress no longer worked alongside her domestic; the mistress had become a supervisor and often did not participate in the actual housework at all.

Mistresses also used two different and contradictory models in dealing with their domestics. One was that of an entrepreneur who looked on the labor of her servant as a commodity, and the other was that of a missionary who looked on the servant as a subject to educate and convert. Mistresses no longer referred to their "help," but to their "domestics." Many domestics, for their part, were quite clear about their attitudes toward their employers and their work: They saw themselves as wage laborers. These different and contradictory images of the employer–employee relationship and the tension arising from having in the home a relationship structured by the ideology of the marketplace resulted in what employers perceived as the "servant problem." Servants were constantly accused of "ingratitude" by their mistresses, but gratitude was not a relevant sentiment from the perspective of most servants, who saw themselves as wage laborers.

The change from "help" to "domestic" occurred unevenly in different parts of the country; it took place relatively early in urban areas in the East, but much later in rural parts of the West. In New York, this restructuring in the relationship between employers and household help began in the 1820s and 1830s and coincided with the influx of Irish girls, who became the city's primary pool of domestic workers for the rest of the century. The very Irishness and Catholicness of these girls further distanced them from their employers, who were primarily Protestant Americans. Many of the Irish girls came directly from a peasant way of life in a rural economy to relatively cosmopolitan New York, and they had had no experience with the domestic amenities that were becoming common in middle-class urban homes in America during this period. The increased social distance between the mistress and her servants was expressed spatially, too. It was at this time that the dichotomy of "upstairs" space for the family and "downstairs" space for the servants (who actually slept above the "upstairs," in the unheated attic at the top of the house) was introduced into some of the city's upper-middle-class homes, and row houses began to be built with a separate, narrow flight of back stairs for servant use (Stansell, 1986:160).

As the city's middle-class wives and daughters withdrew their labor from the family housework pool, and as the redefinition of domestic life required more labor to maintain it, these families hired more "domestics" than they ever had before. In addition, a family's need of household help was more consistent than it had been in the past. Formerly, a family that had teenaged daughters usually had no need to hire help from outside the family. For example, in 1800 the Van Voorhis household included three women and girls. They were probably all family members, as the age categories listed for them in the census returns conform closely to those of the female members of the family: the mistress Catherine Van Voorhis and her two daughters, Susanna, who was 20, and Elizabeth, who was 11. These three on their own probably did most of the mountains of housework required to run this large household of 18 people, with additional "help" being brought into the house only temporarily for a particular task.[9]

In 1820, Dr. Benjamin Robson and his wife, Eliza, apparently also relied on household "help." Their household consisted of six people in that year. In addition to the couple themselves, it included their three children (Mary,

William, and Benjamin, Jr.), who were all under 10, and a young girl who is listed in the census returns as being between 10 and 16 years old. This young girl was probably hired to help Eliza with the housework and with taking care of the children.

Ten years later, by 1830, the Robson household (described in this year at the beginning of this chapter) may have shifted from "help" to "domestics." Even though there were only five family members, and even though their daughter, Mary, was a teenager, the census lists two adult women as part of the household who were not part of the immediate family. One of these women was in her twenties, and the other was listed in the census returns simply as an "alien." The Robson household had changed since 1820. Then, there had been only a girl to "help." Now, the presence of what appear to have been two domestic servants (including one—the "alien"—who was probably Irish) as well as a teenaged daughter suggests that neither Eliza Robson nor her daughter did much of the housework themselves; rather, it seems that Eliza merely supervised the domestics, who did the actual work in her home. The Robsons continued for decades to have two female servants (who were almost always Irish) living in their home.[10]

Before the 1830s, live-in African-American servants were very common in New York. Unlike their white counterparts in the 18th century, black domestics did not work casually and temporarily as "help"; most of them were enslaved. Because of the nature of New York's emancipation laws—emancipation was a gradual process, completed only in 1827—most of the blacks who lived in the homes of the city's white middle-class and wealthy families were slaves in 1790, whereas by 1820 most of them were free (see Figure 4–4).[11]

African-Americans had become much less common as live-in servants by the 1830s. As Thomas Hamilton (1834), one visitor to the city, noted, their places were being supplanted by "natives of the Emerald Isle . . . who come annually in swarms like locusts" (p. 93). Figure 4–5 shows the mean number of blacks listed in the census returns as living in the city's middle-class and elite homes, and it shows that this figure had drastically shrunk by the 1830s.[12]

The decline in the number of black live-in servants was probably related to two factors. First, most black servants (unlike their native-born white counterparts who served as "help" or even most of their Irish counterparts who served as "domestics") did not confine their work as servants to the period before they were married. Assuming that they wished such an arrangement, a black working-class family could not be supported by a black man's wage because of discrimination against free black men in the marketplace. Black women continued to work for wages as domestics after they became wives and mothers. Given these circumstances, they presumably preferred to live out and go home to their families at night. Second, the Irish were not willing to live

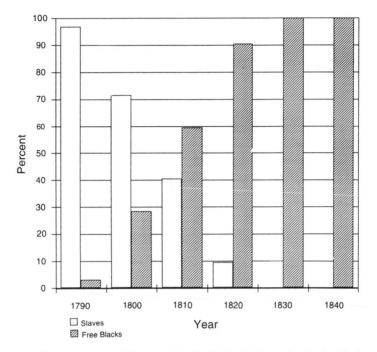

Figure 4–4. The percentages of slave and free-black New Yorkers who lived with the white families in the samples, by year.

and work beside blacks in these middle-class and wealthy homes. Black women who continued to work in domestic service (and they did not have many job options) therefore tended to live with their own families and not the families of their employers. Much of their work in these homes is therefore not visible in the census records for the early part of the 19th century (Dudden, 1983).

Next, we look at when the composition of the adult members of the households in the samples began to change. Did the decline in the number of male workplace employees and the increase in the number of female domestics living in these homes begin before or after the separation of the home and the workplace? Unfortunately, as discussed above and in Appendix A, we have to consider all of the white males and all of the white females who were listed as over 10 years of age in the returns as "men" and "women" for this study because of the nature of the census data. Some of the "men" in this group were actually the apprentices and journeymen who worked in the family business and boarded with the family, whereas others were simply male boarders or male family members. Some of the "women" in this group were the live-in

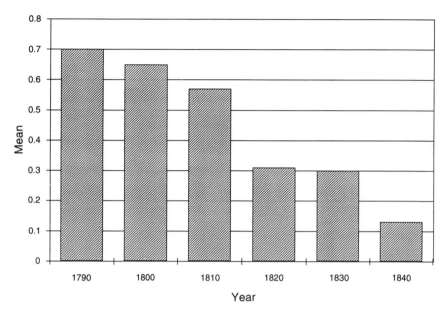

Figure 4–5. The mean number of black New Yorkers who lived with the white families in the samples, by year.

domestic help we are interested in studying, but others were female boarders or adult female family members. Therefore, it is not possible to measure directly the changes in the numbers of female domestic servants and male employees residing in these homes; we can only make inferences about this issue.[13]

One interpretive question that has to be considered here is whether any changes occurred in the ages at which children tended to leave home and to marry. Unfortunately, we have little systematic information on this subject, and none of what we know is quantifiable. During the late 18th and early 19th centuries, many children—both male and female—did leave home well before they married. Some of the sons of the middle class left home early to learn a trade, like Stephen Allen, who was only 12 when he was apprenticed to the sailmaker. Some daughters of the middle class also left home to serve as "help" in other families (like the "help" in the Van Voorhis and Robson households) or to teach in schools that were located far from home. It is thought that between 1750 and 1820, the average age when boys left home dropped from the early 20s to the late teens. By the late 19th century, however, children of both sexes continued to live at home for longer periods than they had earlier in the century. However, we do not know precisely when these shifts occurred.

We also do not know the ages at which middle-class sons and daughters tended to marry, and once they had, whether they tended to set up house on their own or to board with others, either at a boardinghouse or with the parents of one of the couple. Unfortunately, there is little quantifiable information on this subject for most of the period of interest here. However, even with the limits of the data, we can see and interpret certain trends in the composition of the adults in the households in our samples over the period of study (Coontz, 1988:261; Halttunen, 1982:12).[14]

Figure 4–6 shows the average number of white adult men and women in the middle-class households in the samples. Among this group, there was a gradual but steady increase in the average number of men until 1830, followed by a decrease between 1830 and 1840. The shape of this curve suggests that men began to move out of the homes of their employers in that decade, as fewer men were living in these homes in 1840 than had lived there only a decade before. The data suggest that, in terms of male boarders, these homes were becoming privatized in the 1830s, and that this aspect of privatization coincided with the separation of the home and the workplace.

There had been an almost equal number of women and men in these households before 1830, when a decided increase in the number of women appeared. This number remained relatively high through 1840. This curve could well express the presence of an increased number of female domestic servants in these households in the 1820s, and it suggests that the quality of domestic life was becoming an important issue for middle-class women as a whole during this period, a decade before the separation of the home and the workplace occurred in most of these households.

Figure 4–7 shows that there was a roughly equal number of men and women in the elite households in 1800. However, from 1810 to 1840, there were considerably more women than men in these homes. This change is interpreted as an expression of a sharp increase in the number of female domestic servants between 1800 and 1820 in these homes and a relative decrease in the number of male boarders residing in them after approximately 1800.

In addition, the curves representing the number of women and men are roughly parallel to each other from 1810 to 1840, with nadirs in 1810 and peaks in 1820 being followed by gradual but steady declines for the rest of the study period. This pattern of a nadir, a peak, and a subsequent decline for both men and women occurred a decade after the nadir, peak, and decline shown in the number of small children in these households between 1800 and 1830 (see Figure 4–3). This finding suggests that the shape of each of these curves after 1800 expresses the decline in the birthrate and a corresponding decrease in the numbers of older sons and daughters living in these households during this period. The relationship between the curves, however, shows the relative in-

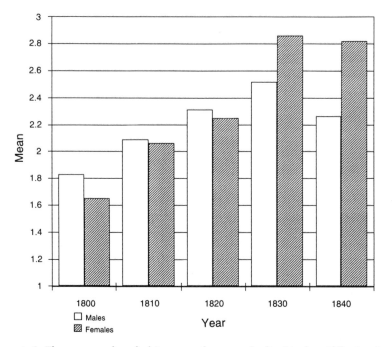

Figure 4–6. The mean number of white men and women who lived in the middle-class house-holds in the samples, by year.

crease in the number of domestic servants and the relative decrease in the number of male boarders in these homes, respectively.

Finally, we must compare the numbers of men and women who lived in middle-class integrated homes and workplaces with those who lived in homes that were separate residences in order to see if there were any correlations between the numbers of men and women in a household and the kind of household that was being maintained. This further division of the data from the census returns resulted in sample sizes that were extremely small for some of the years (see Appendix D), so our inferences here are simply suggestive.

Figures 4–8 and 4–9 show the breakdown for both groups. The number of women in the homes that were combined with workplaces was roughly similar to the number of women living in separate homes (see Figure 4–8); they both increased through the 1820s and leveled off after 1830. This pattern suggests that the enhanced quality of domestic life that these women were hired to maintain developed regardless of whether a home was combined with or separate from its associated workplace.

For the men in these households (Figure 4–9), the curves are quite

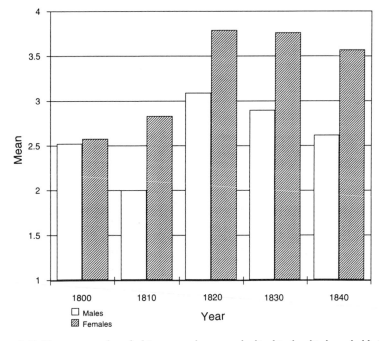

Figure 4–7. The mean number of white men and women who lived in the elite households in the samples, by year.

different. Among the households that were combined with workplaces, there was a gradual increase in the number of men from 1800 through 1830, followed by a leveling off or a slight decline for 1840. This pattern suggests that many male boarders continued to reside in traditionally organized households through the 1830s.

When the households listed with two addresses are examined, the sample sizes are very small for the early years. However, it appears that those employers who had established separate homes and workplaces before 1810 had much larger shops in terms of the number of men they employed and also continued to provide room and board for many of their employees, as the mean number of men in these households was remarkably high for that year.[15] By 1820, this mean had declined markedly, although it continued to be higher than the mean of the number of men living in combined homes and workplaces for both 1820 and 1830. In the 1830s, however, there was another decline in the number of men in these households, so that by 1840 there were fewer men in the households with separate workplaces than there were in the other group.

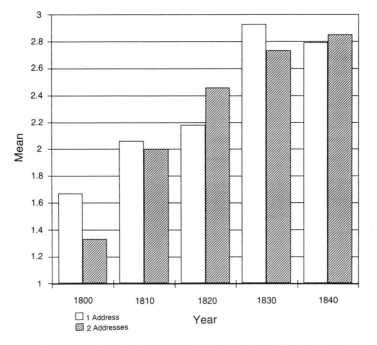

Figure 4–8. The mean number of white women who lived in the middle-class households in the samples, by number of addresses and year.

The data suggest, then, that the separation of the middle-class home and the workplace may have been directly associated with increases in the sizes of the shops and the number of employees in them. Furthermore, many employers with separate workplaces had discontinued the practice of providing accommodation for most of their male employees by 1820, a practice that declined further in the 1830s. As far as male employees were concerned, the home was becoming increasingly privatized.

CONCLUSION

This chapter explored the timing of the changes in the composition of the household that we associate with the beginnings of the modern middle-class family. These changes included decreases both in the number of children that a couple might have and in the number of men who boarded in these homes, as well as an increase in the number of female domestic servants hired to help with the ever-growing load of housework associated with the enhanced quality of domestic life. The question asked in each case was whether these changes

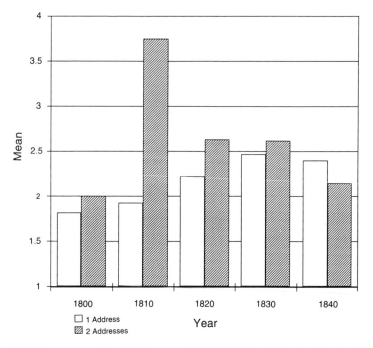

Figure 4–9. The mean number of white men who lived in the middle-class households in the samples, by number of addresses and year.

began in the period of the combined workplace and home, or whether they emerged only after the isolation of the home from the workplace.

For the middle class, the picture is clear-cut. As we saw in Chapter 2, most of the members of this group separated their homes from their workplaces in the 1830s. A decline in the middle-class birthrate began as early as 1810, and there was also a marked increase in the number of domestic servants visible in middle-class households in the 1820s. This finding suggests that the two changes in household composition that we associate with the creation of woman's sphere began in the integrated homes of the middle class well before the separation of the home and the workplace occurred.

The decrease in the number of male boarders began only in the 1830s, however, and co-occurred with the separation of the home and the workplace. This co-occurrence suggests that these phenomena may have been related to each other and that both may have been associated with the growth in the scale of production and the hardening of the lines between the classes in the city's workplaces. This interpretation is supported by the high number of men who lived under the aegis of their masters in some of the shops that were separate from their homes early in the century. We should remember the example of Daniel Van Voorhis, however, as a cautionary tale. He had a large number of men working in his shop and lived in an integrated home and workplace during most of the years of the late 18th century, but he occasionally leased a home that was separate from his workplace as well. The decision of living in a home that was separate from the workplace certainly was not an irrevocable one and did not necessarily mean that one's home was becoming permanently privatized as far as its male boarders were concerned.

The data for the elite support the interpretations for the middle class. The separation of the home and the workplace took place quite early in most of the elite households, before 1810. This is the same decade that saw a marked decline in the number of adult men residing in elite homes. Again, the co-occurrence of these two events supports the interpretation that they may well have been related. An increase in the number of domestic servants became evident in the next decade, before 1820. As among the middle class, the decade ending in 1820 was also the one that saw the beginnings of a fall in the birthrate in the elite group. Both of the changes in social practice that we associate with the beginnings of woman's sphere—a decline in the birthrate and an increase in the number of domestic servants in the household— occurred in the decade that followed the separation of the home and the workplace for wealthier New Yorkers.

The data suggest that the separation of the private home from the commercial workplace was not a precondition for either the decline in the birthrate or an increased number of domestic servants. Among the middle class, both these trends *preceded* the separation of the home and the workplace, whereas in the city's wealthier households, these changes *followed* it.

Next, we continue to look at the elaboration of domesticity inside the homes of the city's middle-class and wealthy families by concentrating on a more quotidian aspect of everyday life: the ritualization of family meals that developed as part of woman's sphere in the early 19th century.

NOTES

1. The information on the size and breakdown of the Van Voorhis household in 1790 is from the U.S. Government, Bureau of the Census (1790); although the nature of the census records from the late 18th and early 19th centuries makes it hard for us to know exactly who lived in a particular household, we can make inferences with the help of additional biographical information. Information on the number, names, and birth years of the children in the Van Voorhis family is from Van Voorhis (1888:192–197); information on Daniel's partner, Garret Schanck, and the latter's brother, John, is from Laidlaw (1986:15–21, 33–36; 1988).

2. The Robsons' wedding was announced in the *Commercial Advertiser* of 29 April 1813; the information on their household composition is from the U.S. Government, Bureau of the Census (1830); information on the ages of the family members is inferred from the State of New York Census (1855).

3. See Appendix A for a fuller description of the advantages and disadvantages of this approach. Unfortunately, the information on black New Yorkers in the census returns is not broken down in a way that is consistent with the information on white New Yorkers for all of the years. For the years before 1820, the black population is not broken down by age or sex at all, and for 1820, the ages used to divide the black population are not comparable to those used for the white population. For this reason, I have considered only white New Yorkers for most of this part of the study.

4. The statistic used here is the mean number of people residing together in the same household. This aggregate figure provides a baseline against which we can examine changes in household composition. People living together in these late-18th- and early-19th-century households were not necessarily related to each other by blood or marriage; rather, they simply lived together and may have participated in common economic activities (Laslett, 1972a:ix; 1972b:126).

5. The figures for Massachusetts are from Greven (1972:550). The figures for New York City in 1703 are from O'Callaghan (1849, I:611–624), and those for the city in 1790 are from Greven (1972:552) and Appendix D of this book; slaves are included in both of these figures.

6. The information on the Bowne marriage and the number of children in the various Bowne families is from Wilson (1987); the information on the number of children in the Hull family is from Hull (1863).

7. The indirect measure of the birthrate used for the 1800 samples through the 1840 samples is the mean number of white children under 10 years old who lived in a household where the oldest white female was still close to childbearing age: under 45 for the 1800, and 1820 samples and under 50 for the 1830 and 1840 samples. The different ages were used as cutoffs for categorizing these groups of women simply because they were the ones used in the census records for the appropriate years (Forster and Turner, 1972:5; Grabil, Kiser, and Whelpton, 1958:14, 17; Wells, 1975:9).

8. Much of the following discussion on the nature of household help and domestics is derived from Dudden (1983).

9. The information on the composition of the Van Voorhis household is derived from the U.S. Government, Bureau of the Census (1800); that on the identity of individual family members is inferred from Van Voorhis (1888:192–197).

10. The information on the composition of the Robson household is inferred from the U.S. Government, Bureau of the Census (1820, 1830).

11. New York's emancipation bills were somewhat convoluted. According to Pomerantz (1965), the bill of 1799 freed not those who were then enslaved, but only their children; it stipulated that of those who were born in slavery after 4 July 1799, the men would be freed at age 28 and the women at age 25. In 1817, another law was passed that stated that slaves born before 4 July 1799 would be freed as of 3 July 1827.

12. Much of the background for this discussion was drawn from Dudden (1983).
13. The nature of the census data is discussed more fully in Appendix A.
14. Cott (1977:14) lamented the lack of information on the ages at which men and women tended to marry; some work has been done on the age of marriage of men and women in particular communities before the turn of the 19th century (see Farber, 1972; D. S. Smith, 1973, 1978). As discussed more fully in Chapter 6, when Elizabeth Bleecker married in New York in 1800, she continued to live in her parents' home with her husband for four months, when they took their own house (diary entries for 8 April through 11 August 1800).
15. We should remember, however, that it is also possible that these employees, like Stephen Allen during part of his apprenticeship as a sailmaker, may have lodged in the shops and not the private homes of their employers' families.

Chapter 5

The Ritualization of Family Meals I

The Van Voorhis Household, 1780s

In the 1780s, when Daniel and Catherine Van Voorhis had their silver and jewelry store on Hanover Square and lived there as well, their shop was located on the first floor at the front of the building, and their workroom was behind it. The couple and their younger children probably slept on the second floor above the store, the older children, apprentices, journeymen, and help sleeping on the third floor or in the attic. The women in the household prepared meals in the kitchen that was in the building's back basement, and household members ate them in the combined dining-and-sitting room in the front basement. They started their day with breakfast and had their main meal—dinner—at midday. After evening supper, they often had their friends in for tea.[1]

The Bowne Household, circa 1805

After Penelope Hull and Richard Bowne married and took over the Hull family drug shop in the first decade of the 19th century, they also lived at the store. They used the private family space in their Pearl Street premises much as the Van Voorhises had done at Hanover Square 20 years before, and they ate similar meals in the combined dining-and-sitting room in their front basement. They also conducted their business from the first floor of the house, displaying and selling their remedies from the front room that looked out on the street. The Bownes may have had two other, smaller

109

rooms on this floor, too: one for consulting with patients about their ailments and one for mixing remedies.[2]

The Robson Household, 1820s

When Benjamin and Eliza Robson moved their family to their new house on East Broadway in 1829, Dr. Robson continued to run his practice out of the first-floor room that fronted on the street. Although the family had their midday dinner and other meals in their dining-and-sitting room in their front basement, opposite the kitchen, they probably also had an upstairs drawing room or parlor for entertaining at evening tea.

When the family moved up to Washington Square 12 years later, Dr. Robson left his practice behind on East Broadway. At this point, the family began to have their dinner in the evening, after the doctor had returned from work.

The first floor of the new house had double parlors connected by folding or sliding doors that the family used for entertaining. The Robsons probably continued to eat their family meals in the front basement room downstairs, however, and used the formal rooms upstairs only for visitors and parties.[3]

* * * * *

During the half century that followed the Revolution, many changes in the arrangements of domestic life occurred inside the homes of the city's middle-class and wealthy families. Unfortunately, however, it is hard to grasp the details and temporal sequences of these changes from contemporary accounts. Travelers who wrote about their visits to America in the early 19th century usually described the homes of the rich and not those of the middle class. In addition, they were often vague and even conflicting in their descriptions of the details of home life that they saw in the new republic. The Englishwoman Frances Trollope (1839/1984), for example, visited New York in the late 1820s and described the homes of the wealthy as:

> extremely handsome, and very richly furnished. Silk or satin furniture is as often, or oftener, seen than chintz; the mirrors are as handsome as in London; the cheffoniers [sic], slabs, and marble tables as elegant; and in addition, they have all the pretty tasteful decoration of French porcelain, and ormolu in much greater abundance, because at a much cheaper rate. (p. 298)

Another visitor, Thomas Hamilton (1834), arrived in New York at around the same time, but his impression of the opulence of the accoutrements of the domestic life of the wealthy was quite different:

> Here are no buhl tables, nor or-molu [sic] clocks, nor gigantic mirrors, nor cabinets of Japan, nor draperies of silk or velvet. . . . In short, the appearance of an American mansion is decidedly republican. (p. 101)

It is not clear whether Trollope and Hamilton were commenting on similar kinds of homes but were using different frames of reference from their own backgrounds, or whether they were seeing the homes of the members of different socioeconomic or ideological groups. In this and the following chapter, we begin to explore when some of the changes in domestic life that we associate with the creation of woman's sphere actually began.

Here, we examine family meals and some of the accoutrements that were used in presenting them as examples of some of the changes in the more quotidian aspects of domestic life that were occurring at this time. The question we are asking is whether or not middle-class women were beginning to enhance this aspect of domestic life inside their combined homes and workplaces, or whether they began to do so only after the separation of the home and workplace.

The family meals that were served inside these homes are an important part of this story because, by the middle of the 19th century, some of them had become secular domestic rituals deeply embedded in middle-class life. As anthropologists Sally Moore and Barbara Myerhoff (1977:2–8) pointed out, ritual can be used to turn new material into tradition as well as to perpetuate old ways of life. They identified six properties of ritual that are relevant in this regard: repetition; acting, as opposed to merely saying or thinking something; special behavior or stylization, in which action or symbols can be used in an unusual way that sets them apart from the mundane; order, in that ritual is an organized event, with a beginning, a middle, and an end; an evocative presentational style or staging through the manipulation of symbols and sensory stimuli; and a "collective dimension," with social meaning and a social message.

Family dinner and other meals had a high potential for ritualization at the beginning of the period of study. They were enacted every day and all family members could participate in them. In addition, meals have the potential of having a highly structured order, with dishes grouped into a number of courses. These courses in turn have the capacity for an evocative presentation both in the arrangement of the dishes in table settings and in the sensory stimulus of the food itself. Meals may also involve stylized special behavior: table manners. Here, the ritualization of family meals is looked on as part of the process of incorporating new material into a new domestic tradition associated with the ideology of woman's sphere. By the middle of the 19th century, some family meals, particularly family dinner, had fulfilled this potential. They had become secular rituals that were presided over by the woman of the house.

Although family meals were important in the 18th century, they were less important as communal ritual events because family members were together regularly in their homes for much of the day anyway. By the mid-19th century, with husbands and older children away from home during the day, some meals had become very important. Family meals, and particularly dinner, were the only daily occasions when all of the members of the family were together as a group in relative leisure. As Calvert Vaux, the 19th-century architect and sometime partner of Frederick Law Olmsted, said in the 1850s in reference to the importance of the dining room, mealtime was a "constant and familiar reunion" (quoted in Clark, 1986:42). Catharine Beecher (1842), one of America's most ardent writers on domestic life, also stressed this "reunion" aspect of meals in explaining to servants (whom she clearly looked on as "domestics" and not "help") why it was not appropriate for them to sit and eat with the family at the table. She stated that "the master of a family is often so engaged in business that the only time he can see his wife and children together is at meals, and then he wishes to be at liberty to talk freely, as he could not do, if every stranger he hires must come to his family meal" (p. 88). Catherine Sedgwick (1837) also described the importance of meals in her novel *Home,* which was set in New York. Family meals were "more than the means of sustaining physical wants." They were "opportunities of improvement and social happiness," as they taught eight lessons three times a day with each enactment: "punctuality, order, neatness, temperance, self-denial, kindness, generosity, and hospitality" (p. 28).[4]

One of the ways that the growth in the importance of family meals was expressed was in the elaboration of the preparation of the food itself. In the late 18th and 19th centuries, American cuisine became significantly more sophisticated and complicated than it had been before. Prior to the 1830s, even in urban areas, most people still cooked at the open hearth. The cast-iron stoves that facilitated the elaboration of cuisine among the middle classes began to be produced on a large scale only in this decade (Strasser, 1982:36).

Cookbooks also eased the trend toward serving more elaborate food. They became increasingly popular after the Revolution, serving as vehicles that enabled women to create more complicated meals. Recipes had formerly been handed down from mother to daughter as part of an oral tradition. The first cookbook published in America was written by Amelia Simmons and appeared in 1796. Simmons described herself as an orphan, thereby implying that she herself had not benefited from this oral tradition. She may in fact have mentioned her orphan status to justify the need for a cookbook in traditional American society (noted by Dickinson, 1985:17).

Richard Cummings (1970:41–42) chronicled this aspect of the ritualization of meals by comparing the number of pages in some of the cookbooks published in America during this period. Simmons's book was small in size, with only 46 pages. It was republished in many editions until it was superseded in 1829 by Lydia Child's cookbook, which contained 95 pages. Mrs. Putnam's cookbook, published in 1858, contained 223 pages. The growing size of these cookbooks documents the elaboration through time of the food that families ate as part of this communion ritual.

The discussion of other aspects of the ritualization of family meals is presented here in two chapters. In this one, we explore the background behind the changing structure of family meals—the content, scheduling, table settings, and types of service that women used—with information gleaned from contemporary primary sources. In the next chapter, the focus shifts to some of the accoutrements that served as symbols that were manipulated during the ritual: the ceramic vessels used to serve these meals. The data for this part of the study are derived from a new source for studying family life: the archaeological materials from late-18th- and early-19th-century homes in New York City.[5]

This discussion focuses on the changing social contexts of the meals that were consumed in the urban middle-class and wealthy households of our study. It uses evidence from the prescriptive literature, diaries, fiction, and contemporary travelers' accounts as well as from secondary works derived from these sources. Primary sources are often quite biased in that they usually detail the more formal aspects, rather than the everyday aspects, of domestic life. The prescriptive literature prescribes what domestic life *should* be like, rather than describing what it *is* like. In fact, the existence of a market for prescriptive literature suggests that there were discrepancies between the way people actually conducted themselves and how they thought they should live. However, the increasing popularity of these works in the 1830s indicates that these books filled a need perceived by the women who bought and read them. Travelers' accounts have another kind of bias. Most of the travelers who wrote these works stayed in boardinghouses and were entertained in elite and wealthier middle-class homes. Therefore, they saw and recorded for the most part only the more formal aspects of domestic life.

Although the evidence is frequently distressingly vague, it nonetheless strongly suggests that, during the period of study, women changed the organization, style of presentation, and scheduling of some meals, while leaving others virtually the same.

BREAKFAST

Breakfast, by definition, was always the first meal of the day. It was usually served at around seven or eight in the morning but could be eaten as early as six or as late as nine (Haswell, 1896:70; Hall in Pope-Hennessy, 1931:43; Scott, 1952:67; Sherrill, 1971:82). Breakfast does not appear to have changed much in either its structure or its content during our period, although meats seem to have been more important components of this meal in the late 18th and early 19th centuries than they are today. People usually had bread and butter, tea or coffee (the latter becoming more popular as the early 19th century progressed), and cold meat, eggs, or cheese (Beecher, 1855:308–309; R. Roberts, 1827:43; Root and Rochemont, 1976:120). When Brissot de Warville visited Boston in the 1780s, he noted that there "breakfast consisted of tea, coffee and meats, both broiled and roasted" (quoted in Sherrill, 1971:81). Margaret Hall, visiting New York in the late 1820s, was impressed by the large size of the breakfasts there. At the American Hotel she was served "beefsteak, mutton chops, shad (a sort of fish somewhat resembling flounder), mackeral [sic], omelet and eggs, besides tea, toast, and rolls, all excellent as far as we could put it to trial" (quoted in Pope-Hennessy, 1931:43). In the 1840s, Phila Williams (diary entries for, e.g., 19 and 22 February and 2 March 1844), the wife of a New York merchant, often had a Graham cracker and beefsteak for breakfast.

In the 1840s, Catharine Beecher (1842) described for domestics how the table should be set both for evening tea and supper:

> For breakfast and tea, set the waiter [tray] on *square,* put the cups and saucers in front, and the sugar and slop bowls, and cream cup the back side. Put a sugar spoon, or tongs, by the sugar bowl. Then set the plates around the table at regular distances with a knife in front, and a napkin on one side and a cup mat the back side of it. Put mats for dishes of food in a regular manner, and set these dishes on, square and orderly. Set the tea or coffee either on the waiter, or on a mat at the right hand. (p. 214)

A table setting for serving breakfast is shown in Figure 5–3.

DINNER

Then, as now, dinner was the main meal of the day. For most of the period, it took place in the afternoon, usually at 2 or 3 P.M. Even after the elite moved their homes across town to the west side of Manhattan (see Chapter 3), this meal continued to be held in the afternoon, with men hurrying home for their dinners and then returning to work in the late afternoon. As late as the 1840s, Daniel Williams, a merchant, walked from his Pearl Street store to his home on Chambers Street every day for his dinner (Arfwedson, 1968, I:232; Hall in Pope-Hennessy, 1931:19, 43, 70, 134; Hamilton, 1834:113; Haswell, 1896:70, 72; Sherrill, 1971:82–83; Phila Williams diary, entry for 22 March 1844). After these wealthy families moved their homes northward to the perimeter of the city (see Chapter 3), they changed this custom and shifted their dinner to the early evening. Presumably, this change occurred among those members of the middle class who traveled long distances to work as well.

The literature documents two different kinds of dinners for the late 18th and early 19th centuries: dinner parties and family dinners. Dinner parties were a common form of socializing among wealthier men—they were not taken up by the middle class until much later, in the 1880s (Clark, 1987:154–155). Elite parties took place either at private homes or at hotels and men's clubs and might be held as part of club activities, to commemorate an event, to honor a visiting dignitary, or simply for socializing.

When male dinner parties took place in private homes, the women of the house where the party was held would be included, but their role was primarily to superintend the serving of the meal. Women, unless they were traveling, rarely dined out at the homes of those who were not family members (Hone in Nevins, 1927, passim; Hall in Pope-Hennessey, 1931:121, 212, 213; Trollope, 1839/1984:256, 299). As Thomas Hamilton (1834) noted on his visit to the city in 1830, "Unfortunately, it is not here the fashion to invite the fairer part of creation to entertainments so gross and substantial; and it rarely happens that any ladies are present on such occasions, except those belonging to the family of the host" (Vol. 1, p. 115). Margaret Hall remarked in a letter to her sister that she wrote while visiting New York in the late 1820s that "I suspect ladies are seldom included in dinner invitations in this ungallant place. Mr. Proctor, a lodger here [at the boardinghouse where the Halls were staying], told me that many ladies of the first families in New York have never dined out" (quoted in Pope-Hennessy, 1931:121, 212, 213). And Catharine Beecher confirmed in the 1840s that "It is generally the case, that, at dinner-parties for gentlemen, no ladies are present but those who are members of the family" (1846:234). When women did appear at these parties, they were not seated among the men as they are today. Rather, the women and men sat separately, in two segregated groups at the table (Belden, 1983:29; Watson, 1856:87, 108; Wright, 1981:34–35).

Although also the focus of male social parties among the elite, dinner continued to be primarily a private, family meal throughout the period of study (see Figure 5–1). Most of those who were not household members who attended family dinners were related to each other by blood or marriage. However, the literature suggests that this family meal became increasingly elaborate and ritualized during the first half of the 19th century. Aspects of the elaboration of this meal include the reorganization and increased specialization of its course structure and changes in the style of presentation of the table settings and in the form of table service used in the ritual.

At the beginning of the period, there was relatively little differentiation in the kinds of dishes that made up the main courses of the meal. Throughout colonial times, for all but the wealthy, dinner usually consisted of ubiquitous "one-pot" dishes of soup or stew and bread. On those relatively infrequent occasions when fresh meat was served instead of the salted and dried varieties that were available throughout the year, it was usually served roasted. Fancier dinners might consist of puddings and pies and meats and vegetables. A first course might be made up primarily of meats and vegetables and the second

Figure 5–1. Family dinner and family tea; woodcuts by Alexander Anderson from Sproat's *The School of Good Manners,* published by Samuel Wood and Sons, New York, c. 1822. (Rare Books and Manuscripts Division, The New York Public Library, Astor, Lenox and Tilden Foundations.)

course mainly of pies and puddings, but, unlike today, there was no strict adherence to this course structure. Again, unlike today, the first course also did not necessarily begin with soup. Rather, a pudding was often the first dish consumed during the meal. After the main course(s), the tablecloth might be removed and a dessert of fruit and nuts served on the bare dining room table (Belden, 1983:5, 207; Carter, 1796:129; Dickinson, 1985; R. J. Hooker, 1981:67).

Examples of elaborate versions of these dinners with a less specialized course structure appear in Susannah Carter's how-to book for housewives, which was first published in Philadelphia in 1796. Carter gave several sample menus for nine-dish, two-course meals for various months of the year. For July, for example, she suggested a first course of mackerel, herb soup, boiled goose and stewed red cabbage, breast of veal *à la braise,* venison pastry, chickens, lemon pudding, neck of venison, and mutton cutlets. The second course included roast turkey, fruit, roast pigeons, stewed peas, sweetbreads, custards, apricot tart, fricasee of rabbits, and cucumbers. Each course contained meat, poultry, sweets, and vegetables.

By the 1820s, the contents of each of these courses had become more specialized. The first, as it does today, usually began with soup and fish and continued with meat and vegetable dishes exclusively, and the second, which Americans now referred to as *dessert,* consisted of sweets like pies and puddings as well as, often, cheese, ice, and fruit. The dinner could be made more formal and elaborate for guests with the addition of other courses, such as a game course after the first main course, a cheese and salad course before the pies and puddings, a separate course of ice cream and preserved fruits after the pies and puddings, and a separate fruit course served on the bare wooden table at the end of the meal. More informal family meals could be further simplified with the omission of the soup and the reduction of the number of dishes and courses (Belden, 1983:35; Hall in Pope-Hennessy, 1931:19, 65, 149; R. J. Hooker, 1981:121; Sherrill, 1971:74, 83–85). The importance of each meal could be measured by the number of the dishes within a course and by the number of courses within the meal. This pattern persisted at least to the mid-19th century. The meal had become a highly organized and ritualized event, with a beginning, a middle, and an end.

Margaret Hall described a "family dinner" that she had in the late 1820s in Albany at the home of Governor and Mrs. Clinton. Needless to say, as Hall noted, a family dinner with such a family had to be considered "a family dinner in the first style." The dinner consisted of two courses. The first included boiled mutton, roast beef, mashed turnips, a slaw, beans, potatoes, roast duck, and cauliflower. The second course included bread pudding, ice in a pyramid "rivalling those of Egypt," "a very unseemly piece of cheese," sweetmeats, biscuits, and fruits like melon, peaches, grapes, and plums. Elsewhere, Hall noted that Americans had "no meat along with the sweet things" but often grouped together different categories of foods into a sweet course that in England would have been confined to separate courses, such as tarts, fruit, and cheese (quoted in Pope-Hennessy, 1931:65). Henry Unwin Addington, an Englishman who also visited America in the 1820s, confirmed this course structure of a meat and a sweet and further noted that this was the form of dinner which had been common in England 30 years ago, "in the days of our ancestors" (quoted in Perkins, 1960:33).

There was also a significant change in the presentation of the meal during this period. Although the table setting used was consistently called the Old English or covered-table plan, Americans began to change their interpretation of the plan in the 1830s. According to the Old English plan, all the dishes that made up the first course were placed together on the table in shared serving platters when the diners sat down for the meal. All of the food for each subsequent course was also laid out on the table at the beginning of that course. Nancy Dickinson (1985) pointed out that this arrangement stressed corporate and communal values at the table.

In the early version of this presentation, the focus was on the food rather than on a decorative centerpiece. The serving dishes were often left uncovered so that the food itself was visible. They covered the table in a balanced and symmetrical arrangement, none of them constituting a visual focal point for

ARRANGEMENT

OF A DINNER OR SUPPER TABLE,

CONSISTING OF NINE DISHES.

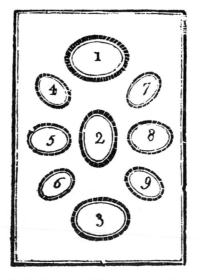

Figure 5–2. Setting the table for dinner, c. 1802, from Susannah Carter's *The Frugal Housewife* (1802). (Rare Books and Manuscripts Division, The New York Public Library, Astor, Lenox and Tilden Foundations.)

the table. Their placement was often discussed in the prescriptive literature, which stressed symmetry and order in the placement of these dishes. The diagram in Figure 5–2 is from Susannah Carter's cookbook and shows how to place the platters and dishes on the table for the nine-dish courses described above. Travelers also occasionally included diagrams of these arrangements in their accounts. The abundance of the food was a measure of the social status of the family that was holding the dinner. The adults at the table carved and served portions of food from the serving dishes nearest them and then either passed the plate directly to the individual who had requested it or, more formally, handed it to a servant, who would take it to its destination.[6]

By the 1840s, however, there was a change of emphasis in the table settings, and a "less cluttered" style became popular. Although all of the food was still on display when the diners sat down to dinner and at the beginning of each subsequent course, the table now had a centerpiece, or a visual focal point at the center of the table, that was not one of the main dishes being served. The centerpiece tended to stand higher than the surrounding platters and dishes. A caster or cruet stand (an ornate metal stand, its set of glass bottles and jars holding the condiments for the meal) might be used for this purpose, or a salad, or even (especially when guests were present) an epergne or flowers. The centerpiece was surrounded by the serving dishes, which were still laid in a regular pattern and placed symmetrically to match on the diagonal or "cross corners." The serving dishes, in turn, were encircled by the individual place settings. The less cluttered style required that fewer dishes be used to make up each course. This aspect of the change was probably related in part to contemporary food reform movements that encouraged a decrease in the consumption of meats and fried foods and smaller portions in general (Beecher, 1855:309; Belden, 1983:28–29, 33; Hooker, 1981:103; Leslie, 1844:257).

Catharine Beecher (1842) described this new method of setting a table for a main course in one of her domestic advice books:

> For *dinner*, set the caster exactly in the middle of the table, and put the salts at two oblique corners of the table between two large spoons crossed. If more spoons are needed lay them each side the caster. Lay the salt spoons across the salt dishes, and the mustard spoon beside its cup. Place the knives and forks at regular distances, so the knife will be at the right hand and the fork at the left. Place a tumbler and napkin so that they will be at the right hand side of each plate. . . . Place the two largest mats opposite the master and mistress of the family, and the others in regular order. Put the two principal dishes on these largest mats. (p. 215)

Figure 5–3 shows a diagram of a similar table setting for a main course from the mid-1840s. The platters and serving dishes are now all covered (Beecher, 1846, e.g., p. 239).

The mistress and master served the soup and the fish, respectively—the dishes that began the meal. The master also carved and served the main meat dish. The servant might hold and serve the plates that were filled by the carver. At formal dinners, servants also carried the vegetable dishes (which had been placed on the table at the beginning of the course) to each of the individual diners as well (Beecher, 1846:236; Dickinson, 1985:13; Leslie, 1844:263; R. Roberts, 1827:54). Some people began to keep the casters and vegetables on a side table and had them handed around by the waiter or servant, as was common in England at this time. The verdict on this practice, according to Eliza Leslie's contribution (1844) to the prescriptive literature, was that "We think this custom too tedious and too troublesome to become very general in America" (p. 263).

Another important difference between family dinners of the 18th century and those of the 19th century was in the composition of the diners: In the late-18th-century middle-class home, the help ate with the family, whereas in the mid-19th-century she usually waited on them at the table and ate separately at another time. Eliza Leslie, in a prescriptive work published in 1844, encouraged the family to have their domestic wait on them at dinner so that

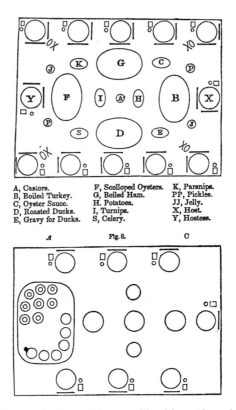

A, Castors.
B, Boiled Turkey.
C, Oyster Sauce.
D, Roasted Ducks.
E, Gravy for Ducks.

F, Scolloped Oysters.
G, Boiled Ham.
H, Potatoes.
I, Turnips.
S, Celery.

K, Parsnips.
PP, Pickles.
JJ, Jelly.
X, Host.
Y, Hostess.

A   Fig. 8.   C

Figure 5–3. Setting the table for dinner (above) and breakfast and tea (below), c. 1846, from Catharine Beecher's *Domestic Receipt-Book* (1846). (Rare Books and Manuscripts Division, The New York Public Library, Astor, Lenox and Tilden Foundations.)

she would not get out of practice or lose respect for them as she presumably would if she sat down at the table with them (p. 267). Other authors of the late 1820s and later were especially specific about the duties of the waiter or servant, implying that this information might not be common knowledge among their middle-class readers. At least two American guides were written for the domestics themselves (Beecher, 1842; R. Roberts, 1827).

It is interesting to note that a new form of dinner service, called service à la française, which was already popular in England and on the Continent, was introduced into New York in the late 1830s but was rejected there. In this form of service, the serving dishes were set on the sideboard, rather than on the table. The set table no longer included the food itself or the shared serving dishes as part of the display. Rather, the sole focal point of the table was an elaborately arranged centerpiece, which was surrounded by the individual place settings. The roasts were carved by the servants at the sideboard, and with the other dishes passed round by the servant one at a time, each dish constituting a course. The master and mistress no longer carved the roasts and served the meats and soups, and the diners could no longer choose the dishes they wished to eat (Belden, 1983:33–34; Dickinson, 1985:2, 5; Williams, 1985:152).

Philip Hone, the former mayor of New York, was quite outspoken in his reaction when he first encountered this new form of service in 1838:

> The dinner was quite à la française. The table, covered with confectionary and gew-gaws, looked like one of the shops down Broadway in the Christmas holidays, but not an eatable thing. The dishes were all handed round; in my opinion a most unsatisfactory mode of proceeding in relation to this important part of the business of a man's life. One does not know how to choose, because you are ignorant of what is coming next, or whether anything more is coming. . . . It will not do. (quoted in Nevins, 1927:299–300)

Only in the late 19th century was this form of service accepted, first for dinner parties and later, in a streamlined version, for family dinners (Belden, 1983:35; Dickinson, 1985; S. Williams, 1985).

The rejection of service à la française and the subsequent acceptance of the less cluttered form of the Old English plan of service are interesting in light of the changing social meaning of this meal. In service à la française, the servant mediated between all of the food that was served and the individual diners, and the shared serving dishes were not even present on the table; only the individual place settings and the elaborate, formal centerpiece were there. The communal aspects of eating together were lost (Dickinson, 1985).

With the less cluttered form of the Old English plan, the central focus of the caster or flowers allowed the elaboration of the material culture of the dining ritual. In addition, however, the master and mistress still directly served the main or "stressed" meat dish and the first dish (soup) of the meal onto the plates of the diners. In this form of service, the servant might mediate only between the less important, "unstressed" dishes and the plates of the diners in passing around only the vegetable dishes. The unity of the group continued to be emphasized by the presence of the shared serving dishes on the table. The communal aspects of eating together continued to be underlined (Douglas, 1975).

We observe this same dichotomy in our more formal dinners today. The service we use at our dinners celebrating holidays that emphasize the values of family and community—such as Thanksgiving and Christmas—is basically the Old English plan. On more formal occasions, where ties of association (rather than ties of community) are stressed, we still use French service.

In addition, it is possible that the adoption of service à la française may have had ramifications that were unacceptable to American culture during this period. The reason given by travelers from overseas for the rejection of this form of service was that there were not enough well-trained servants in America to be able to execute it properly, and there was probably some truth in this explanation. However, there may have been more to it than that. An American traveler in France during the Revolution marveled that the men and women mingled and cheerfully conversed together at the mixed-sex dinner parties there. The lady of the house participated with her guests in the meal's enjoyment, instead of merely superintending the serving of the dinner.[7]

Furthermore, of all the myriad dinner parties that Hone attended in the city and mentioned in his diary for the period of study, he noted taking his "womenfolk" to only two. Both of these dinners occurred toward the end of the period of study and were the only meals that he also recorded as being served à la française (quoted in Nevins, 1927:299–300, 462). Thus, dinner à la française may have connoted a different definition of community: It may have assumed that both men and women sat at the table and socialized together, and this pattern may well have violated the structural opposition of man's sphere and woman's sphere in the United States.

The arrangement of the individual place settings themselves remained relatively unchanged throughout the period of study. Each diner was provided with a plate, with a napkin and a fork placed to its left and a knife (with its sharp side facing inward) and a soup spoon to its right, with glasses (which might include both wineglasses and tumblers for beer, cider, or water) placed to the upper right of the plate. Some 19th-century variations on this plan consisted of placing either the knife or the soup spoon at the top or bottom of the setting, parallel to the table's edge, and the napkin to the right of the plate, as shown in Figure 5–3. Two-pronged forks (used for holding meat while it was cut) were commonly used in the United States well into the nineteenth century, and during the first quarter of the century, most people continued to eat with their knives. The flatware and china for the meal's subsequent courses were displayed on the sideboard or on a side table (Belden, 1983:21, 39; Hall, quoted in Pope-Hennessy, 1931:21, 37; Hooker, 1981:97; Leslie, 1844:257; P. E. Roberts, 1967:169–171; R. Roberts, 1827; Williams, 1985:150).

TEA

Before the mid-18th century, the consumption of tea was confined to wealthier households because of the high cost of the tea itself, the accoutrements needed to serve it, and the leisure time needed to consume it. Around 1750, however, the price of tea came down, and the middle classes began to indulge in it as well. By the late 18th and early 19th centuries, the beverage might be served in three different social contexts in middle-class and wealthier homes: informally as part of breakfast (described above) and high tea (described below), and as the focus of a "tea," which could be a formal evening or afternoon party (Roth, 1961: 64–66; Williams, 1987).

"Tea" was a late-afternoon or evening meal in which the whole family participated and to which outsiders (friends and acquaintances) were invited. In the 1780s, Brissot de Warville noted that "As in England, tea forms the basis of the principal parties in [New York]. It is to tea that a stranger is invited" (quoted in T. E. V. Smith, 1972:116–117). Late-afternoon and evening parties that featured tea as well as buttered bread and cakes or, more elaborately, dessert courses and possibly supper as well as wine were the primary arenas for socializing through the 1840s (Hall in Pope-Hennessy, 1931:168; Perkins, 1960:33; Scott, 1952:124).

Tea was usually served at a small tea table in the sitting room or parlor (see Figures 5–1 and 5–3). Only women served the tea; the mistress or daughter of the house sat at this table, pouring the tea and handing it to those present. In the 18th century, teatime behavior was apparently somewhat unstructured: The tea drinkers could stand or sit around the tea table or elsewhere in the room and could chat, gossip, or play games (Roth, 1961:70–71). By the end of the century, some of these parties had become much more formidable, and the separation of the sexes apparent in other aspects of American culture in the 19th century had already begun at tea parties, as a Frenchman visiting America observed:

> At five o'clock all betake themselves to tea-parties, where everything is conducted with the greatest ceremony. On the right of the mistress of the house are ranged in a half circle all the women, as well attired as possible. A profound silence follows the arrival of each guest, and all the ladies maintain the gravity of judges sitting on the bench. (Quoted in Sherrill, 1971:92)

In the 1820s, some of these evening parties continued to be extremely formal. The English traveler Margaret Hall described one in a letter to her sister:

> I do not remember whether I have described to you at any time the extreme stiffness of an American party. . . . We were last night at one at Mrs. Clinton's. We were invited to tea and went at eight o'clock. On entering the first drawing room both Basil [Hall's husband] and I started back, for we saw none but gentlemen, not a single lady, and we thought there must be some mistake . . . , but in a moment the Governor came forward and giving me his arm hurried me into the adjoining room at the top of which sat Mrs. Clinton. . . . Round the room were placed as many chairs as could be crammed in and a lady upon each, a most formidable circle. . . . In the course of the evening the gentlemen did venture into the room and stood for a short time talking to one or other of the

ladies, . . . and altho' occasionally the ladies had courage to cross the room and change places with each other I never saw any lady standing during the whole evening. (Quoted in Pope-Hennessy, 1931:63)

Later, Hall described a wedding that she attended in Mount Holyoke, Massachusetts, by saying that "[t]he company were seated according to the American fashion as if they were pinned to the wall, and the gentlemen divided from the ladies" (quoted in Pope-Hennessy, 1931:81).

By the 1840s, people no longer regularly served tea as part of their evening parties. Rather, they served wines and lemonade along with dessert courses and sandwiches. Tea parties now took place in the late afternoon. They were primarily social events designed for women because they began while the men were away at work, although men often stopped by them after work as well (Beecher, 1846:241; Williams, 1985:10).

LUNCH, SUPPER, AND HIGH TEA

As some households moved their midday dinners to the evening, they adopted a new midday meal—lunch—which took place at 12 or 1 o'clock. When served at home for women and small children, this was an informal meal that might consist of heated up leftovers, cold meat, bread, soup, or stew. The men working in the business district who no longer returned home for their midday dinners began to frequent downtown restaurants that offered quick lunches. Later in the century, lunches, segregated by sex, developed into important social events for both women and men (Hooker, 1981:145; S. Williams, 1985:146, 147, 165).

Supper was the final meal of the day for all socioeconomic groups in the 18th century. Among the poor, it was served relatively early in the evening, at around 6 or 7, while the wealthy might have this meal later, at around 9 or 10. It was a relatively informal, light meal: As Chastellux reported in the late 18th century, supper "is not the important meal of the Americans" (quoted in Sherrill, 1971:96). The dishes that composed it were often similar to those served at breakfast. Fancier suppers might also be served as the culmination of evening parties. As dinner shifted to the evening in many elite and middle-class households in the 19th century, it replaced the early supper. However, among the fashionable, a late supper might still be served toward the end of an evening party or ball. Among those who continued to have their main meal in the early afternoon, supper continued to be the final meal of the day (Belden, 1983:91; Hall, quoted in Pope-Hennessy, 1931:134; Haswell, 1896:70; R. J. Hooker, 1981:67; S. Williams, 1985:148, 191–192).

For those who continued to have their dinners at midday, late-afternoon tea might be expanded with the addition of cold dishes to a high or family tea that substituted for supper. Apparently, if hot food was served at this early-evening meal, it was referred to as *supper,* whereas if only cold dishes were served, it was called *high tea* (Belden, 1983:251; Hooker, 1981:157; S. Williams, 1985:148–149, 191).

DISCUSSION

This background shows that during the late 18th and early 19th centuries, the social context of different family meals varied and the social meaning of some of them changed. Breakfast and family supper (as opposed to a supper that might be served as part of an evening party) continued to be somewhat informal meals. Lunch became the midday meal in those homes where dinner shifted to the evening; it was segregated by sex, with men eating downtown in the business district and women eating at home. This meal developed into an important social event for men and women as the century progressed.

Whether they occurred in the late afternoon or evening, teas conducted by women continued to be the setting for social gatherings for both sexes and for the display of household status throughout the late 18th and early 19th centuries. For the elite and most members of the middle class, tea was the primary meal at which nonfamily visitors were entertained. By the middle of the century, however, this meal had become feminized into an afternoon social ritual, conducted by and for women.

Dinner, whether held in the afternoon or the evening, was primarily a family meal among the middle class. During the half century following the Revolution, it began to exhibit many of the properties of a ritual. Its course structure became more highly ordered and specialized, and both the food and the table settings became more elaborate. By the middle of the century, this meal, with its daily enactment involving all family members, had become ritualized as a daily family reunion and was a focal point of woman's sphere.

Unfortunately, it is not possible to tell from contemporary written sources if this elaboration occurred in the combined homes and workplaces of the city's wealthy and middle class, or whether it happened only later, after the home had separated from the workplace. In the next chapter, we will explore this issue by analyzing a set of information derived from archaeological materials. These materials consist of the ceramic dishes that were used for serving these meals in the wealthy and middle-class homes of the city.

NOTES

1. These descriptions of the use of space in the Van Voorhis, Bowne, and Robson homes are reconstructed from contemporary accounts and modern interpretations. The reconstruction of the use of space in the Van Voorhis home and workplace is further enhanced by Laidlaw's interpretation (1986:18–19; 1988:32) of the inventory for

the shop and dwelling of Garret Schanck, the silversmith who was Van Voorhis's third cousin, who was, at different times, his apprentice and partner, and who died intestate in New York in 1795. This reconstruction of the use of space in the Van Voorhis shop and dwelling is derived from her interpretation of the inventory in combination with that of Wright (1981:34–36) and Blackmar (1989:47–48).

2. Reconstructed from Blackmar (1989:47–48), Wright (1981:34–36), and Gill (1972:67).

3. Reconstructed from Blackmar (1989:48), Hamilton (1834:100), Trollope (1984:299), and Wright (1981:34–36).

4. See also Strasser (1982:296) and S. Williams (1985:52) on the importance of family meals.

5. Barbara Carson (1990) uses written sources similar to the ones used in this chapter in her rich examination of social life in Washington, D.C., during the same period. Her research on meals, conducted completely independently, generally confirms the interpretations made here. The approach for the next chapter is adapted from Douglas and Isherwood (1979:74, 76) and Hodder (1982:10).

6. Hall (in Pope-Hennessy, 1931:19) noted that the dishes were uncovered; Belden (1983:5, 41) and S. Williams (1985:152) both noted that the amount of food was a measure of a meal's importance. Diagrams of the table are included in Belden (1983:20), Carter (1796:256–260), Pope-Hennessy (1931:66), and Rundell (1823: facing p. 8); the service is described in Belden (1983:21, 35) and by Hall in Pope-Hennessy (1931:21).

7. Hall remarked on the problems of French service and servants in America (quoted in Pope-Hennessy, 1931:188); see also Watson (1856:87).

Chapter 6

The Ritualization of Family Meals II

The Van Voorhis Household, 1780s

In the 1780s, Catherine and Daniel Van Voorhis and their family, apprentices, journeymen, and help all ate their meals together in their front basement room from plates of plain white earthenware with simple molded rims (see Figure 6–1). When their friends joined them for evening parties, they drank their tea from Chinese porcelain tea bowls decorated with painted Chinese landscapes and floral motifs (see Figure 6–2).[1]

The Bowne Household, circa 1805

Around 1810, Richard and Penelope Bowne also ate their meals in their front basement room, but the dishes they used were quite different from the ones in the Van Voorhis home. Instead of the simple, all-white earthenware with molded rims popular two decades earlier, Penelope Bowne had two contrasting sets of dishes. One was all white like the Van Voorhis earthenware but was completely plain, with no molded decoration at all (see Figure 6–3). The other set was also made of earthenware but was more elaborately decorated with a shell-edged pattern that was molded around the rim and was colored bright green (see Figure 6–4). The Bownes probably used earthenware tea bowls for their tea at breakfast and Chinese porcelain tea bowls for company at evening tea. Many of their tea vessels were decorated with floral motifs (see Figure 6–5).[2]

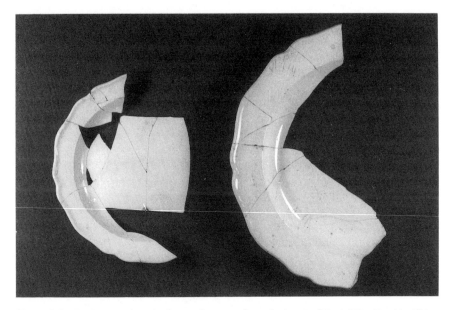

Figure 6–1. Creamware plates in the royal pattern, from the home of Daniel Van Voorhis. This pattern was very popular with New Yorkers in the 1780s. (Small plate 6¹/₈″ diameter; South Street Seaport Museum.)

Figure 6–2. Blue-on-white Chinese export porcelain tea bowl and saucer decorated with Chinese landscapes. These vessels, from the home of Daniel Van Voorhis, the silversmith, are typical of those used in New York in the 1780s. (The bowl is 2³/₈″ high; South Street Seaport Museum.)

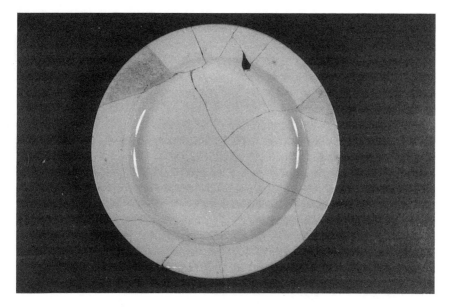

Figure 6–3. Creamware plate in the plain or Paris pattern, from the home of Richard Bowne, the Pearl Street druggist, c. 1810. (The plate is 9⁹/₁₆″ in diameter; South Street Seaport Museum.)

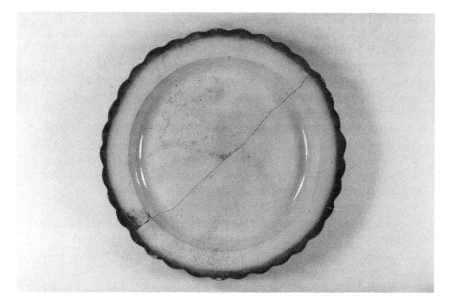

Figure 6–4. Pearlware plate with green shell-edged decoration, from the home of Richard Bowne, the Pearl Street druggist, c. 1810. (The plate is 8³/₈″ in diameter; South Street Seaport Museum.)

Figure 6–5. Enamel-painted Chinese export porcelain tea bowl and saucer. Chinese-style tea bowls like this one were popular from the 17th through the early 19th centuries. These tea vessels from the Bowne household typify the decorative styles popular in wealthier households during the first decade of the 19th century. (The bowl is 2¼″ high; South Street Seaport Museum.)

Figure 6–6. Blue transfer-printed pearlware plate with a Chinese landscape in the willow pattern. This plate, from the Robson home, typifies those popular among New Yorkers in the 1820s. (The plate is 10″ in diameter; South Street Seaport Museum.)

The Robson Household, 1820s

Two decades later, the Robsons ate their dinners and drank their teas from dishes that were quite different from those of the Bownes. Although they had some shell-edged plates, most of their table dishes came from two blue-on-white sets that were busily decorated with Chinese landscapes. One set was made of relatively inexpensive, transfer-printed British earthenware decorated in the popular willow pattern (see Figure 6–6), and the other was made of more expensive Chinese export porcelain decorated in the Canton style (see Figure 6–7). Their teacups were made of British earthenware and were decorated for the most part with Western floral motifs (see Figure 6–8).[3]

* * * * *

In the last chapter, we saw from contemporary accounts how middle-class and wealthy New Yorkers ritualized their dinners into family reunions during the late 18th and early 19th centuries. Unfortunately, however, contemporary accounts do not tell us whether the elaboration of this aspect of domesticity took place relatively early, within the city's combined homes and workplaces, or only later, after people had moved their homes away from their businesses. One way to resolve this question is to look at the actual ceramic dishes that women used in presenting and serving these meals to their families. The dishes played an important role in the ritualization of these meals; they were the physical symbols that were manipulated as part of the ritual (see Geertz, 1973:91). In looking at them, we can see if women like Penelope Bowne and Eliza Robson began to ritualize their meals in the front basement rooms of their combined homes and workplaces, or if they waited until their families had moved their homes away from their workplaces, as the Robsons did later, in the 19th century.

In this chapter, we begin by looking at the ceramic dishes available to New York families during the period of study. Next, we discuss the new data source used here to examine the dishes that these families were actually using in their homes: the ceramic dishes excavated at archaeological sites in the city. Some of these dishes were actually used in the Van Voorhis, Bowne, and Robson homes. Then, we look at changes first in the decorative style and then in the relative cost of these dishes. Finally, we explore the development of the use of contrasting sets of tableware within these middle-class households in the city.

THE AVAILABILITY OF CERAMIC VESSELS

From the 17th through the mid-18th centuries, New Yorkers bought ceramic dishes imported from a wide variety of places: porcelains from East

Figure 6–7. Chinese export porcelain soup bowl painted in blue-on-white with a Chinese landscape in the Canton pattern, from the Robson home, c. 1825. (The bowl is 8⅞″ in diameter; South Street Seaport Museum.)

Figure 6–8. Blue transfer-printed whiteware tea cup and saucer, made at the Spode pottery and decorated in the geranium pattern. Tea cups with handles like this one became popular in the 1820s. This cup and saucer are part of a set from the Robson home. The cup is 2¼″ high; South Street Seaport Museum.)

Asia and earthenwares and stonewares from Britain and the Continent. Beginning in the third quarter of the 18th century, however, mass-produced British earthenwares and Chinese porcelains made for export to the West began to be extremely popular in the United States and Britain and on the Continent. These ceramics continued to dominate the U.S. market until the middle of the 19th century (Miller, Martin, and Dickinson, 1989:3).

The British Staffordshire potteries began to industrialize in the late 18th century. At first, the U.S. market played a relatively minor role in the British potters' marketing efforts. After the British lost access to markets on the Continent because of the Napoleonic Wars and European tariffs, however, the U.S. market became more and more important to the British potters and their agents. From the end of the War of 1812 through the mid-19th century, the U.S. market absorbed almost half of the ceramics exported from England. During this later period, the Staffordshire potters were extremely sensitive to the needs and preferences of the U.S. market. They also began to discount the price of their wares, so that the cost of the dishes dropped during the early 19th century (Miller et al., 1989).

Most of the dishes that New Yorkers bought were earthenwares produced at the Staffordshire potteries. Creamware, a cream-colored earthenware that was sold plain or with molded, enamel-painted, or transfer-printed decoration, was introduced in the 1760s. Pearlware, with its blue-painted designs on a bluish-cast ground in obvious imitation of Chinese porcelain, was introduced around 1780, and blue transfer-printed designs on pearlware followed in the 1790s. In the 1820s, white wares, with a true white cast, were introduced and remained popular for the rest of the century. Transfer-printed patterns in other colors, such as red, brown, green, black, and purple, were also introduced in that decade and were used to embellish the white wares (Miller et al., 1989:4–7).

Porcelains from China were also available for purchase throughout the period. Direct trade between the United States and China began immediately after the Revolution. Both tablewares and teawares were produced for export by the Chinese. Some were painted in blue under the glaze, and others were painted over the glaze in a host of bright enamel colors. These wares were either mass-produced for the lower-income market or decorated to order for wealthier customers (Mudge, 1981: 1986).

Contemporary accounts give us a general idea of the vessels that were used in more elegant homes in the United States during this period. In the 1820s, Margaret Hall, the British traveler who ridiculed so many aspects of the domestic arrangements of the Americans in her letters to her sister, consistently admired the china and glassware that she saw on their tables—"they have the most beautiful china," she wrote. In the course of an evening party at Governor Clinton's, for example, she remarked on the "beautiful, [sic] china plates" that were handed around. In describing her dinner with the same family, she emphasized, "I must first premise that we had beautiful china and cut glass an inch thick." At a party in New England, she noted that "there was the most beautiful set of Sevres [sic] dessert china that I ever saw with ice pails to match" (quoted in Pope-Hennessy, 1931:63, 65, 89).

We also know about the forms of the ceramic vessels that were available on the U.S. market. Dishes used for serving dinner usually included plates in several sizes, with large soup plates and table plates for the meals' main meat and pudding courses and smaller plates for dessert and cheese. The forms of the tableware used at lunch and supper were similar to those used for dinner. There were serving dishes like butter and sauce boats and tureens with covers and stands, as well as deep dishes and platters in a variety of sizes. Serving dishes might be made of ceramic, silver, or silver plate, whereas the plates were almost always made of ceramic (Dickinson, n.d.; Mudge, 1981:150, 258–260).[4]

Evidently, silver serving dishes were not very common in the United States, however, even in the homes of the rich. Margaret Hall (quoted in Pope-Hennessy, 1931:88, 147) noted at one point during her trip here that she had "not yet seen any plate at the tables of those we have dined with." Later in her trip, when she went to Philadelphia, she dined at the home of a man who was "said to live in the best style of anyone in Philadelphia, and most assuredly [she] had a grand dinner, such heaps of plate, silver and gold, such beautiful French china, and such heaps of dinner, well-dressed, however." This was the only plate that she mentioned encountering in her visits into America's more elegant homes. Less expensive silver-plated wares became common only later, in the mid-19th century, after the refinement of the electroplating process in the 1840s and the lowering of the price of silver with the discovery of the Comstock lode in Nevada in the late 1850s (Rainwater, 1987).

The types of dishes used to set the table for tea and breakfast were quite similar to each other. They might include cups and saucers, small plates, tea and coffee pots, a cream pot, a sugar bowl or pot, and a slop bowl (which was used for disposing of the dregs of tea that were left in the bottom of the cups). For tea, a tea cannister to hold the dry tea leaves was also brought to the table, and a cake plate might be used, too. At breakfast, a butter boat was often placed on the table as well (Mudge, 1981:150, 258–259; Roth, 1961:74, 80).

All of the vessels on the breakfast table were made of ceramic, usually a simple earthenware. For tea and evening parties, however, the serving vessels in wealthy homes might be made of silver or later, in middle-class homes, of silver plate, but the cups and saucers and the cake plates were always made of ceramic, and often of porcelain. As early as the late 18th century, a French traveler to the United States made the exaggerated remark that "there is not a single citizen who does not drink [tea] from porcelain cups" (quoted in Sherrill, 1971:94). By 1820, a British traveler noted that "although it should require the united exertions of the family to effect the object, few young girls, at the present day, enter into the marriage state, without contributing their respective China Ware Tea Setts to the general concern" (quoted in Mudge, 1981:146).

Before the War of 1812, New Yorkers usually purchased their ceramics at the shops of the merchants who imported them. When Elizabeth Bleecker (1799–1806) was in her late teens, she recorded in her diary on several occasions the ceramic purchases she made for her mother. On 16 January 1799, for example, she reported that she "went to Mrs. Christie's for Mama & bought 1 Cup & 1 Bowl." On 24 August 1799, she wrote that

> after tea Mary and I went to look for a Tea-Pot and brought one home for to shew Mama—it did not suit & we were going back with it, when I broke the spout. I was of course oblig'd to pay for it—I paid ten shillings for carelessness.

After her marriage to Alexander MacDonald in 1800, Bleecker recorded the purchases of ceramics and other household goods that she made for her first home. The entries (2, 8, and 14 May 1800) provide an idea of how the daughter of a wealthy family went about setting up house at the turn of the 19th century. After her April marriage, she and her husband continued to live with her family for several months while they went about setting up their own home. Her husband first took a house in Broad Street, but as she did not like it ("It has been left in a very dirty situation, and is very much out of repair"), he rented that house out, and together the couple chose and rented a house in William Street.

Between the time when they took the house in May and the time when they finally moved into it in August, Bleecker recorded in her diary (3, 14, 16, and 17 July and 9 August 1800) some of the purchases of household goods that she made for her new home. These purchases included carpeting both for the rooms and for the stairs, wallpaper, chairs, and other furniture, as well as dishes and kitchen equipment. In July, she and her mother went shopping in Broad Street, where her mother bought her some "Cups and Saucers," presumably for tea. Later in the month she went out again with her mother to shop for "Pots and Kettles." She also went alone on three separate occasions to shop for "Plates and Dishes." In August, just before the couple moved into their new house, she and her sister Mary went again to Mrs. Christie's shop in Maiden Lane to "look for Tea Pots." They evidently did not find any that suited, because she continued to shop for one (2 September 1800). She finally reported (5 September 1800) that she had bought "a Tea-Pot, Sugar Pot, and Milk Pot at Mr. Peter's," another china-and-glass dealer who also had his shop in Maiden Lane.

Elizabeth Bleecker's diary entries suggest that women took an active role and used a lot of thought in choosing dishes to grace their tables. It is only unfortunate that she and her contemporaries did not describe their purchases in greater detail. We therefore have to look to other sources to find out about the ceramics that were used in New York during this period.

THE CERAMIC VESSELS

As noted above, unfortunately, contemporary observers did not describe the dishes that were used to enhance the tables of late-18th- and early-19th-century New Yorkers. Merchants' records also tell us only about the vessels that a particular merchant had in stock at a particular time. Dishes in museum collections can give us only a biased view of the material life at the tables of the past. The reason is that most of the dishes that have survived to make up these collections are the relatively valuable, rarely used pieces that belonged to the elite. These pieces were not subjected to the high rate of breakage of the dishes in everyday use; instead, they survived to become the heirlooms that were ultimately donated to a museum. The dishes shown in paintings from this period are usually those used in the more formal meals that were depicted.

Archaeological collections, on the other hand, provide not only our best but perhaps our only source for examining the dishes that were in daily use in late-18th- and early-19th-century homes. These dishes were used in individual and often identifiable households and might have been acquired from a number of sources over a long period of time. The dishes were often broken in the course of everyday use and then discarded. They then became part of the archaeological record that, centuries later, can be examined by archaeologists for information on the poorly understood aspects of daily life in New York in the early 19th century.

I looked at the dishes that were used in 11 late-18th- and early-19th-century New York households in order to see whether the elaboration of this aspect of domesticity occurred earlier, in the combined homes and workplaces of the city's middle and wealthier class, or whether this elaboration occurred only later, after the separation of the home and the workplace. The dishes were unearthed in the course of archaeological excavations at six different sites in Manhattan. The ceramic assemblages and the archaeological features and the sites where they were found are all discussed in Appendix E; Figure 6–9 shows the location of each of the archaeological sites.

I place the 11 assemblages of dishes in three chronological groups based on the average date of purchase of the vessels in each assemblage. The assemblages in the early group date to the 1780s, those in the middle group date to the first decade of the 19th century, and those in the later group date to the 1820s. Because we can assume that these dishes continued to be used for at

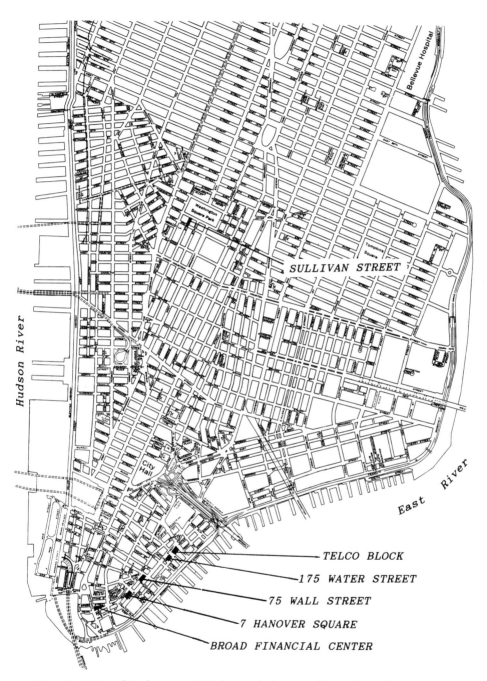

Figure 6–9. Map of Manhattan, c. 1980, showing the location of the archaeological sites where the ceramics used in this study were found. (Courtesy of the Department of City Planning, City of New York.)

137

least a decade after purchase, together the assemblages can tell us about the ceramics that were in use in homes dating from the 1780s to the 1830s. There are four assemblages in both the early and the middle groups and three in the later group. The methods used to assign these assemblages of dishes to particular time periods and in some cases to identified households are described in Appendix E.

Table 6–1 presents a summary of the information on the households where the dishes were used. The occupations of the heads of the households represent both the manufacturing and the commercial sectors of the economy. Two artisans (including the jeweler and silversmith Daniel Van Voorhis), several merchants (including the druggist Richard N. Bowne), and the doctor Benjamin Robson are included here. All of the assemblages of dishes in the early and middle groups and one of those in the later group probably originated in combined homes and workplaces, whereas only one of those in the later group came from a home that had definitely separated from its associated workplace. The provenience of two of the assemblages (Sets 7 and 10) is unclear.

In the next three sections of this chapter, I discuss various aspects of the ceramics from these households: their style of decoration, their relative cost, and their occurrence in matched sets. The data are presented in greater detail in Appendix E.

STYLES OF DECORATION

Recently, many archaeologists have begun to look at the style of objects as a way of exploring the definition and maintenance of social boundaries between social groups. The rationale behind this approach is that individuals use the style of material objects to mark their group identity or membership in a group.[5] Differences in style can also be used to mark the definition of boundaries between social arenas, where different messages are being conveyed, within the same social group. By extension, changes through time in an object's style also express changes in the social meaning of that object and in the social context in which it was used.

Here, we look at the styles of the motifs that embellished the ceramic dishes used in the homes of middle-class New Yorkers in the late 18th and early 19th centuries. Historical accounts suggest that some meals, like dinner, were predominantly private family occasions, whereas others, such as tea, were more public events. The individuals who participated in these different meals were therefore acting in different social arenas, where different kinds of messages were being conveyed to the participants. Tea provided an arena for social interaction between the members of a household and outsiders. As the

Table 6–1. Information on Households Where Sets of Ceramic Dishes in Archae-ological Collections Were Used, Including Occupation of the Household Heads and Whether or Not Homes Were Integrated with Commercial Workplaces.

Vessel Set	Occupation of household head	Separate home and workplace		Combined home and workplace
Early Group, 1780s				
1.	Daniel Van Voorhis, jeweler and silversmith			x
2.	Artisan: hatter			x
3.	Merchant			x
4.	Merchant			x
Middle Group, 1800s				
5.	Richard N. Bowne, druggist			x
6.	Grocer			x
7.	Merchant or artisan	x	(or)	x
8.	Merchant			x
Later Group, 1820s				
9.	Benjamin Robson, physician			x
10.	Druggist or boardinghouse keeper	x	(or)	x
11.	Commission merchant	x		

19th century progressed, tea also became feminized as a social ritual for women. Dinner and other family meals, on the other hand, became more important as family rituals, as they were the only daily occasions when the entire family was together. If this interpretation is true, we would expect the styles of the motifs used to decorate the teawares and tablewares to be consistently different from each other during each period, because the social meaning of these meals was different. Furthermore, we would expect the decorative styles of the vessels used at each of these meals to change through time as the social meaning of their contexts or arenas of use changed.

If we can see changes in the styles used in the decoration of the tableware dishes from the households in early, middle, and later groups, these changes would suggest that the social meaning of dinner and other private meals changed during this period. Furthermore, stylistic differences between the dinnerwares dating from the early and middle periods would indicate that changes in the social meaning of this meal were already under way in the combined homes and workplaces where these ceramics were used.

Here, the decorative styles of the tablewares and teawares from the assemblages are classified into four broad groups. These groups encompass most of the styles that were available during the period: minimally decorated all-white neoclassical vessels (which may or may not have molded decoration at the rim; see Figures 6–1 and 6–3), neoclassical shell-edged wares (which are decorated with molded rims painted in either green or blue; see Figure 6–4), wares that are decorated with romantic Chinese landscapes (see Figures 6–2, 6–6, and 6–7), and wares decorated with neoclassical and romantic floral motifs (see Figures 6–5 and 6–8). Throughout the entire period of study, vessels could be purchased with most of these different kinds of decoration: plain white tableware and teaware; tableware and teaware decorated with painted or transferprinted Chinese landscapes and floral motifs; and shell-edged creamware, pearlware, and whiteware plates. The only combination of style and vessel form that was not available throughout the period was teaware dishes decorated in the shell-edged pattern. Teaware vessels decorated in this style were produced in the 1770s, but they were not available later on, presumably because they were not popular.[6]

Figure 6–10 shows the mean percentages of the tableware and teaware dishes decorated with these different styles of motifs for each of the chronological groups. The kinds of motifs on both the teawares and the tablewares are consistently different from each other within each of the chronological groups, and the kinds of motifs popular for both the tableware and the teaware changed through time as well.

For the early group, dating to the 1780s, most of the tablewares are minimally decorated white vessels with molded rims like the ones that were used in the Van Voorhis household (see Figure 6–1). Vessels in the royal pattern predominated in all four of the households in this group (see Table 6–2). The teawares, on the other hand, are evenly represented by those decorated with Chinese landscapes (like those from the Van Voorhis household shown in Figure 6–2) and those decorated with floral motifs.

For the middle group, dating to the first decade of the 19th century, most of the tableware vessels are decorated with shell-edged motifs painted in blue or green (see Figure 6–4). Green shell-edge predominated in two of the households—including the Bowne home—and blue shell edge in the other two. Each household had plain white vessels as well. However, the most popular style for plain white plates in the Bowne and other middle-period households was no longer the royal pattern popular in the early period, but the Paris pattern, which has no molded decoration at all (see Figure 6–3).

The teawares in these middle-period households had also changed. Tea cups and saucers with floral motifs (see Figure 6–5) were now more popular, and they predominate over those decorated with Chinese landscapes in three of the four households.

Finally, for the later group dating to the 1820s, there is a marked and clear-cut change in the motifs preferred in both the tablewares and the teawares: Most of the tablewares from the households in this group are decorated with Chinese landscapes like those the Robsons used (see Figures 6–6 and 6–7), whereas most of the teawares are embellished differently, with floral motifs (see Figure 6–8).

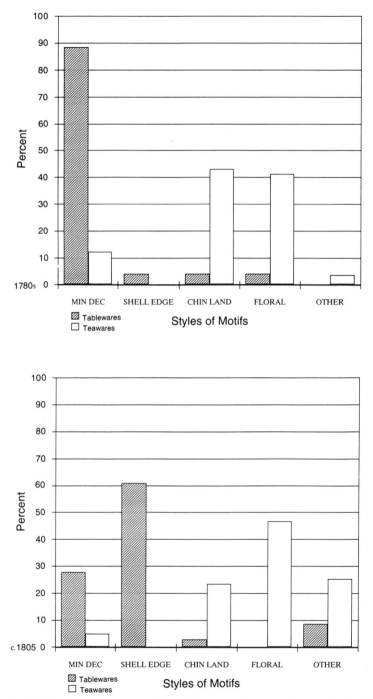

Figure 6–10. The mean percentages of the tablewares and teawares decorated with different styles of motifs, by chronological group.

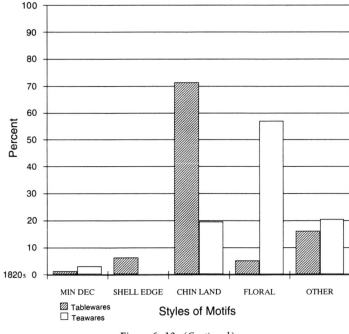

Figure 6–10. (*Continued*)

The changes in the kinds of decorative motifs on the tablewares and teawares throughout the period suggest that the women who were buying them to serve dinner and tea were redefining the meaning of these meals. Furthermore, the differences that we can see between the tableware dishes in the early and middle groups tells us that women began this redefinition before the first decade of the 19th century, in the combined homes and workplaces of the city's middle class.

THE RELATIVE COST OF THE TABLEWARES AND TEAWARES

We also might be able to see changes in the social meaning of these meals by looking at the monetary value of the dishes that were used to present them. We would expect that, as dinner and other family meals became more important as ritualized family reunions, families would be willing to spend more money to buy the dishes used to present them. On the other hand, we would not expect to see a similar increase in the value of the teaware dishes that people were buying. Although one of the social contexts in which tea was served changed (from its being the keystone of evening parties to its being the focus of women's afternoon parties), nevertheless tea continued to be the focus of the meal to which outsiders were invited into the home. We would expect the tea dishes used at these tea parties to be quite expensive. Tea also continued to be served at relatively informal, private meals like breakfast and supper throughout the period. We would expect the tea dishes used at these meals to be less expensive. We would therefore expect the value of the dishes used to serve these two kinds of teas to average out to be relatively high, and to remain consistently high throughout the period of study.

Figure 6–11 shows the mean relative monetary values of the tableware and teaware dishes from the 11 households by chronological period. The method used to compute the relative values was adapted from the work of George Miller (1980, 1988) and is discussed in Appendix E. The figure shows that the curves of the mean values for the different kinds of dishes are quite different from each other and that they change through time. The values for the teawares increased but only very slightly during the period. The shape of that curve suggests that the goal of the mistress of the house was always to have a showy teaset, and she continued to be able to achieve this goal through-

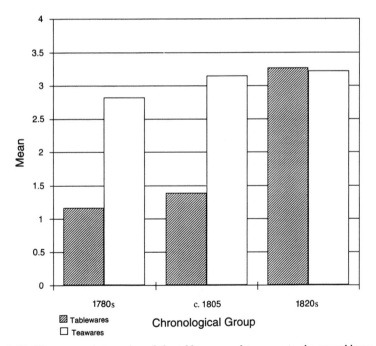

Figure 6–11. The mean relative value of the tablewares and teawares in the assemblages, by chronological group.

out the period. This is what we might expect for dishes used in a social ceremony like tea, which was consistently used to display a household's socio-economic status to outsiders.

The tableware dishes used at family meals, on the other hand, show a marked increase in value relative to the teaware dishes during the same period: They started out at less than half the value of the teawares for the early period and ended up being equal to them in value for the later period. The increase was relatively modest between the vessels in the early 1780s group and the middle circa-1805 group, but there was a quantum leap of well over 100% between the value of the vessels in the middle circa-1805 group and the later 1820s group. This jump shows that during the first three decades of the century, New Yorkers were willing to spend ever-increasing amounts of money on the dishes that they used at family meals.

By the 1820s, the mistresses of these households were willing to spend as much for their tableware dishes, which were usually seen and used only by household members, as for their teaware dishes, which were used to entertain outsiders. This consumer decision suggests that the social context of family meals and the meaning of family life were changing as well: Family meals and domestic life were becoming more and more important inside the combined homes and workplaces of the city's middle class.

THE USE OF MATCHED DISHES

Finally, we look at the use of matched dishes for presenting family dinners and social teas in these Federal households. If we look on differences in style as expressing social boundaries, the unity of style expressed by the use of a matched set of dishes emphasizes the community of a group, rather than the differences among its individual members. We would therefore expect that matched dishes were used at family meals throughout the whole period, and that, in fact, is what we find (see Table 6–2).

In addition, there is enormous standardization in the tableware patterns that were popular in each of the periods. All of the households in each chronological group had tableware dishes made of matching wares decorated with matching designs (see Table 6–2), with relatively little variation in the details of the decoration on even the hand-painted wares. All of the households in the early group had plates decorated in the royal pattern, all of those in the middle group had plates decorated with shell-edged motifs, and all of those in the later group had porcelain dishes decorated in the Canton pattern.

The development of the use of different and contrasting tableware sets within each individual household also suggests an elaboration through time. All of the sets from the early group are made up of minimally decorated, plain

Table 6–2. Sets of Tableware Vessels in Archaeological
Assemblages from All Households

Assemblages	Tableware sets	
	Pattern	n
Early group, 1780s		
1. Daniel Van Voorhis,	Royal	15
jeweler and silversmith	Diamond/beaded	2
	Feather	7
2. Artisan: hatter	Royal	5
	Plain	2
	Shell-edged (uncolored)	2
3. Merchant	Royal	2
4. Merchant	Royal	10
	Plain	2
Middle group, c. 1805		
5. Richard N. Bowne,	Plain	7
druggist	Shell-edged—blue	6
	Shell-edged—green	14
	Willow	2
6. Grocer	Royal	4
	Plain	6
	Shell-edged—blue	8
	Shell-edged—green	2
7. Merchant or artisan	Royal	4
	Shell-edged—blue	15
	Shell-edged—green	3
8. Merchant	Royal	2
	Plain	2
	Shell-edged—blue	3
	Shell-edged—green	5
	Western landscape	4
Later group, 1820s		
9. Benjamin Robson,	Plain	2
physician	Shell-edged—blue	6
	Shell-edged—green	3
	Canton porcelain	12
	Willow	14
	Unidentified Chinese porcelain	7
	(3 different patterns)	
	Fitzhugh porcelain	4
	Western landscape	2
10. Druggist or	Canton porcelain	8
boardinghouse keeper	Willow	3
11. Commission merchant	Canton porcelain	3

white vessels. It is hard for us today to imagine which set was used to mark the rank of more and less important meals. Even though we can assume that contrasting sets of pewter plates could have been used as alternatives to these plain white dishes, they are similar in style to the ceramic plates.[7] The larger collections from the households from the two later periods contain contrasting sets of ceramic plates that can be differentiated either on the basis of their degree of decoration (the sets of decorated shell-edged and plain Paris plates of the middle period, for example, or the shell-edged and fancier chinoiserie willow and Canton plates of the later period), or on the basis of their relative cost (the sets of cheaper plain white and more expensive shell-edged earthenware of the middle period and the sets of expensive Canton porcelains and cheaper willow-patterned and shell-edged earthenwares of the later period). The finding of contrasting sets suggests that, at least as early as the middle period around 1805, New Yorkers had elaborated their system of family meals into more and less important events, and that they used contrasting sets of ceramic dishes as markers to rank the different level of importance of each meal—perhaps to contrast, for example, Sunday dinner to weekday dinner, or to mark the importance of family dinner as opposed to other meals.

The meaning of the contrasting blue- and green-painted trim on the shell-edged plates that were popular in the middle period (see Figure 6–4) is not clear: Blue trim was most popular in two of the households and green in the other two. Were these contrasting colors used interchangeably for the same course of the same meal? Or were they used to mark different courses of a meal? Was one color more popular first, and then the other (with green being replaced by blue, as the latter continued to be popular later in the 19th century)? Or were plates in one color ranked more highly than those in the other and used only for special occasions?

The standardization among the tablewares from all of the households for the later period is particularly striking when we take into account the efforts of the Staffordshire potters to compete for the U.S. market after the War of 1812. The potters began to produce large numbers of vessels decorated with U.S. views and national heroes, which were apparently not very popular, as they almost never turn up in archaeological assemblages dating from this period (Miller *et al.*:14). The consistency of the tableware patterns from the New York City households during the three chronological periods indicates that, like Elizabeth Bleecker, most women had very precise ideas about what was suitable when they went shopping for their dishes.

The matched teaware cups and saucers are quite different in this regard and are not standardized at all. The most popular pattern in tewares from each of the households is depicted on an average of only about a third of the tea vessels in each assemblage, and very few of these patterns turn up in the assemblages from more than one household.

The lady of the house may well have used the standardization of the tablewares in each period to emphasize to the members of her household the importance and universality of the community values of the family. As the social meaning of home life and family dinner was rapidly changing, the standardization of these dishes was important, so that their message came through loud and clear. This standardization is particularly striking when we remember that these objects were seen regularly primarily by household members and kin.

The mistress used the teaware dishes, on other hand, in two very different arenas: for entertaining friends of the same class from outside the home at tea parties and for other, more intimate meals. The diversity of the patterns on the tea cups expresses both the differences between these two arenas and the different messages that different households were sending out about their position in this highly diversified society. In addition, the hostess did not use matched sets of teawares because she did not care to stress the communal values shared by household members and their guests.

CONCLUSION

We can learn a great deal about changes in family dinner and other meals and, by extension, about the development of woman's sphere itself during this period by combining the information learned from contemporary accounts (outlined in the last chapter) with the information gleaned from the dishes in the archaeological collections.

During the early part of the period, in the 1780s, the sensory stimulus of the food was the primary focus of family dinner and other private meals. The food was highly visible: It was presented in serving dishes that were often uncovered and that were arranged in a highly structured and symmetrical pattern, following the Old English plan. As in the Van Voorhis home, the dishes and plates, whether made of ceramic or pewter, were plain, and their simple molded decorations were confined to their rims (see Figure 6–1). The dishes simply provided a frame for the important item, the food itself. Furthermore, the importance of a dinner was simply measured by the quantity of the food, by the number of different dishes that were placed on the table in each course, and by the number of courses in which the dishes were presented.

There was little differentiation in the structure of the main courses: Pies and puddings and meats and vegetables could be placed on the table together, and the pudding was often the first dish consumed at the meal. The master and the mistress and the other adults at the table served each other, themselves, and the children from the common serving dishes.

During the middle period, in the first decade of the 19th century, the food at family meals continued to be a primary focus, and the dishes were still presented according to the Old English plan. However, women had instituted an important change in the staging of these meals. This change embodied the elaboration and specialization of family meals and marked the beginning of the ritualization process. The importance of a meal could now be marked by the elaboration of the ceramic vessels that were used in its presentation as well as by the number of dishes and courses it contained. Plain white, completely undecorated china plates (see Figure 6–3) were used, but presumably only for the most mundane of meals. These dishes, with their plain, unmolded rims, stood in stark contrast to the more highly decorated sets that were also popular. More important occasions were marked by the use of the more highly decorated and costly shell-edged vessels, which were brightly trimmed in blue or green (see Figure 6–4). These dishes did not detract from the importance of the food, however; rather, the confinement of the decoration to the vessel's rim served only to enhance the food's importance. Such contrasting sets of dishes were used in the Bowne home.

By the later period, in the 1820s, women had instituted further elaborations in the staging of these meals. First, the number of courses in which the meals were presented was still used to mark their rank, but the courses had become much more specialized. Family dinner was now composed of two or more main courses. The first was made up of meats and vegetables and might begin with soup and fish. Pies and puddings were confined to the second course, which might also include ice creams and other sweets as well as cheese and fruit. For more elaborate dinners, these foods could be presented separately in additional courses.

There was also a change in how the meal was served. Domestics often handed around some of the dishes, but these were only the dishes that were not regarded as the most important ones. Instead, the master and the mistress served the more important dishes. The mistress served the soup, the dish that opened the meal, and thus emphasized her role as family nurturer, whereas the master served the roast or main meat dish, the most stressed item on the menu, and thus underlined his role as family provider.

Finally, the meal's focus was no longer on the food alone; it was also on the dishes that served as symbols in this ritual and were used to present the meal. Serving dishes were still displayed symmetrically on the table, but these serving dishes were now covered, so that the ceramic covers, rather than the food itself, were visible to the diners when they sat down to eat. Furthermore, the patterns of the dishes used in the homes of the Robsons and their contemporaries had dramatically changed. The busy blue chinoiserie decorations on the most popular kinds of china sets did not simply serve to enhance the food but almost replaced it in importance (see Figures 6–6 and 6–7). Whether these sets were used in the most quotidian of meals (like the cheaper willow earthenwares), or whether they were reserved for special occasions (like the more costly Chinese Canton porcelains), the blue-on-white Chinese landscapes used to decorate them covered almost all of the available space on each vessel. This intensification in decoration expressed the changes in the meaning of this meal.

This study of household dishes indicates that the mistresses of these families were well on their way to elaborating dinner and other family meals into the secular rituals of woman's sphere by the 1820s. Furthermore, it suggests that they began this ritualization process even earlier, in the first decade of the 19th century, in the integrated homes and workplaces of the city's middle class, well before the separation of the home and the workplace.

NOTES

1. The kinds of dishes used in the Van Voorhis home are inferred from the archaeological materials found on an old basement floor at the 75 Wall Street site. The materials date from the 1780s and include a great number of crucibles and other items from a silver- and goldsmith shop as well as domestic materials. The property's address was 27 Hanover Square in the 1780s. Daniel Van Voorhis is the only silversmith documented as working at this address during this period; he lived and worked there from about 1784 until about 1787 (Wall, 1987:363). Therefore, I have inferred that the crucibles and, by extension, the domestic materials associated with them were used in his home. The archaeological materials are in the 75 Wall Street collection at the South Street Seaport Museum.

2. The kinds of dishes used in the Bowne home are inferred from the archaeological materials found in a privy at the 75 Wall Street site. Based on their date of manufacture, the materials are thought to have been deposited in the ground about 1810. The privy straddled a property line dividing one house lot from another and included several items from a druggist's shop. The materials are interpreted as having been used in the Bowne household because theirs was the only druggist's shop on either of the two properties during the appropriate period (see Wall, 1987:365–367). The archaeological materials are in the 75 Wall Street collection at the South Street Seaport Museum.

3. The kinds of dishes used in the Robson home are interpreted from the archaeological materials found in a privy at the Sullivan Street site. Based on their period of manufacture, the materials are interpreted as having been deposited in the ground in the mid to late 1840s. The privy was on the property where the Robson family lived from 1841 until Benjamin Robson's death in the late 19th century. Therefore, the materials are inferred to have been used in the Robson home. The archaeological materials are in the Sullivan Street collection at the South Street Seaport Museum.

4. As Ann Smart Martin (1989) discussed, pewter plates had been important components in setting 18th-century tables, but apparently, by the turn of the 19th century, they were still common only in rural areas.

5. Archaeologists who have looked at style in this way include Wobst (1977), Conkey (1978, 1982), and Hodder (1979); see Plog (1983) for a review of archaeological approaches to the interpretation of style and some caveats for this kind of analysis.
6. The following table documents the availability of tablewares and teawares in the various styles discussed here at the beginning of the period of study:

Stylistic group	Vessel type	Reference
1. Minimally decorated	Dinnerwares	Noel Hume (1969, pp. 125–126)
	Teawares	Godden (1965, p. 113)
2. Shell-edged	Dinnerwares	Noel Hume (1969, pp. 116, 131)
	Teawares	Towner (1978, p. 68)
3. Chinese landscape	Dinnerwares	Towner (1978, p. 144); Howard (1984, p. 68); Noel Hume (1969, pp. 127, 129, 260); Godden (1965, p. 194)
	Teawares	Towner (1978, p. 123)
4. Floral	Dinnerwares	Howard (1984, p. 64); Towner (1978, pp. 107, 175)
	Teawares	Howard (1984, p. 64); Towner (1978, pp. 48, 57, 93, 95, 98, 99, 145)

7. In her study using probate inventories in Virginia, Martin (1989) showed the importance of pewter vessels in households there and emphasized their invisibility to archaeologists because they were recycled rather than thrown away.

Chapter 7

Conclusion

> [O]ur furniture was a bed and bedstead, one pine table (value of fifty cents), three Windsor chairs, a soup-pot, tea-kettle, six cups and saucers, a griddle, frying-pan and brander. It was enough—it was all we wanted. . . . Now we have carpets to shake, brasses to scour, stairs to scrub, mahogany to polish, china to break, servants to scold; and what does it all amount to?
>
> GRANT THORBURN (1834), comparing his
> household goods at the time of
> his marriage in 1797 with those of 1834

This study has explored whether middle-class and elite New York women, acting within the framework of contemporary American culture, contributed through their actions to the structural transformation that resulted in the division of this culture into man's and woman's spheres. In exploring this issue we have looked on the separation of the home and the workplace—the spatial expression of the division of the spheres—as a watershed. I have argued that, if we could see the social practices associated with woman's sphere beginning in the combined homes and workplaces of these groups, this finding would indicate that the women, through their practices, actively contributed to the development of woman's sphere and to the transformation itself. If we could not see these changes beginning before the home separated from the workplace, this finding would suggest that women simply reacted or adapted to changes that were initiated in the larger society. The evidence presented in this study indicates that many of these changes did indeed begin before the separation of the home and the workplace and therefore suggests that women must be regarded as active agents in the redefinition of gender and the transformation itself.

This concluding chapter is divided into three sections. First, I summarize the scenario of the changes in social practice that led to the transformation and compare how they occurred in the homes of middle-class and wealthy New

Yorkers. Then, we take a brief look at the middle class during the period immediately following these changes. This period, extending from the 1840s to the 1870s, marked the beginning of the era when middle-class values became the major influence in American culture, an era that we are still in today. Finally, I discuss some of the implications that explanations of cultural change that are based on social practice have for the lives of men and women both in the 19th century and today.

SUMMARY

The American Revolution, marking America's transition from a colony to an independent republic, accelerated the transformation to modern life by opening up a myriad of possibilities. Whether these possibilities were acted on by men or by women was related to their roles in colonial society. Some possibilities pertained primarily to the political and economic arenas and were acted on primarily by men; others were related to concerns about social reproduction and were acted on primarily by women. The ways in which these possibilities were acted on by men and by women had ramifications that resulted in a structural transformation that deeply affected urban life in the new nation.

After the Revolution, New York's merchants were challenged by a whole new set of possibilities created by the removal of Britain's mercantilist restrictions, and accordingly, they developed new trading ties in different parts of the world. They also benefited from the European wars, during which their ships became the primary neutral carriers in the 1790s. In order to take advantage of the possibility of controlling this larger market, the merchants transformed the role of the colonial general merchant into a number of new, specialized roles. This specialization contributed to an important change in the marketplace itself, which became more impersonal and highly competitive. In order to succeed in this world, the merchants redefined the market as an arena in which their actions became almost completely cut off from moral considerations. Although these changes occurred over a long period of time, they were under way in the 1790s.

The artisans emerged from the Revolution with an egalitarian political identity that was shared by masters and journeymen alike and that was distinct from and often in conflict with that of the merchants. An obvious source of friction was the issue of encouraging American manufacturers by restricting the importation of British manufactured goods. Trade restrictions would naturally help the artisans at the expense of the merchants who traditionally imported these goods. Needless to say, the merchants, who had the capital, were not willing to invest in manufactures that would compete with the goods that they imported. It was only after about 1800 that some masters were able to act on the possibilities of the expanding market by breaking their clientage ties with the merchants and beginning to compete with them in the growing and impersonal marketplace.

In order to compete successfully, the productive process in some artisan shops was reorganized and broken down into simplified and routinized tasks. Semiskilled workers were hired in these shops in place of trained journeymen. These changes in the social relations of production were part of a long-term and uneven process that began in the late 18th century and continued well after the period of study. However, by the 1830s, the solidarity of masters and journeymen had been seriously weakened: Some masters had adopted the *laissez-faire* ideology of the merchants, while the journeymen were developing their own identity as members of a wage-earning working class.

After the Revolution, wives and mothers were able to change and enhance their position in society because the quality of family and home life was looked on as extremely important for ensuring social stability in the new republic. While middle-class men spent more of their time and energy competing in the impersonal marketplace, their wives continued in their household role at home. With the growth of the market economy, these women spent less time in household production and turned their attention instead to the enhancement of home life. They raised the standard of the quality of domestic life and elaborated on their role as the mothers of the future citizens who would be responsible for the success of the new nation.

One important aspect of the enhancement of the quality of home life was the elaboration of domestic furnishings, a process that Grant Thorburn commented on (see the beginning of this chapter). Family meals, for example, became ritualized as the 19th century progressed and began to serve as family reunions. We saw this ritualization process expressed in the ceramics that women used for setting their tables: As the social meanings of the meals changed, women chose ceramics in different and more elaborately decorated styles to express these new meanings. The women were also willing to spend more and more money on each of the ceramic dishes they bought to grace their tables. They began this elaboration process in the combined homes and workplaces of the city's middle class at least as early as the first decade of the nineteenth century.

The elaboration of domestic life also involved an increase in the number of domestic servants who were hired to do the labor-intensive housework necessary to maintain these homes. The rise in the number of domestic servants began in wealthier households in the first decade of the 19th century, at the same time these wealthier families separated their homes from their workplaces. Among the middle class, this increase became visible somewhat later, in the 1820s, but clearly preceded this group's separation of the home and the workplace, which occurred in the 1830s.

Middle-class and wealthy women also began to have fewer children, presumably so they could concentrate more time, energy, and money on raising each one of them. We have seen that this decline in the birthrate for these women began at least as early as 1810 and continued to at least 1830 in wealthy families and to at least 1840 among the members of the middle class. While enhancing the importance of the individual child, these women also enhanced their own roles as the mothers who supplied the greater amounts of nurturing required to raise tomorrow's republican citizens.

Two other related phenomena occurred in these homes during the period of study: the separation of the home and the workplace and the discontinuation of the related practice of having the men and boys who worked in the family trade board in the home. Social relations among men who were not related to each other were becoming increasingly strained by the competitive capitalist marketplace and were out of place in the home, where (except for the relations between a mistress and her domestics) social relations were becoming increasingly structured by the affective ties of domestic life.

For most of the middle class, both of these phenomena occurred in the 1830s and followed the introduction of all of the changes in social practice marking the development of woman's sphere examined here. For most of the elite, they occurred together much earlier, before 1810, coinciding with the appearance of the practices marking woman's sphere.

This sequence of events indicates that woman's sphere did not simply develop in a vacuum after the separation of the home and the workplace, when the commercial and productive activities of men had left the home. Instead, it suggests that, just as changes in man's sphere both allowed and facilitated the development of woman's sphere, the development of woman's sphere, in turn, may have encouraged the continuing redefinition of man's sphere.

Finally, these changes in the definition of class and gender were graphically expressed in the transformation of the social landscape of the city. At the end of the Revolution, the social geography of the city continued to emphasize a more egalitarian way of life. New Yorkers tended to house their homes and workplaces in single, integrated structures. Those of the poor and the middle class were distributed side by side throughout the city; only those of the elite tended to cluster at the city's center. Early New Yorkers also used architectural style as an integrating device; the structures for the poor and for most of the rich were executed in a similar, small-scale Federal style, while a different version of this style was used for the city's monumental structures: its churches and the city hall (see Plates 3 and 4).

By 1840, the social landscape of the city had markedly changed. There was a well-defined commercial district at the center of the city, in the area of the port. Some of the men and women of the poor continued to live here, but for members of the middle class, this area had become man's sphere (see Plates 7, 8, and 15). In addition, the homes of many of the members of all the classes were now confined to relatively class-exclusive neighborhoods, which in the middle and wealthy classes constituted woman's sphere. The wealthy residential neighborhood was secluded on the outer edge of the city, where members of both the middle class and the working class had little occasion to see it (see Plates 11, 12, and 13). The homes of the middle class were, for the most part, on the eastern and western edges of the city, out of the way of the working class (see Plate 5). Many wealthy and middle-class men traveled to work on omnibuses that traversed the shop-lined streets of working-class neighborhoods and never had occasion to see the hearts of these neighborhoods at all (see Plates 14 and 16).

New Yorkers began to use architectural style in a new way in the 1830s city: The popular Greek Revival style made explicit statements about function, gender, and class that had been masked by the earlier Federal style. It was executed differently in the commercial structures of man's sphere than it was in the domestic structures of woman's sphere (see Plates 11, 13, and 15). Furthermore, it was also executed differently in the neighborhoods of the wealthy, the middle class, and the poor (see Plates 11 through 14). Finally, yet another version of this style was used for the monumental structures associated with man's sphere (politics and the economy), whereas the monumental structures associated with woman's sphere (the city's churches) began to be built in a new and quite different Gothic Revival style (see Plates 10 and 15).

I see these changes in the social landscape of the city as being directly related to the development of the separate ideologies of man's and woman's spheres. As relations between the classes came to be structured more and more by the capitalist social relations of man's sphere and those among family members in middle-class and wealthy homes became structured more and more by the affective social relations of woman's sphere, the juxtaposition of these different arenas in the same social space became less tenable.

By 1840, gender and class had become the primary cultural categories used to organize the social space of the city. But for the members of the middle class and the elite, the visible cultural category was the "natural" one of gender, which veiled the importance of the "pernicious" category of class in a city that was supposed to be egalitarian.[1]

THE VIEW AT MIDCENTURY

Although the middle-class vision of domesticity and the family has been predominant in American culture since the 1840s, this vision has not been static since that time. Instead, American men and women have continued to act in terms of the possibilities and constraints they perceived, and middle-class culture has continued to change. The developments that took place in the succeeding period, in the three decades between the 1840s and the 1870s, provide a glimpse of how the middle class continued to redefine itself as the 19th century progressed (Coontz, 1988).

The mid-19th century saw the beginnings of the growth of industrial capitalism, and the corporations that were first created in the early 19th century were the vehicles of its success. Originally, these corporations had been conceived of as public or quasipublic institutions created for the public interest. Starting in the 1850s, however, with the beginning of the extension of the railroads into the western territories and the rise of a factory system serving a national market, these corporations took on a life of their own. Particularly after the Civil War and throughout the Gilded Age, small groups of managing directors began to gain both vertical and horizontal control of many developing industries by pooling the capital of thousands of investors. Although we tend to associate this period of industrial expansion with the names of individual "robber barons"—Rockefellers, Carnegies, Swifts, and Goulds—it was, in fact, the groups of anonymous capitalists who controlled the corporations who seized the opportunities afforded by the unprecedented growth of the national market. By the 1870s, corporate control of business had become commonplace, succeeding the partnerships and family businesses that had characterized the structure of the American economy earlier in the century. And of course, this trend has only continued to grow; in this century, corporations have taken over the world economy: By 1900, America's 100 largest corporations controlled one-third of the country's production, and by 1974, 51 multinational corporations controlled over half of the 100 largest economic units in the world (the other 49 of them were nations) (Coontz, 1988:332; Trachtenberg, 1982).

By the 1850s, New York City was the unquestioned economic hub of the country and its center of commerce, manufacturing, banking, and finance. In 1860, one-third of the nation's exports and over two-thirds of its imports passed through the port of New York. The value of goods manufactured in the city more than tripled in two decades, from $105 million in 1850 to $333 million in 1870. And most significantly, the city also began its role as the site of the headquarters of the new corporations that were beginning to take over the economy (Albion, 1939:390–391; Lockwood, 1972:126–127).

Needless to say, the class structure in New York and other American cities became increasingly rigid during the mid-19th century. By the last decades of the century, conflicts between capitalists and labor were increasingly being acted out with violence; strikes and protests were the only means that labor had to counteract the manipulations of the capitalists. Class conflict was compounded by the cultural differences between these groups. Second only to the issue of wealth was that of ethnicity. The capitalists, on the one hand, were perceived ethnically as "Americans," that is, white Anglo-Saxon Protestants.

Labor, on the other hand, was increasingly regarded as "foreign." With the growth of the American economy and of unrest overseas, more and more European immigrants flocked to the United States, and many of them settled in the cities. The population of New York more than tripled in the three decades between 1840 and 1870 (from 312,710 to 942,292), and a large part of this increase was due to immigration. By 1870, 45% (or 419,094) of the city's population had been born outside the country. Many of these immigrants were unskilled laborers from Europe who became part of the city's industrial work force. By 1870, one out of every three industrial workers in the nation was foreign-born (Rosenwaike, 1972:32, 42, 67; Trachtenberg, 1982:87–88).

The nature of work for middle-class men in urban centers changed dramatically. Whereas earlier in the century most could hope to establish their own businesses as entrepreneurs, as time went on business became a riskier undertaking (some contemporary observers estimated that, in the 1870s and 1880s, 95% of all businesses failed), and as the century progressed, more and more middle-class men found themselves working in the corporations. There, they became white-collar salary earners working as clerks, accountants, middle managers, and salesmen, as well as in marketing and advertising. Although they may have had more economic security than they would have had as entrepreneurs, they lost a good deal of their independence. In order to succeed in this environment, middle-class values had to undergo a change. Earlier in the century, individualism and entrepreneurship had been looked on as the means to success for middle-class men in the workplace. Now, although the ideal image of the risk-taking, self-made man persisted, most middle-class men found themselves increasingly in situations where organizational and administrative skills were becoming more valued, as were obedience and loyalty to the firm (Trachtenberg, 1982:84).

In the corporations and in industry, middle-class men often found themselves caught in the middle, serving as intermediaries between capitalists and labor, two worlds that many of them found alien. They could not identify with the interests of the industrial workers, a large proportion of whom were foreign-born, and many were also stunned by the growing power of the capitalists and even of money itself. The middle class, caught between, solidified its identity as a class vis-à-vis the capitalists and the working class (Trachtenberg, 1982:71, 73, 80, 84).

The increasing alienation among the classes played itself out in the social geography of the city. In New York, the Wall Street district continued to be devoted to business, and wealthy, middle-class, and working-class New Yorkers intensified their earlier pattern of establishing their homes in residential neighborhoods that were segregated by class. The pattern of wealthy families' living at the city's edge continued, as the rich moved farther and farther uptown along the central spine of Manhattan on a strip that focused on Fifth

Avenue. Before the Civil War, some wealthy New Yorkers began to move their homes out of the city entirely, to the new suburbs that were being established in New Jersey and upstate New York. The middle class followed them later in the century, beginning in the late 1870s (Lockwood, 1972:200; Marsh, 1990; Wright, 1981:96).

As men's roles and the values of the workplace continued to change, the roles of women and the significance of the homes they created changed as well. Through the 1830s, middle-class women had successfully enhanced their position by fulfilling the image of nurturing republican mothers who could guarantee the success of the new nation by raising the citizens of tomorrow. By mid-century, however, their role had changed and now encompassed two different, and in some ways conflicting, aspects of social reproduction. On the one hand, their role became sentimentalized and even sanctified as the homes that they ran came to be perceived as sanctuaries from the heartless world of the marketplace. On the other, they were also responsible for negotiating the family's position in the perilous class structure so that family members (and particularly daughters as they reached marriageable age) would continue to have access to the middle class. They did this by promoting their home's and the family's image of refinement, gentility, and fashion among friends and acquaintances (Blumin, 1989:183–185; Coontz, 1988:211, 230; Marsh, 1990:9, 13).[2]

Both of these aspects of women's roles were evident in different features of the homes they created: in the architecture and organization of the houses themselves and in the style of the material culture that they used inside them. The uncertainties of the mid-19th century saw the introduction of a profusion of nostalgic styles in architecture and home furnishings. It was during the 1840s that the Gothic style was introduced into American architecture. In fact, its religious associations made it extremely popular for middle-class homes in small towns because it embodied the home's role as a sanctuary from the heartless world of business. As mentioned in Chapter 3, however, although a profusion of churches was built in this style in New York, Gothic never became popular for domestic buildings in the city. Instead, the romantic palazzo style that was introduced into the city for commercial and public buildings and the mansions of the very wealthy in the 1840s became extremely popular in its domestic Italianate form for the row houses of the middle class. This style, with its elegance of height and allowance for rich architectural detail, allowed householders to make statements about wealth, fashion, and taste on an unprecedented scale—statements that were much more obvious than those made by the Greek Revival style that this style supplanted. Block-long rows of these houses created class-consistent uniform street fronts on a much broader scale than ever before. From our perspective here, these homes emphasized the role of the woman of the house as social negotiator in making a visible, public statement of the family's class position (Lockwood, 1972:131–132, 143–155).[3]

Style was also used in a similar way inside these homes. First of all, changes were made in the functions of some of the rooms inside the house. During the 1850s, many of the upper-middle-class families who lived in these row houses abandoned their basements and moved to the first floor. As described in Chapters 5 and 6, the front room in the basement in the early-19th-century New York home had served as a "family room"; it was here that family members spent their time together and ate their meals. They occupied the first floor of the house only when they entertained guests in their double parlors. Around mid-century, however, many of these families moved their dining rooms away from their basements and up to the first floor. Some wealthier families with larger houses added a dining room behind the first-floor double parlor, and others simply converted the back parlor into a dining room. The family had moved "upstairs." The basement was now for the most part "downstairs": the domain of domestics. This separation between "upstairs" and "downstairs" was underscored by the two sets of stairs that were installed in some of the new homes that were built for wealthier families at this time. One elaborate set of stairs was located in the middle of the house, to be seen by guests and for the family to use, and another, narrower set was installed in the back of the house, to be used by the domestics. Now, the family spent much of its time on the first floor (Lockwood, 1972:167–168).

It was on the first floor that the woman of the house used material goods to exercise both aspects of her role most visibly. The first floor of the row house consisted minimally of three rooms: the hall, where visitors and the family entered the house; the front parlor, where guests were entertained; and the back dining room, where the family and close friends took their meals. The parlor and the hall were arenas where the woman of the house negotiated her family's position in the class structure by her show of fashion and gentility to formal guests, and the dining room was the arena for exercising her role as moral guardian.

The differences in the stress of the meaning of these rooms and the corresponding differences in women's responsibilities are evident in the differences in the styles of the objects that were used to furnish the parlor and the dining room, respectively, and even in the differences in the ceramics that were used to present the meals that were served in these two rooms. The writers of the house-plan books, who began their contribution to the prescriptive literature in the 1850s, directed attention to the importance of the home as an influence in building character. Although their plans were almost always of homes in the country (they assumed that it was impossible to create a home encompassing middle-class values in the sin-filled city), they did discuss the style of the furnishings of these rooms so that the rooms would embody the values that were being emphasized in them and the activities for which they were used. In 1850, for example, Andrew Jackson Downing wrote that "the prevailing character of the Grecian and Italian styles partakes of the gay spirit of the drawing-room and social life; that of the Gothic, of the quiet, domestic feeling of the library and the family circle" (pp. 23–24).

That these differences in style were used to express the different functions of these rooms and, by extension, different aspects of women's roles in the city as well as in the country is evident in a growing body of archaeological data that is emerging from excavations in New York City. The data from the ceramics that were used in these homes allow us to see how women set their tables for the teas that graced their parlors as well as for the dinners that they served in their dining rooms. The ceramics even allow us to see variation in the emphasis of these roles of women among families that were at the wealthier and poorer ends of the middle-class spectrum.

One set of ceramics comes from one of the homes described in Chapters 2 through 6, that of the Robsons, who moved to Washington Square South in Greenwich Village in 1841. As we saw in Chapter 6, in the 1820s and 1830s, Eliza Robson used two different kinds of ceramics to serve her meals: earthenware and porcelain plates heavily decorated in blue-on-white chinoiserie patterns for use at her dinner table and teacups in a myriad of floral and other patterns to serve her teas. By the 1840s, however, her china dishes had undergone a dramatic change. Although the patterns of the dishes that she used for serving teas and family dinners were markedly different from each other, both sets were predominantly white. Most of her plates were made of ironstone and were completely white; their only decoration consisted of molded panels around the edge (see Figure 7–1). This style of vessel is referred to as *Gothic* in the ceramics literature. She also had some paneled cups and saucers that matched this pattern; they were probably used for drinking morning tea and coffee at the breakfast table. Eliza Robson presumably used her Gothic dishes for the family meals that she served in her first-floor dining room, which may well also have been furnished in a corresponding Gothic style. It was there that she exercised her almost sacred role as moral guardian of family members (Wall, 1991).

Although some of Eliza Robson's teacups were in the paneled Gothic pattern, over a third of them were in a quite different style. These cups were made of white European porcelain molded into a pedestaled shape and decorated with gilt flowers and leaves, reminiscent of the French Second Empire style (see Figure 7–2). Eliza Robson presumably used these porcelain vessels to serve tea to her friends and acquaintances in her parlor, which was probably decorated in a corresponding French or Italian style. It was in the parlor that she negotiated her family's position in the city's class structure (Wall, 1991).

As we might expect, not all middle-class women had ceramics in these two contrasting patterns. The archaeological data suggest that women at the

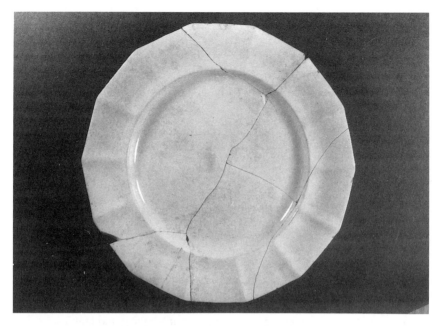

Figure 7–1. Ironstone table plate in the Gothic pattern, 1840s, part of a set from the Robson home. (The plate is 10¼″ in diameter; South Street Seaport Museum.)

Figure 7–2. Gilded and pedestaled European porcelain teacup and saucer, 1840s, part of a set from the Robson home. (The saucer is 5½″ in diameter; South Street Seaport Museum.)

poorer end of the middle-class spectrum exercised their moral leadership at the dinner table but relinquished the competitive social displays of the parlor. Ceramics from poorer middle-class households show that these women purchased and used Gothic-styled ironstone dinner plates but eschewed the fancier porcelains. Furthermore, by the 1860s, many of these families lived in apartments and not houses and presumably did not even have parlors in which to do formal entertaining. The competitive displays of tea parties were probably not relevant to their way of life (Bodie, 1992; Wall, 1991).

This glimpse of women's roles in the mid to late 19th century shows how middle-class women continued to use material goods to create and re-create their role to take advantage of the possibilities that they perceived as the century progressed.

CONCLUSION

This study suggests that women and men were both active agents in the creation of the complementary worlds of woman's sphere and man's sphere in the half century that followed the Revolution. It also indicates that women, in creating woman's sphere, did not simply react or adapt to the withdrawal of production from the home after the home and the workplace had become separated. Rather, these often contradictory but complementary ideologies apparently developed in counterpoint to one another in the integrated homes and workplaces of the city's middle class. These changes in social practice began well before they ultimately coalesced into the ideology of woman's sphere, as articulated in the popular prescriptive literature of the 1830s.

This study does not imply, however, that women had the same degree of choice in changing their social practices as men of the same class. It also does not mean that the middle class simply followed, or emulated, the elite in undergoing this transformation. Rather, it suggests that the men and women of these classes worked out their own but similar solutions to the problems posed by their actions vis-à-vis a new set of conditions—America's new status as an independent republic—within the framework of contemporary U.S. culture. The actions of men in regard to the politics and economy of an emerging nation resulted in the development of man's sphere and also contributed to the creation of woman's sphere. Conversely, the actions of women in regard to the new concerns about social reproduction in the new republic resulted in the development of woman's sphere and also facilitated the definition of man's sphere. In other words, the new content that men's and women's practices acquired in acting on the possibilities of a new nation resulted in cultural tensions. The resolution of these tensions changed the relationship between men and women and their relationships to other cultural categories as well. As

Marshall Sahlins (1981) put it in describing another cultural transformation, "The structure, as a set of relationships among relationships, [was] transformed" (p. 37).

The position of urban middle-class and wealthy families was enhanced in many ways by this transformation. However, in the long run, the division of American culture into man's sphere and woman's sphere also diminished the position of both men and women (see Weiner, 1982:52). Most obviously, middle-class and elite women were barred from direct participation in economic and political life, that is, the public arena. They were clearly subordinate to men in the context of the large society. However, men also became limited, though more subtly, in their participation in the private arena, that is, the world of morality, affect, home, and family. The implications of these limitations for both women and men are still of great concern to us today.

Finally, the acceptance of the interpretation that women, as well as men, actively contributed through their social actions to the separation of the spheres has ironic implications. Looking on this structural transformation as a consequence (although unintended) of changing social practices on the part of both men *and women* implies that women were at least in part responsible for their own ultimate seclusion in the home.[4] And therein lies a cautionary tale for us today. As Michel Foucault noted, "People know what they do; they frequently know why they do what they do; but what they don't know is what what they do does" (personal communication in Dreyfus and Rabinow, 1982:187).

NOTES

1. This perceptive distinction was made by Sklar (1973:211) and refers to American attitudes toward gender and race.
2. Halttunen (1982) and McDannell (1986) have provided complementary views of these aspects of women's roles as the arbiters of fashion and morality, respectively.
3. The 19th-century authors of the prescriptive literature were explicitly aware of the appropriateness of different styles of architecture and objects to convey different messages and to reinforce different kinds of behavior. Clark (1986) provided a good introduction to the prescriptive literature on architecture.
4. This irony was noted by Ortner (1984:157) for this kind of interpretation in general and by Ryan (1979) for the restructuring of the gender system in 19th-century America in particular.

Appendix *A*

The Documentary Data

The samples described in this appendix provide the data for Chapters 2, 3, and 4 of this study. These chapters look at the separation of the home and the workplace and at the associated changes both in the social landscape of the city and in the composition of the household in late-18th- and early 19th-century New York. In order to examine some of the variables relevant to these changes, I collected information on the people who lived and/or worked in New York during the half century after the Revolution by constructing a series of samples of this population.

I drew the samples from the New York City directories and culled additional information on the people in the samples from contemporary maps, tax records, and federal census returns. I ended up with information on the people's names, on their occupations, on the locations of their homes and/or workplaces, on the value of some of their property holdings, and on the composition of their households.

This appendix is divided in two sections. The first consists of a discussion of the nature of the samples (including a description of the data, the rationale behind their use, how they were gathered, and possible sources of error), and the second describes how I organized the data in order to analyze the research questions.

THE NATURE OF THE SAMPLES

I began the sampling procedure by drawing a 2% random sample from each of the city directories at 10-year intervals for each of six years, from 1790 through 1840. The directories, which served a function similar to that of our telephone books today, were published annually from the late 1780s through the end of the 19th century. During the period under study, work was begun on collecting the names for the directories at the beginning of May, and the directories were published during the summer. The listings in the directories include the names of a business and/or household head, his or her occupation, and either a single address (usually referring to a combined home and workplace) or the addresses of separate homes and businesses.[1]

I used the directory listings as the sampling universe for this part of the study because they contained more identifying items about each individual than any of the other available data sources. Thus they ensured that individuals could be linked from data source to data source with the least chance of errors. I discuss the linkage problem more fully below. The numbers of names in each of the 2% samples ranged from 86 for 1790 to 720 for 1840, with a combined total of 2,396 individuals for all of the sample years.

There are a number of problems in using the directories as a sampling universe for heads of households living and/or working in the city. The stated purpose of the directories was to list the names of "all persons doing business, heads of families, whether journeymen or master mechanics, editors of newspapers, clerks, colored people, gentlemen and commoners . . . all indiscriminately" (T. Longworth, 1830:673). Some groups, however, tended to be excluded.

The directories, like other records, tended to be biased against including information on the poor, the highly mobile (or less stable) parts of the population, the female, and the young (Wrigley, 1973:12). Unskilled workers (except those, like cartmen, who were licensed by the city) also tended to be underrepresented (Blumin, 1969:170). For example, the 1810 directory listed only 43 (or 14%) of the 295 families or individuals listed as receiving public assistance in an account book for that year (Mohl, 1971:22). It has also been estimated that fewer than one-third of the journeymen working in unlicensed artisan trades were listed in the directories (Rock, 1979). This problem was minimized in the present study because the focus here is on the middle class and the elite, groups whose members the directories tended, for the most part, to list.

Another problem arose from the listings of the occupations in the directories. The occupations, which could serve as marks of status, were often self-ascribed. The designation "merchant," for example, could include both those in control of vast wholesale operations and small retail dealers with relatively small capital investments (Pessen, 1973:49). Those described as "grocers" could include, on the one hand, those in control of wholesale warehouses and, on the other, the proprietors of neighborhood stores (Johnson, 1978:143). Similar problems occurred among the members of the artisan trades; for example, both those who owned shoe factories and their employees described themselves as shoemakers in the directories. I therefore combined the data from the directories with those providing information on wealth (following Johnson) to help resolve some of the problems of ascertaining the socioeconomic position of the people in the directory samples.

The New York City tax assessment records were the source that provided information on the wealth of those who lived and/or worked in the city during the period under study. The city was authorized by the state to levy taxes for the support of the poor and other purposes in 1786. Taxes were levied on both real and personal estates, and the items taxed included "all real estate, and all personal estate of whatsoever description, household furniture . . . , goods, chattels, debts due from solvent debtors, notes, bonds, mortgages, bank stocks, and all other kinds of stock; and all such property real and personal, as is not exempted by some law of the United States" (State of New York, 1827:137) or of New York State. Corporate wealth, however, was not included in the assessment records (Wilentz, 1984:397). Property was assessed annually, during the summer (Stokes, 1915–1928, vol. 5, pp. 1211, 1233), and for at least part of the period under study, the assessments were made in May and June and were based on property possessed as of 1 May (State of New York, 1827:138).

The tax assessment records were organized by ward, and by house and street address within the ward. Therefore, each of the addresses listed in the directory samples had to be assigned to its ward. In doing this, I followed one of two procedures, depending on the sample year. For the sample years before 1830, I used contemporary maps.[2] I found the street from the listing in the directory sample on the appropriate map, and I recorded the ward(s) through which the street ran. I then looked up the street address in the appropriate ward book(s) in the tax assessment records.

For the later sample years (1830 and 1840), I used a special feature of the directories to locate the street addresses. The directories for each of these years include a "Runner's Vade Mecum," which consists of a guide to the block location of the numbered houses on each of the city's streets. I used this feature to find the block on which each address listed in the directory samples was located, and I then looked up the ward location of the block on the appropriate map (W. Hooker, 1831; T. Longworth, 1830, 1840; J. C. Smith, 1839).

I looked up each of the addresses associated with each of the names pulled in the samples from the directories in the tax records for the appropriate year (City of Brooklyn, 1841; City of New York, Tax Assessment Records, 1790, 1799, 1802, 1810, 1820, 1830, 1840), and I recorded the assessments of personal and real property for each of the names. When I could not find the name in the tax records at the appropriate address for the appropriate year, I assumed that the person had no assessable wealth.

It should be noted that there were several problems in using the tax records for this purpose. First, the assessors were widely believed to under-assess the estates of the wealthy who wielded governmental influence (Pessen,

1973). Second, because the properties were assessed by address, the real properties owned by a particular individual were listed not in one place, but by
their locations all over the city. Therefore, for an evaluation of the holdings of
each person, every address of every ward should be scanned. However, the
problem was even more complex than this. It was not simply the owner of each
property who was assessed for its value. Rather, the tax records described the
name associated with each property as either its owner *or* its occupant (or
tenant) and did not specify which; the lease on each property usually designated who was to pay the real estate taxes. In fact, the "person in possession"
of the property, rather than its owner, was the one who was legally liable for
paying the taxes on the property (State of New York, 1827:138). Therefore, it
was not possible simply to scan the listings in every ward in order to determine
the value of a particular person's holdings in the city.

For this study, I looked up each person listed in the directory samples in
the tax records only at the address(es) where he or she was listed in the
directory, following Wilentz (1984:397). It should be remembered that the real
estate values included here may be either inflated (if the person was in fact
only the tenant of the property) or deflated (if the person had extensive real
estate holdings throughout or outside the city). The variable of wealth is
therefore used only to place people in broad ordinal categories, rather than as
interval data.

Finally, I should note that all of the tax assessment records for one of the
years, and for several of the wards and for Brooklyn (where some of the people
who worked in New York lived) for other years, are not available. None of the
records from 1800 has survived, so the samples drawn from the directory for
that year were limited to names that were also listed in the directories for the
years 1799 and/or 1802, the years closest to 1800 for which the tax records
have survived. These names were then looked up in the tax records for the
appropriate year. The 1800 sample therefore includes a more stable segment of
the population than the samples for the other years.

In addition, the books for the 10th ward for 1810 and for the 11th and
15th wards for 1840 are also missing. The names listed in these wards were
looked up first in the directories for the years immediately before and after the
study year and, if listed, were looked up in the tax records for the appropriate
year. Here again, the people in the samples from these wards and years represented a more stable segment of the population than those from the other
wards in the samples. Finally, those listed in the 1830 directory sample as
working in New York and living in Brooklyn were dropped from the sample
and replaced, as no Brooklyn tax records are available for that year or for any
year close to 1830. I used the 1841 Brooklyn tax assessment records to check
the wealth of the Brooklynites listed in the 1840 directory sample.

I used the U.S. manuscript census returns for the sample years to provide information on the composition of the households of those included in the directory samples who were "family heads." The federal census was initiated as a result of Article 1, Section 2 of the Constitution, to provide information for apportioning representatives and taxes. The enumerations are made at 10-year intervals. Throughout the study period, Native Americans, who were not taxed, were also excluded from the enumeration.

The target date for the census enumeration was in the warmer months throughout the period under study. For the years 1790 through 1820, the population was counted as of the first Monday in August, whereas for the 1830 and 1840 census, the target date was the first day of June (Jackson and Teeples, 1978).

The information provided in the census returns for the sample years is relatively sparse compared to that provided later in the 19th century. Throughout the study period, the census returns were organized by ward, but in most cases, no addresses or even streets within the wards were given. The names were listed in the original order in which they were entered, reflecting the enumerator's path through the ward, which was roughly house-by-house down each street. Furthermore, each of the entries was listed under the name of the "family head" and consisted of a single line of information for each household. Neither the names of other household members nor their relationship (if any) to the "family head" were given.

The line entry for each of the households consisted of various kinds of information about household members, mostly concerned with the number of household members in various age, sex, and racial categories. The returns for the later sample years also included information on the numbers of household members who were employed in various sectors of the economy (for 1820 and 1840) and who were infirm in any of a number of ways (for 1830 and 1840), as well as some information on literacy (for 1840). The categories of information requested for each household ranged in number from 6 for 1790 to 78 for 1840. It should be understood that the census schedules were not strictly comparable for all of the sample years. I discuss this problem, and how it was dealt with, more fully below.

I looked up each of the names in the samples from the directories in the census index for the appropriate year (Jackson and Teeples, 1976, 1977, 1978; Jackson, Teeples, and Schaefermeyer, 1977; McMullin, 1971) Those names found in the appropriate ward for the appropriate year were then sought in the manuscript census returns (U.S. Government, Bureau of the Census, 1790, 1800, 1810, 1820, 1830, 1840). If only one similarly spelled forename and surname was listed for the appropriate ward for a sample year, I assumed that this listing in the census in fact referred to the target individual listed in the directory sample. If more than one similarly spelled name was listed for the appropriate ward, I did further research to be sure that the person referred to in the census returns was in fact the target individual listed in the sample from the directory.

For each of the similarly spelled names listed for the appropriate ward, I looked up the three names listed both before and after the target name in the census returns in the directories. If the address of at least one of these names was listed on the same street and in a house near that of the target individual, I concluded that this was the correct "family head." If none of the addresses was listed as being on the same street as the target individual's address, I assumed that the target individual was not a household head listed in the census returns, and that no census information was recorded for that individual's household.

It should be noted that only approximately half to three-quarters of the names in the directory samples were found in the census records. An obvious explanation is that not all of those listed in the directories were "family heads," and the latter, of course, were the only ones listed by name in the census returns. In addition, some of the "family heads" in the directory samples were probably (as is true today) simply missed by the census enumerators, by those who copied the returns, or by those who made up the census index. Finally, variations in the spelling of names may have made it impossible to link a name in the directory with the appropriate one in the census index, although I also checked reasonable alternative spellings.

The problem of linkages must be discussed more explicitly here. Nominal record linkage has attracted a great deal of the attention of historians in recent years. *Nominal record linkage* has been defined as "the process by which items of information about a particular named individual are associated with each other into a coherent whole in accordance with certain rules" (Wrigley, 1973:1). The question as applied to this study is: How can we be sure that the William Smith pulled in the directory sample is the same William Smith about whom information was found in the tax and census records? Although some of the rules for making these decisions have already been touched on, this issue warrants a somewhat more formal discussion (Macfarlane, 1977; Wrigley, 1973).

The linkage problem is greatly reduced for this project because the data are handled as a series of six synchronic sets rather than as a single diachronic one. The problem of tracing people through time in early nineteenth-century New York would be extremely difficult.

All of the data on each of the sampled individuals were originally recorded within periods that were about four months long. The process of gathering names for the directories was begun shortly after 1 May, the traditional moving day in early-19th century New York, when annual leases expired. The tax assessments were also recorded in the summer months throughout the study period (Stokes, 1915–1928, V, p. 1233) and for at least part of the time, the assessments were made of property held as of 1 May. The information gathered for the census returns was also gathered during the warmer months: Information was requested about the composition of the household as of the first Monday in August for the years 1790 through 1820, and for 1 June for 1830 and 1840. Therefore, the likelihood that people either moved away or died between the time their names were recorded for the directories and the time they could be recorded in the tax assessment or census records has been minimized as much as one could reasonably hope.

In general, three items of information about the target individual had to match before I accepted a linkage from one record to another. In all cases, one of these items consisted of a similarly spelled surname. The second item consisted of either a similarly spelled forename or the sex of the individual. For example, Widow Greene could be linked with Abigail Greene, assuming that the third item of information matched as well. The third item was locational information and consisted of either the street address (for linking with the tax records) or simply the ward (for most of the linking with the census records). As discussed more fully above, in cases where several individuals with similarly spelled names were listed in the appropriate ward in the census record index, I looked up some of the adjacent names in the census listings in the directories and matched the addresses with the target individual's address. In these cases, street addresses were used as relevant items of information in matchings with the census records as well.

ORGANIZING THE DATA

After the samples of individuals and the relevant information about them from the directories, tax records, and census lists were compiled, I coded the data so that the information would be as comparable as possible for each of the years under study.

I divided the occupations of the people in the samples into eight somewhat arbitrary categories so that the sector of the economy in which they were working could be considered. The categories, which were broadly adapted from the work of Ryan (1981:244–246) and Johnson (1978:142–151), consisted of merchants and financiers; others working in the commercial sector; white-collar and public-service workers; professionals; semiskilled workers; skilled workers, artisans, and manufacturers; and those for whom no occupation was listed. This last category included "gentlemen," retirees, widows, the unemployed, and those who chose not to include an occupational listing. The distribution of the people in the directory samples by occupational category and sample year is shown in Table A–1.

I also included information on the value of property holdings. Combining

Table A–1. Distribution of People in Directory Samples by Year
and Occupational Category

Sample year	1790		1800		1810		1820		1830		1840	
Occupation	n	%	n	%	n	%	n	%	n	%	n	%
Semiskilled	16	18.6	32	15.7	40	13.3	62	13.5	73	11.7	33	4.6
Artisans, manufacturers	23	26.7	76	37.3	87	29.0	171	37.2	229	36.6	246	34.2
White collar, public service	3	3.5	3	5.7	17	5.7	13	2.8	20	3.2	36	5.0
Services	4	4.7	8	3.9	9	3.0	11	2.4	23	3.7	41	5.7
Professionals	2	2.3	15	7.4	23	7.7	26	5.7	45	7.2	51	7.1
Others in commerce	15	17.4	23	11.3	34	11.3	68	14.8	87	13.9	140	19.4
Merchants, financiers	7	8.1	27	13.2	26	8.7	35	7.6	63	10.1	71	9.9
No occupation	16	18.6	20	9.8	64	21.3	74	16.1	86	13.7	102	14.2
Total	86	100	204	100	300	100	460	100	626	100	720	100

the value of personal wealth and real estate holdings yielded the value of the total wealth of each individual. All of these data, which were listed in the directories and the tax records, were comparable for all of the individuals for all of the sample years.

I also coded information from the manuscript census returns on the individuals making up the households, so that I could examine changes in household composition through time. As mentioned above, these records consisted of only a single line entry under the name of each household head for all of the years under study. Neither the names of other household members nor their relationship (if any) to the household head was included. Here, I coded information on the race and the number of household members for all of the sample years. However, the data on the age, sex, and race of the various household members were not comparable for all of the census years.

For most of the samples, the number of household members under 10 years old and of the males and females 10 years old and older was recorded so that inferences about the composition of these households could be drawn. However, neither those listed in the 1790 sample nor the free-black and slave populations for 1800 and 1810 could be included here because of the lack of breakdown into these categories in the census data. In addition, I had to divide the free-black and slave populations in the 1820 samples at 14 years, because of the age categories used in recording the 1820 census.

Finally, an age category for the oldest male and the oldest female in each household was recorded, so that a household's stage in the developmental cycle could be inferred. For example, the age of the wife/mother in a household allows one to make inferences about changes in the birthrate. Therefore, only households with "oldest females" who were close to childbearing age were included in explorations of this issue. However, the definitions of these age categories varied because of the nature of the census data for the various years. Again, the 1790 samples could not be used in this breakdown. For the white population, the age of 45 was used as a cutoff for the 1800, 1810, and 1820 samples, and age 50 was used for the 1830 and 1840 samples.

THE DIVISION OF THE SAMPLES INTO "CLASSES"

In order to begin to look at social change in late-18th- and early-19th-century New York, I also had to assign the individuals in the samples to socioeconomic groups that could be roughly equated with classes. Mills (1951:5) described the class structure in the early-19th-century American city as consisting of three broad occupational groups: merchants, mastercraftsmen and shopkeepers, and laborers. The merchants continued to constitute the social and economic elite of New York until after the mid-19th century (Pessen, 1973). Many of the middle-class artisans and shopkeepers, who had tended to own the property on which they worked early in the century, became salaried managerial employees later in the century (Braverman, 1974). As the century progressed, laborers and journeymen, who could no longer look forward to becoming masters in their own right, came to make up a wage-carning working class.

It would have been ideal to be able to take three variables into account in assigning the sampled individuals to classes: income level; nature of occupation; and, most important, identity. Unfortunately, none of these variables could be used directly with the available data, and I could make inferences about only two of them. Because of the nature of the samples, we have no idea at all about the class identity of any of the individuals included in them.

We know the occupations of most of the individuals in the samples from the listings in the directories. However, we do not know the "nature" of these occupations. For example, as mentioned above, we do not know if an individual listed as a "shoemaker" in the directories worked as a mastercraftsman, a journeyman, or a wage earner in a shoe factory. The same is true of a "grocer": It is unclear if such an individual was a merchant who imported foods or the operator of a small retail store. The occupations as listed in the directories could therefore not be used in assigning an individual to a class.

"Income" per se is not listed in any of the available sources. Instead, I used the sum of both real and personal property as listed in the tax records to infer income levels for this study.

In order to place the individuals in the samples in the three-class framework, I ranked the individuals in each of the samples for each of the years in the order of the value of their total property holdings. Then, I divided each of the samples into three groups, designated as the wealthy, the middle class, and the working class. The lines marking the boundaries between these wealth categories or "classes" was drawn arbitrarily and judgmentally. Two criteria were taken into consideration in making these decisions.

First, the criteria used in other studies on New York City were considered. For example, Sean Wilentz (1984:398) in his study of the formation of the working class in early-19th-century New York, used the arbitrary dividing line of $150 in discriminating between mastercraftsmen and journeymen in 1816. The same dividing line was used in this study to discriminate between the middle class and the working class in 1820, the sample year closest to 1816.

Second, I took care that the majority of each of the "classes" was made up of people working in the occupations that scholars (Mills, 1951; Pessen, 1973) have identified as characterizing each of these groups, because there is no reason to doubt these interpretations. The majority of those with identified occupations in the elite group have been defined as "merchants and financiers" and "others working in the commercial sector" of the economy. Those in the latter category have been assumed to be merchants specializing in particular kinds of goods. The majority of the "middle class" have been described as "artisans and manufacturers" (assumed here to be masters) and "others working in the commercial sector" (assumed here to be shopkeepers). The majority of those in the working-class group have been identified as "semiskilled" and "artisans and manufacturers" (assumed here to be journeymen). The occupational breakdowns of each group and the wealth values used to define them are shown in Tables A–2 through A–4.

It should be stressed that, given the nature of the data, as discussed above, these categories can be viewed as being only roughly correlated with classes. In fact, successful shopkeepers dealing in the retail trade may have been included in the elite category, and less financially successful members of the city's "first families" may have been included in the middle group. Successful working-class people who owned some property have probably been included in the middle class, and less successful masters in the working class. Finally, a few people described as merchants may have fallen into the working-class category. These may have been either people who worked in the commercial sector and chose to give themselves high-status occupational titles or the sons of successful merchants, working as junior partners or clerks in mercantile houses. Their family wealth would have been assessed under their fathers' names. However, these exceptions can safely be assumed to include only a relatively small proportion of the individuals in the samples.

Table A–2. Distribution of Individuals in Elite Group by Level of Wealth
and Occupation for All Sample Years

Sample year	1790		1800		1810		1820		1830		1840	
Wealth (in pounds)	> £399		> £2,999		> £3,499		> £5,999		> £5,999		> £10,000	
Occupation	n	%	n	%	n	%	n	%	n	%	n	%
Semiskilled	0	0	0	0	0	0	0	0	0	0	0	0
Artisans, manufacturers	2	16.7	3	8.1	3	9.4	8	15.7	5	10.6	10	13.9
White collar, public service	0	0	1	2.7	1	3.1	2	3.9	1	2.1	1	1.4
Services	0	0	1	2.7	0	0	2	3.9	0	0	5	6.9
Professionals	0	0	4	10.8	1	3.1	3	5.9	4	8.5	4	5.5
Others in commerce	5	41.7	5	13.5	3	9.4	14	27.5	12	25.5	21	29.2
Merchants	3	25.0	18	48.6	15	46.9	14	27.5	19	40.4	23	31.9
No occupation	2	16.7	5	13.5	9	28.1	8	15.7	6	12.8	8	11.1
Total	12	100	37	100	32	100	51	100	47	100	72	100

Table A–3. Distribution of Individuals in Middle-Class Group by Level of Wealth
and Occupation for All Sample Years

Sample year	1790		1800		1810		1820		1830		1840	
Wealth (in pounds)	£25– £399		£100– £2,999		£101– £3,499		£151– £5,999		£200– £5,999		£250– £9,999	
Occupation	n	%	n	%	n	%	n	%	n	%	n	%
Semiskilled	7	13.7	15	13.3	10	9.0	12	7.7	16	7.4	2	0.8
Artisans, manufacturers	15	29.4	49	43.4	26	23.4	55	35.5	64	29.5	79	32.1
White collar public service	1	2.0	2	1.8	8	7.2	7	4.5	10	4.6	14	5.7
Services	3	5.9	5	4.4	5	4.5	6	3.9	11	5.1	5	2.0
Professionals	1	2.0	8	7.1	14	12.6	13	8.4	23	10.6	24	9.8
Others in commerce	9	17.6	16	14.2	19	17.1	35	22.6	35	16.1	59	24.0
Merchants, financiers	4	7.8	8	7.1	5	4.5	12	7.7	30	13.8	26	10.6
No occupation	11	21.6	10	8.8	24	21.6	15	9.7	28	12.9	37	15.0
Total	51	100	113	100	111	100	155	100	217	100	246	100

Table A–4. Distribution of Individuals in Working-Class Group by Level
of Wealth and Occupation for All Sample Years

Sample year	1790		1800		1810		1820		1830		1840	
Wealth (in pounds)	< £25		< £100		< £101		< £151		< £200		< £250	
Occupation	n	%	n	%	n	%	n	%	n	%	n	%
Semiskilled	9	39.1	17	31.5	30	19.1	50	19.7	57	15.7	31	7.7
Artisans, manufacturers	6	26.1	24	44.4	58	36.9	108	42.5	160	44.2	157	39.1
White collar, public service	2	8.7	0	0	8	5.1	4	1.6	9	2.5	21	5.2
Services	1	4.3	2	3.7	4	2.5	3	1.2	12	3.3	31	7.7
Professionals	1	4.3	3	5.6	8	5.1	10	3.9	18	5.0	23	5.7
Others in commerce	1	4.3	2	3.7	12	7.6	19	7.5	40	11.0	60	14.9
Merchants, financiers	0	0	1	1.9	6	3.8	10	3.9	14	3.9	22	5.5
No occupation	3	13.0	5	9.3	31	19.7	50	19.7	52	14.4	57	14.2
Total	23	100	54	100	157	100	254	100	362	100	402	100

NOTES

1. The directories used for pulling the samples are Hodge, Allen, and Campbell (1790), D. Longworth (1800), David Longworth (1810), and T. Longworth (1820, 1830, and 1840). Information about the directories is included in D. Longworth (1800:390) and T. Longworth (1830:670; 1840:729).
2. The maps used were Hills (1785); Hodge, Allen, and Campbell (1789); Taylor and Roberts (1797); Anonymous (1804); David Longworth (1808); and Poppleton (1817).

Appendix **B**

The Data on the Separation of the Home and the Workplace

In this appendix, the data summarized in the figures in Chapter 2 on the separation of the home and workplace are presented more fully in Tables B–1 through B–5. The data are based on the 2% samples of the entries in the New York City directories for 1790, 1800, 1810, 1820, 1830, and 1840, discussed in Appendix A. Those listed with one address in the directories were interpreted as having kept integrated homes and workplaces, and those listed with two or more addresses were inferred to have maintained separate homes and workplaces.[1]

Table B–1. Percentages of Members of Middle Class and Elite in Directory Samples Who Maintained Separate as Opposed to Integrated Homes and Workplaces, by Year

Year	Separate home and workplace		Integrated home and workplace		Total	
	n	%	n	%	n	%
1790	1	2.0	48	98.0	50	100
1800	6	4.4	129	95.6	135	100
1810	24	21.8	86	78.2	110	100
1820	59	32.2	124	67.8	183	100
1830	109	46.0	128	54.0	237	100
1840	201	69.8	87	30.2	288	100

Table B–2. Percentages of Members of Elite in Directory Samples Who Maintained Separate as Opposed to Integrated Homes and Workplaces, by Year

Year	Separate home and workplace		Integrated home and workplace		Total	
	n	%	n	%	n	%
1790	0	0	10	100.0	10	100
1800	3	9.4	29	90.6	32	100
1810	12	52.2	11	47.8	23	100
1820	22	51.2	21	48.8	43	100
1830	34	79.1	9	20.9	43	100
1840	46	69.7	20	30.3	66	100

Table B–3. Percentages of Members of Middle Class in Directory Samples Who Maintained Separate as Opposed to Integrated Homes and Workplaces, by Year

Year	Separate home and workplace		Integrated home and workplace		Total	
	n	%	n	%	n	%
1790	1	2.5	39	97.5	40	100
1800	3	2.9	100	97.1	103	100
1810	12	13.8	75	86.2	87	100
1820	37	26.4	103	73.6	140	100
1830	75	38.7	119	61.3	194	100
1840	155	69.8	67	30.2	222	100

Table B–4. Percentages of Members of Middle Class Listed as Artisans in Directory Samples Who Maintained Separate as Opposed to Integrated Homes and Workplaces, by Year

Year	Separate home and workplace		Integrated home and workplace		Total	
	n	%	n	%	n	%
1790	0	0	15	100	15	100
1800	2	4.1	47	95.9	49	100
1810	6	23.1	20	76.9	26	100
1820	16	29.1	39	70.9	55	100
1830	21	32.8	43	67.2	64	100
1840	51	64.6	28	35.4	79	100

Table B–5. Percentages of Members of Middle Class Listed with
Commercial Occupations in Directory Samples Who Maintained Separate
as Opposed to Integrated Homes and Workplaces, by Year

Year	Separate home and workplace		Integrated home and workplace		Total	
	n	%	*n*	%	*n*	%
1790	1	7.7	12	92.3	13	100
1800	1	4.2	23	95.8	24	100
1810	3	12.5	21	87.5	24	100
1820	15	32.6	31	67.4	46	100
1830	35	53.8	30	46.2	65	100
1840	64	75.3	21	24.7	85	100

NOTE

1. The directories used as sources for these data are Hodge, Allen, and Campbell
(1790); D. Longworth (1800); David Longworth (1810); and T. Longworth (1820,
1830, 1840). The people listed without an occupation and with only one address in
the directories were excluded from these figures, so that the retired and the unemployed (who had no workplaces at all) would not bias the results.

Appendix C

The Geographical Data

In this appendix, the data used to explore the changing social landscape of the city in Chapter 3 are presented in Tables C–1 through C–3. The data were derived by plotting the addresses of the people listed in the directory samples on contemporary maps of the city. This procedure is outlined more fully in Appendix A. The chi-square tests indicated that, in all three cases, the distributions of the members of the different social groups in the various zones of the city were significantly different from each other at the .01 level of significance.

Table C–1. Distribution of Different Groups in 1790 City by Zone, and Results of Chi-Square Test

| Zone | Group | | | |
	Elite	Middle class	Poor	Total
Core	10	17	7	34
Periphery	2	34	16	52
Total	12	51	23	86

Chi square = 11.47
$df = 2$
$\alpha = .01$
$p < .01$

Table C–2. Distributions of Different Groups and Separate
Workplaces in 1810 City by Zone, and Results of Chi-Square Test

Zone	Group				
	Elite	Middle class	Poor	Workplace	Total
Business district	4	3	2	7	16
Core	21	25	28	12	86
Periphery	7	84	122	5	218
Total	32	112	152	24	320

Chi square = 86.53
$df = 6$
$\alpha = .01$
$p = < .001$

Table C–3. Distributions of Different Groups and Separate Workplaces in 1840
City by Zone, and Results of Chi-Square Test

Zone	Group				
	Elite	Middle class	Poor	Workplace	Total
Business district	22	18	71	127	238
Inner middle-class area	0	21	6	11	38
Working-class area	16	36	90	23	165
Outer middle-class area	4	40	23	8	75
Periphery	16	123	208	28	375
Suburb	10	6	2	1	19
Total	68	244	400	198	910

Chi square = 330.76
$df = 15$
$\alpha = .01$
$p < .001$

Appendix D

The Data on Household Composition

In this appendix, the data on household composition shown in the figures in Chapter 4 are presented in tabular form (Tables D–1 through D–7). The data are based on the U.S. manuscript census returns for those listed in the directory samples. The age breakdowns used here are dependent on those used in the original manuscript census returns; these are discussed in Appendix A.

Table D–1. Mean Number of People Living in Middle-Class and Elite Households in Samples, by Year

	Middle Class			Elite		
Year	Mean	SD	n	Mean	SD	n
1790	6.29	2.91	35	7.33	2.15	12
1800	5.25	2.64	81	7.73	3.48	33
1810	6.28	2.71	89	8.13	2.44	23
1820	6.67	3.33	102	9.52	4.20	33
1830	7.31	3.63	127	8.83	3.46	29
1840	6.69	2.84	137	8.05	3.22	42

Table D–2. Mean Number of White Children Younger Than 10 Living in Sample Households Where Oldest White Female Was Younger Than 45 (1800–1820) or 50 (1830–1840), by Year

Year	Mean	Standard deviation	Sample size
1800	1.56	1.36	101
1810	2.10	1.71	146
1820	1.88	1.56	170
1830	1.62	1.52	242
1840	1.66	1.48	261

Table D–3. Mean Number of White Children Younger Than 10 Living in Middle-Class and Elite Households in Samples Where Oldest White Female Was Younger Than 45 (1800–1820) or 50 (1830–1840), by Socioeconomic Group and Year

Year	Middle Class			Elite		
	Mean	SD	n	Mean	SD	n
1800	1.65	1.34	51	1.18	1.40	22
1810	2.30	1.93	63	2.63	1.82	16
1820	1.99	1.67	73	2.30	1.79	23
1830	1.91	1.76	100	1.70	1.49	20
1840	1.73	1.47	107	1.90	1.80	29

Table D–4. Percentages of Enslaved and Free Blacks Living in Middle-Class and Elite Households in Samples, by Year

Year	Slaves		Free blacks	
	%	n	%	n
1790	96.9	32	3.0	1
1800	71.6	53	28.4	21
1810	40.6	26	59.4	38
1820	9.5	4	90.5	38
1830	0	0	100.0	46
1840	0	0	100.0	24

Table D–5. Mean Number of Black New Yorkers Living in White Middle-Class and Elite Households in Samples, by Year

Year	Blacks	Households	Mean
1790	33	47	.70
1800	74	114	.65
1810	64	112	.57
1820	42	135	.31
1830	46	155	.30
1840	24	179	.13

Table D–6. Mean Number of White Males and Females 10 Years or Older Living in Middle-Class and Elite Households in Samples, by Year

	Males						
	Middle Class				Elite		
Year	Mean	SD	n		Mean	SD	n
1800	1.83	1.58	81		2.52	1.92	33
1810	2.09	1.30	89		2.0	1.24	23
1820	2.31	1.90	102		3.09	2.02	33
1830	2.52	2.02	126		2.90	1.99	29
1840	2.26	1.50	137		2.62	1.74	42
	Females						
	Middle Class				Elite		
Year	Mean	SD	n		Mean	SD	n
1800	1.65	1.01	81		2.58	1.68	33
1810	2.06	1.29	89		2.83	1.47	23
1820	2.25	1.25	102		3.79	1.95	33
1830	2.86	2.0	126		3.76	1.84	29
1840	2.82	1.60	137		3.57	1.82	42

Table D–7. Mean Number of White Males and Females 10 Years or Older Living in Middle-Class Households in Samples, by Number of Addresses and Year

	Males						
	One address				Two addresses		
Year	Mean	SD	n		Mean	SD	n
1800	1.82	1.60	78		2.0	1.0	3
1810	1.93	1.03	81		3.75	2.38	8
1820	2.22	1.52	78		2.63	2.84	24
1830	2.47	2.27	81		2.62	1.50	45
1840	2.40	1.35	57		2.15	1.60	80
	Females						
	One address				Two addresses		
Year	Mean	SD	n		Mean	SD	n
1800	1.67	1.03	78		1.33	.58	3
1810	2.06	1.26	81		2.0	1.69	8
1820	2.18	1.22	78		2.46	1.35	24
1830	2.93	2.27	81		2.73	1.42	45
1840	2.79	1.62	57		2.85	1.60	80

Appendix *E*
The Archaeological Data

This appendix presents the methods used in analyzing the ceramic dishes from the archaeological contexts that provided the data for Chapter 6, the second chapter on the ritualization of family meals. The appendix is divided into six parts. First, I describe how I chose the particular archaeological assemblages to analyze for the study. Then, I describe the three techniques I used to date the materials and, third, how I ascribed a particular set or assemblage of artifacts to a particular household. Fourth, I discuss the process of extrapolating the number of vessels (referred to as the *minimum number of vessels* in the archaeological literature) from the sherds that were most frequently found in these deposits. Fifth, I present the data that were used to analyze the dishes in Chapter 6. Finally, I consider some sampling problems.

CHOOSING THE ARCHAEOLOGICAL ASSEMBLAGES

I used three criteria in choosing materials to analyze for this study. First, each set of materials had to be from a domestic assemblage; that is, it had to include samples of ceramic vessels that had been used to present meals. Second, the assemblages had to date to the target period of time—the late 18th or early 19th century—and had to have been excavated in an area that was part of New York City during the target period. Finally, each assemblage had to come from a deposit that was relatively unmixed with earlier or later materials, so that we could infer that the materials had been used in a single household at a particular time. In all, 11 assemblages in collections from six archaeological sites in New York met all of these criteria.

DATING THE ARCHAEOLOGICAL ASSEMBLAGES

I used several different dating techniques for each of the assemblages so that I could find out more about the ceramics and the people who had used them. These are the mean ceramic dating technique and the *terminus post quem* and *terminus ante quem* techniques. Stanley South (1977:217) developed the concept of mean ceramic dates in working with 18th-century ceramics in order to identify the occupation period represented by an archaeological site or deposit. This index is a mean date weighted by the frequency of the ceramic sherds of those ceramic types that have a known period of manufacture and/or popularity. The formula used to derive the mean ceramic date is

$$Y = \frac{\sum_{i=1}^{n} x_i f_i}{\sum_{i=1}^{n} f_i}$$

where x_i is the mean date for the manufacture and/or popularity of each ceramic type, f_i is the frequency or number of sherds in each ceramic type, and n is the number of ceramic sherds in the sample. Sherds of ceramic types whose dates of manufacture are not known or that were made over long periods of time are not used in the calculation. The assumption behind this technique is that the life cycle of the popularity of a ceramic type (or style) follows a battleship curve: new styles are introduced, slowly become popular and replace earlier styles, and then gradually fall into disuse, being replaced in their turn by newer styles.

For this study, I ran the formula on the vessels, rather than the sherds, in each assemblage. I also interpreted the date somewhat differently from South's original idea of extrapolating a mean date of occupation for a site. Instead, I assumed that the consumer patterns of those buying different kinds of ceramic vessels also follow a battleship curve, and I used the index to provide a mean date for when the ceramic vessels in a particular assemblage were acquired by a household. After they were acquired, they were used in the household for a number of years before they ended up in the ground to form part of the archaeological record.

I used the mean ceramic date to place the 11 assemblages in temporal groups that could then be placed in chronological order, so that changes through time in the quality of the ceramics could be analyzed and information on the relative prices of different kinds of vessels could be studied. These prices changed throughout the period of study.

The 11 assemblages come from six archaeological sites. The location of each site is shown in Figure 6–9. There are four assemblages in the early chronological group that dates to the 1780s: the materials from Test Cut J, a privy at the 7 Hanover Square Site (Rothschild and Pickman, 1990);[1] the materials from the home and workshop of the Van Voorhis family, which were found on a cobble floor at the 75 Wall Street Site (Berger and Associates, 1987);[2] and the materials from Feature 51 (a privy) and Feature 49 (a wooden box) at the 175 Water Street Site (Geismar, 1983).[3] There are also four assemblages in the middle chronological group, which dates to about 1805: the materials associated with the home and shop of the Bowne family, the Pearl Street druggists, from Feature 48, a privy at the 75 Wall Street Site (Berger and Associates, 1987);[4] the materials from Test Cut AX (a wooden box) and Test Cut AT (a privy) from the Telco Block Site (Rockman, Harris, and Levin, 1983);[5] and those from Feature 43, a privy at the 175 Water Street Site (Geismar, 1983).[6] There are three assemblages in the later group, which dates to the 1820s: the materials from the home of the family of Benjamin Robson, the physician, from Feature 9, and the assemblage from Feature 11, both privies at the Sullivan Street Site (Salwen and Yamin, 1990),[7] and the materials from Component 15, a cistern at the Broad Financial Square Site (Grossman, 1985).[8] Table E–1 presents a summary of the information about the sites, the kinds of deposits where each assemblage was found, and its mean ceramic date.

Table E–1. Contexts of Ceramic Assemblages

Assemblage	Site	Feature type	Mean ceramic date	Period of deposition (approximate)
Early Group				
Test Cut J	7 Hanover Square	Privy nightsoil	1783	1795–1805
Cobble Floor	75 Wall Street	Basement deposit	1787	1780–1788
Feature 51	175 Water Street	Privy nightsoil	1789	1780–1797
Feature 49	175 Water Street	Wooden box fill	1789	1795–1805
Middle Group				
Feature 48	75 Wall Street	Privy nightsoil	1803	1800–1820
Test Cut Ax	Telco Block	Wooden box	1804	1805–1816
Feature 43	175 Water Street	Privy fill	1804	1795–1820
Test Cut AT	Telco Block	Privy fill	1810	1820–1826
Later Group				
Feature 11	Sullivan Street	Privy fill	1818	1849–1855
Component 15	Broad Financial Center	Cistern fill	1820	1842–1847
Feature 9	Sullivan Street	Privy fill	1823	1849–1855

I used the two other dating methods—the *terminus post quem* and *terminus ante quem* techniques—to bracket the period when the archæological materials had been deposited in the ground. The principle behind the *terminus post quem* (or "limit after which") technique is that the date of the deposition of the materials in the ground (as opposed to the date of the acquisition of the ceramics by the household, which I infer from the mean ceramic date) is the same as or later than the date of the introduction of the latest artifact type represented in the deposit (Noel Hume, 1968:69). An obvious example is the use of dated coins to provide this information. If a coin inscribed with the date of 1832 is found in an undisturbed deposit, the archæological materials must have been deposited either during or after that year. However, based on this information, the materials could have been deposited at any time from 1832 to the present. The introductory dates for various types of ceramics and bottles are commonly used to deduce these dates.

A date derived by the *terminus ante quem* (or "limit before which") technique can sometimes be used to infer the latest time that a set of archæological materials could have been deposited in the ground (Noel Hume, 1968:67). For example, if a layer of soil was cut through by a builder's trench for the foundation wall of the most recent building on the property, and if we know from historical records that this structure was build in 1836, then the assemblage must have been deposited in that layer of soil before the 1836 structure was built. These dates can also sometimes be inferred from the absence of popular kinds of artifacts that have known dates of introduction.

Ideally, information derived from the *terminus post quem* and *terminus ante quem* techniques can be combined to bracket the period during which an assemblage of archæological materials was deposited in the ground. When we combine the examples used above, if a layer of soil containing a coin with a date of 1832 was cut through by a foundation wall dating to 1836, we can infer that the materials in the layer were deposited during this five-year period.

Unfortunately, however, the interpretation of these dates is seldom so simple, and they have to be used with caution. Given the complex stratigraphic relationships among the layers of soil in urban sites, it is sometimes extremely difficult to tell whether the deposit has been disturbed and whether the artifact used for deriving the *terminus post quem* is intrusive. Furthermore, a variety of factors can account for the absence of the kinds of artifacts that are used to derive *terminus ante quem* dates (Deetz, 1977:16–17). Table E–1 shows the period when each of the assemblages is thought to have been deposited in the ground.

ASCRIBING THE ARCHAEOLOGICAL ASSEMBLAGES TO PARTICULAR HOUSEHOLDS

In this study, I use the dates derived from *terminus post quem* and *terminus ante quem* techniques for a particular purpose: to ascribe particular assemblages to the particular people who lived on the property when the archaeological materials were deposited in the ground. These people were presumably the ones who actually used the artifacts in question in their households, and their identity is helpful in placing them in their cultural context. In order to identify these households, I intensively researched each of the properties where the assemblages were found for the period when I thought that the materials had been deposited in the ground.[9] During the period of study, there was a relatively high turnover rate among the people who lived on some of the properties. In many cases, I could identify a series of households that might have used the domestic materials found in an archaeological deposit, but I could not identify one particular household where the materials were definitely used. Table 6–1 shows the occupation of the heads of the households where the sets of ceramic dishes were used and information on whether or not each home was combined with or separate from its associated workplace.

COUNTING THE VESSELS

The data for the present study are the *vessels* that were used in these households rather than the bits and pieces or sherds that were excavated. Therefore, I had to extrapolate or estimate the presence of particular vessels from the sherds that were retrieved. To do this, I mended all of the sherds that could be fitted back together so that the vessels were physically reconstructed to the extent possible. Then, I considered the problem of estimating the number and kinds of vessels in the assemblage from the reconstructed vessels and residual sherds. This problem was particularly difficult in this study because of the nature of urban sites. All but one of the sites were in areas of the city that had been intensively occupied both before and after the materials of interest were deposited. In addition, all but one of the sites were located on landfill, which often includes domestic garbage as part of its soil matrix. Therefore, most of the deposits also contained a number of residual sherds that were present in the deposit as part of the soil matrix. Some deposits were also slightly disturbed by the inclusion of intrusive materials from later strata that covered the primary materials.

The problem of extrapolating vessel distributions was further compounded because some of the deposits were partially destroyed by later construction activities on the properties. For example, the tops of many deposits were removed when later basement floors were laid on top of them, and later foundation walls were built through some of the other deposits. In addition, many of the deposits were sampled only during excavation by the archaeologists, and considerably less than 100% of the deposit was excavated.

I had two major concerns in extrapolating the vessels represented by the sherds in each deposit. First, it was important not to overestimate the number of vessels by inferring the presence of a vessel from the presence of sherds that were included in the deposit only incidentally (either from landfill or from other people who had lived on the site either before or after the target period). Second, it was also important not to underestimate the number of vessels in the features, so that those vessels that were only partially retrieved in the course of excavation (because of disposal history, sampling on the part of archaeologists, or later disturbance of the deposit) could be considered.

For this study, I followed a series of somewhat arbitrary rules for determining the minimum number of vessels in each assemblage. In most cases, at least one-quarter of the vessel had to be present in the materials retrieved from the deposit. If two-quarters or more of a vessel matched in pattern and ware, and if, because of how the fragments fit together, they could not have come from the same vessel, these two quarters were interpreted as representing two vessels. The only exception to this rule was in those cases where a vessel fragment that constituted less than a quarter of a vessel was part of a matching set and other members of the set were represented by larger pieces in the assemblage. These small fragments were recorded as separate vessels. Again, care had to be taken so that a small fragment was not counted as a separate vessel when in fact it might have been part of the missing portion of a vessel that had been recorded separately.

After the vessels were assembled and recorded, I placed each of them in one of three different categories, which I chose because of their relevance to the present study: tablewares, teawares, and "other." Vessels in the tableware category include plates of various sizes and serving vessels, like platters, deep dishes, boats, and tureens. Those in the teaware category include teabowls and teacups, saucers, coffee cups, tea- and coffeepots, tea canisters, and sugar bowls. The vessels placed in these two categories were analyzed further as described below and in Chapter 6; those in the "other" category were not analyzed further for this study.

THE ARCHAEOLOGICAL DATA

Next, in Tables E–2 through E–4, I present the data on the dishes in the tableware and teaware assemblage that are analyzed in Chapter 6. The assemblages are organized by chronological group and by the mean ceramic date of the assemblage within each group (the order used in Table E–1).

Five items of information are presented for each type of vessel listed in the tables. The pattern or style is named (e.g., royal or willow) or described (e.g., landscape—Chinese) in the first column. The vessels described as "minimally decorated" in Chapter 6 include those patterns referred to here as plain, royal, diamond/beaded, feather, and barley. An asterisk in the pattern column indicates that the pattern is represented by a "set," or more than one matching vessel, in the assemblage.

The kind of ware the vessel is made from and its type of decoration are listed in the second column. If no ware type is listed, the vessel is made of earthenware; the initials *Cc* indicate that the vessel is made of cream-colored earthenware; "Chinese export porcelain" is abbreviated here by *CEP*. The vessel's form or function (e.g., saucer; table plate, twiffler, and muffin for different sizes of plates [after Miller 1980, 1991]) is listed in the third column. The numbers in the fourth column refer to the number of vessels of that particular type in the assemblage.

Finally, in the fifth column, an "index value" is listed. This value is used to compute the mean relative cost of each of the tableware and teaware assemblages at the time that it was bought as estimated by its mean ceramic date; this value is derived from the work of George L. Miller.

Several years ago, Miller (1980, 1991) developed a method for exploring the relative costs of British ceramic vessels. In studying potters' price lists for refined earthenwares in the late 18th and early-19th centuries, he noted that vessels made of plain, undecorated (cream-colored or cc) earthenware were priced the lowest of all the vessels, and that the prices for these vessels were exceptionally stable from the 1790s through the 1850s. Furthermore, he noted that the prices of wares decorated by various production techniques (such as dipping, edging with color, painting, and transfer printing) maintained the same price relationship to each other and to the plain cream-colored wares until the 1850s. However, the relative cost of many of the decorated wares declined relative to the cost of cc ware (particularly after around 1830), and the prices were further discounted by the potters at ever-increasing rates throughout the period. This decline in the value of the ceramics was offset somewhat by the tariffs that were imposed on the vessels when they were imported into this country. Using the potters' price lists and taking all of this information into account, Miller provided a method for calculating the relative value of the Staffordshire-made vessels in an archaeological assemblage.

Originally, one of the problems with this method of scaling the value of ceramics was that the Chinese export porcelains, which are prevalent in many assemblages from late-18th- and early-19th-century households, could not be included because their prices relative to cc ware were not known. More recent-

Table E–2. Ceramics in Tableware and Teaware Assemblages: Early Group[a]

Table E–2a: Test Cut J

Tablewares

Pattern	Decoration/ware	Vessel form	n	Index value
Royal*	cc	Table plate	4	1
		Platter	1	—
Plain*	cc	Table plate	1	1
		Muffin	1	1
Shell-edged*	Edged	Table plate	2	1.67
Landscape—Chinese	Blue CEP	Table plate	1	3
Landscape—Chinese	Blue CEP	Soup plate	1	3
Floral	Blue CEP	Soup plate	1	3
Floral	Blue CEP	Table plate	1	3
Total			13	

Sum index value: European ceramics 9.34 − 10% = 8.41
          Chinese porcelain = 12.
Sum index value: 20.41 + 5% = 21.43
Mean index value: 1.79

Teawares

Pattern	Decoration/ware	Vessel form	n	Index value
Fluted, scalloped	cc	Teabowl	1	2.6[a]
Landscape—Chinese	Blue CEP	Teabowl	1	3
Landscape—Chinese	Painted	Teapot lid	1	—
Floral*	Overglaze CEP	Teabowl	2	4.5
		Saucer	1	—
Floral	Soft paste	Teabowl	1	4**
Floral	Painted	Teabowl	1	2.5
Floral	Painted	Teabowl	1	3.4*
Total			9	

*1796 potters' price list (Miller, 1991).
**1824 potters' price list (Miller, 1980).
Sum index value: European ceramics 12.5 − 10% = 11.25
          Chinese porcelain = 12
Sum index value: 23.25 + 5% = 24.41
Mean index value: 3.49

(*continued*)

Table E–2b: Cobble Floor

Tablewares

Pattern	Decoration/ware	Vessel form	n	Index value
Royal*	cc	Table plate	9	1
		Muffin	1	1
		Soup	3	1
		Dish	1	—
		Boat	1	—
Diamond/beaded*	cc	Table plate	2	1
Feather	cc	Table plate	5	1
		Soup	1	1
		Boat	1	—
Unidentified	cc	Drainer	1	—
Total			25	

Sum index value: European ceramics $21 - 10\% = 18.9$
Sum index value: $18.9 + 5\% = 19.85$
Mean index value: .95

Teawares

Pattern	Decoration/ware	Vessel form	n	Index value
Landscape—Chinese	Overglaze CEP	Saucer	1	4.5
Landscape—Chinese	Blue CEP	Teabowl	1	3
Landscape—Chinese	Blue CEP	Teabowl	2	3
Landscape—Chinese	Blue CEP	Saucer	1	3
Landscape—Chinese	Blue CEP	Teabowl	1	3
Floral	Blue CEP	Saucer	1	3
Floral	Blue CEP	Saucer	1	3
Floral	Blue CEP	Teabowl	1	3
Floral*	Soft paste	Teabowl	2	4*
Floral	Painted	Teapot lid	1	—
Total			12	

*1824 potters' price list (Miller, 1980).
Sum index value: European ceramics $8 - 10\% = 7.2$
                 Chinese porcelain $= 28.5$
Sum index value: $35.7 + 5\% = 37.5$
Mean index value: 3.41

(*continued*)

Table E–2c: Feature 51

Tablewares

Pattern	Decoration/ware	Vessel form	n	Index value
Royal*	cc	Table plate	1	1
		Twiffler	1	1
Diamond/beaded	cc	Table plate	1	1
Feather	cc	Table plate	1	1
Barley, etc.	White stoneware	Soup	1	—
Total			5	

Sum index value: European ceramics 4 − 10% = 3.6
Sum index value: 3.6 + 5% = 3.78
Mean index value: .95

Teawares

Pattern	Decoration/ware	Vessel form	n	Index value
Plain	cc	Saucer	1	1
Landscape—Chinese	Blue CEP	Teabowl	1	3
Landscape—Chinese	Painted	Saucer	2	2.5
Floral*	Painted	Saucer	2	2.5
Total			6	

Sum index value: European ceramics 11 − 10% = 9.9
                        Chinese ceramics = 3
Sum index value: 12.9 + 5% = 13.55
Mean index value: 2.26

Table E–2d: Feature 49

Tablewares

Pattern	Decoration/ware	Vessel form	n	Index value
Royal*	cc	Table plate	5	1
		Twiffler	1	1
		Muffin	2	1
		Soup	2	1
Plain*	cc	Muffin	2	1
Plain-molded	cc	Boat	1	—
Total			13	

Sum index value: European ceramics 12 − 10% = 10.8
Sum index value: 10.8 + 5% = 11.34
Mean index value: .95

(continued)

Table E–2d: Feature 49 (*Continued*)

Teawares

Pattern	Decoration/ware	Vessel form	n	Index value
Plain*	cc	Teabowl	2	1
		Saucer	2	—
		Teapot	2	—
Landscape—Chinese	Painted	Saucer	6	2.5
		Teabowl	3	—
Landscape—Chinese	Painted	Teabowl	5	2.5
Floral	Blue CEP	Teabowl	1	3
Floral*	Painted	Saucer	2	2.5
Floral	Painted	Coffeepot	1	—
Other—checkered*	Dipped	Saucer	3	1.5*
		Teabowl	1	—
Total			28	

*1825 potters' price list (Miller, 1991).
Sum index value: European ceramics 39 − 10% = 35.1
                         Chinese ceramics = 3
Sum index value: 38.1 + 5% = 40.01
Mean index value: 2.11

[a]Unless otherwise noted by an asterisk in the index value column, the prices used for computing these index values are those from George L. Miller's 1787 price lists (Miller, 1980, 1991). The asterisks in the pattern column indicate that the pattern is represented by a "set," or more than one matching vessel, in the assemblage.

ly, however, Miller (personal communication, 1986) has suggested that, through the 1820s, the relative cost of the blue-underglaze-decorated Chinese porcelains can be estimated at three times the value of the same vessel form made in cc ware. Furthermore, contemporary price lists show that the overglaze-decorated Chinese export porcelains can be conservatively estimated at a value of approximately 1.5 times that of the blue-underglaze-decorated porcelains (Mudge, 1981:100, 166–167), or at 4.5 times that of cc ware. However, Miller noted that overglaze-decorated porcelain vessels might be relatively even more expensive if they were decorated to order.

    The index values for each vessel type are given in the column to the right in Tables E–2 through E–4. Each of these values is multiplied by the number of vessels for that line entry, and the products are added together for a sum index value. Then, the sum index values of the British wares are adjusted for the potters' discounts of 10% for the assemblages in the early and middle groups (before the War of 1812) and of 28.8% for the assemblages in the later group. Then, the sum index values for both the British and the Chinese ceramics are adjusted to take into account the tariffs that were imposed on

Table E–3. Ceramics in Tableware and Teaware Assemblages: Middle Group[a]

Table E–3a: Feature 48

Tablewares

Pattern ware	Decoration/ware	Vessel form	n	Index value
Plain*	cc	Plate	2	1
		Twiffler	1	1
		Soup	3	1
		Platter	1	—
Shell-edged—blue*	Edged	Twiffler	1	1.5
		Muffin (7″)	3	1.51
		Tureen	1	—
		Platter	1	—
Shell-edged—green*	Edged	Table plate	6	1.33
		Twiffler	2	1.5
		Muffin (7″)	1	1.51
		Tureen	1	—
		Platter	2	—
		Deep dish	1	—
		Boat	1	—
Landscape—Chinese*	Willow	Muffins (6″)	2	3.01*
Total			29	

*1814 potters' price list (Miller 1991)
Sum index value: European ceramics 30.54 − 10% = 27.49
Sum index value: 27.49 + 5% = 28.86
Mean index value: 1.37

Teawares

Pattern	Decoration/ware	Vessel form	n	Index value
Landscape—Chinese	Blue CEP	Sugarbowl	1	—
Floral	Painted	Teabowl	1	1.71
Floral	Painted	Sugarbowl	1	—
Floral	Painted	Teabowl	1	1.71
Floral	Painted	Teabowl	1	1.71
Floral*	Overglaze CEP	Saucer	1	4.5
		Teabowl	1	—
Floral*	Overglaze CEP	Saucer	1	4.5
		Teabowl	1	—
Floral*	Overglaze CEP	Saucer	3	4.5
Floral*	Overglaze CEP	Saucer	1	4.5
		Teabowl	1	—

(continued)

Table E–3a: Feature 48 (*Continued*)

Teawares (Continued)

Pattern	Decoration/ware	Vessel form	n	Index value
Other—"sawtooth"*	Overglaze CEP	Saucer	2	—
		Teabowl	3	4.5
		Canister	1	—
		Coffee cup	1	4.5
Other—"lovebirds"*	Overglaze CEP	Saucer	3	4.5
		Teabowl	2	—
Other—pseudo armorial	Overglaze CEP	Teabowl	1	4.5
Other—unidentified	Blue CEP	Teabowl	1	3
Total			28	

Sum index value: European ceramics 5.13 − 10% = 4.62
Chinese porcelain = 66
Sum index value: 70.62 + 5% = 74.15
Mean index value: 4.12

Table E–3b: Test Cut AX

Tablewares

Pattern	Decoration/ware	Vessel form	n	Index value
Royal*	cc	Table plate	1	1
		Soup	2	1
		Platter	1	—
Plain*	cc	Table plate	2	1
		Soup	1	1
		Deep dish	2	—
		Platter	1	—
Shell-edged—blue*	Edged	Table plate	3	1.33
		Twiffler	2	1.5
		Muffin (6")	1	1.49
		Soup	2	1.33
Shell-edged—green*	Edged	Soup	1	1.33
		Platter	1	—
Landscape—Chinese	Blue CEP	Platter	1	—
Other—underglaze-lined	Painted	Platter	1	—
Total			22	

Sum index value: European ceramics 18.47 − 10% = 16.62
Sum index value: 16.62 + 5% = 17.45
Mean index value: 1.16

(*continued*)

Table E–3b: Test Cut AX (*Continued*)

Teawares

Pattern	Decoration/ware	Vessel form	n	Index value
Plain	cc	Coffee pot	1	—
Landscape—Chinese	Overglaze CEP	Teabowl	1	4.5
Floral*	Printed, scalloped	Saucer	1	4.29
		Slop bowl	1	—
Floral	Printed	Saucer	1	3.42
Floral*	Painted	Teabowl	2	1.71
Floral	Overglaze CEP	Teabowl	1	4.5
		Saucer	1	—
Floral	Overglaze CEP	Teabowl	1	4.5
		Saucer	1	—
Other—pseudo armorial	Overglaze CEP	Teapot	1	—
Other—unidentified	Painted	Teabowl	1	1.71
Total			13	

Sum index value: European ceramics 12.84 − 10% = 11.56
              Chinese porcelain = 13.5
Sum index value: 25.06 + 5% = 26.31
Mean index value: 3.29

Table E–3c: Feature 43

Tablewares

Pattern	Decoration/ware	Vessel form	n	Index value
Royal*	cc	Table plate	1	1
		Soup	3	1
Shell-edged—blue*	Edged	Table plate	8	1.33
		Muffin (6″)	1	1.49
		Muffin (7″)	1	1.51
		Soup	1	1.33
		Deep dish	1	—
		Deep dish	2	—
		Platter	1	—
Shell-edged—green*	Edged	Table plate	2	1.33
		Twiffler	1	1.5
Total			22	

Sum index value: European ceramics 23.13 − 10% = 20.82
Sum index value: 20.82 + 5% = 21.86
Mean index value: 1.21

(*continued*)

Table E–3c: Feature 43 (*Continued*)

Teawares

Pattern	Decoration/ware	Vessel form	n	Index value
Plain	cc	Saucer	1	1
Landscape—Chinese	Printed	Saucer	1	3.42
Landscape—Chinese	Printed	Teabowl	1	3.42
Landscape—western	Printed	Saucer	1	3.42
Floral	Painted	Teabowl	1	1.71
Floral	Painted	Teabowl	1	1.71
Floral	Painted	Teabowl	1	1.71
Floral	Painted	Saucer	1	1.71
Floral*	Painted	Saucer	2	1.71
Floral	Painted	Teabowl	1	1.71
Floral*	Painted	Slop bowl	1	—
		Saucer	1	1.71
Floral	Overglaze CEP	Saucer	1	4.5
Other—"star"*	Painted	Teabowl	1	1.71
		Saucer	1	—
Other—unidentified	Overglaze CEP	Teabowl	1	4.5
Total			17	

Sum index value: European ceramics 26.65 − 10% = 23.99

Chinese porcelain = 9

Sum index value: 32.99 + 5% = 34.63

Mean index value: 2.31

Table E–3d: Test Cut AT

Tablewares

Pattern	Decoration/ware	Vessel form	n	Index value
Royal*	cc	Table plate	1	1
		Muffin	1	1
Plain*	cc	Table plate	1	1
		Muffin	1	1
Shell-edged—blue*	Edged	Twiffler	2	1.28
		Muffin (7")	1	1.33
Shell-edged—green*	Edged	Table plate	2	1.33
		Twiffler	1	1.28
		Deep dish	1	—
		Tureen	1	—
Landscape—western*	Printed	Table plate	3	3.33
		Muffin (6")	1	3.61

(*continued*)

Table E–3d: Test Cut AT (*Continued*)

Tablewares (Continued)

Pattern	Decoration/ware	Vessel form	*n*	Index value
Landscape—western	Printed	Muffin (7″)	1	3.5
Total			17	

Sum index value: European ceramics 28.93 − 10% = 26.04
Sum index value: 26.04 + 5% = 27.34
Mean index value: 1.82

Teawares

Pattern	Decoration/ware	Vessel form	*n*	Index value
Plain	Red earthenware	Teapot	1	—
Landscape—Chinese—	Blue CEP	Teabowl	3	—
Nanking*		Saucer	9	3
Landscape—western*	Printed	Saucer	2	3
Floral	Painted, fluted scalloped	Saucer	1	1.5
Floral	Painted	Teabowl	1	2.17
Total			17	

Sum index value: European ceramics 9.67 − 10% = 8.7
                           Chinese porcelains: 27
Sum index value: 35.7 + 5% = 37.49
Mean index value: 2.88

[a]Unless otherwise noted, the prices used for computing the index values for the ceramics in the middle group are those from the 1804 price lists (Miller, 1980, 1991). The asterisks in the pattern column indicate that the pattern is represented by a "set," on more than one matching vessel, in the assemblage.

them. These tariffs raise the prices by 5% for the assemblages in the early and middle groups (before the War of 1812) and by 20% for the assemblages in the later group. Finally, the adjusted sum index values are divided by the number of ceramics that were used in computing the figures to derive a mean index value for each tableware and teaware assemblage. These mean index values form the basis of the discussion of the cost of the tablewares and teawares in Chapter 6.[10]

SAMPLING PROBLEMS

The use of archaeological samples presents a series of problems that need to be considered explicitly. One problem is that of sample bias, and others have to do with sample size.

Table E–4. Ceramics in Tableware and Teaware Assemblages: Later Group[a]

Table E–4a: Feature 11

Tablewares

Pattern	Decoration/ware	Vessel form	n	Index value
Landscape—Chinese—Canton*	Blue CEP	Table plate	2	3
		Deep dish	1	—
Landscape—Chinese	Blue CEP	Table plate	1	3
Landscape—western	Printed	Muffin (5″)	1	3.01
Other—pseudo armorial	Overglaze CEP	Muffin (6″)	1	4.5
Total			6	

Sum index value: European ceramics 3.01 − 28.8% = 2.14
      Chinese porcelain = 13.5
Sum index value: 15.64 + 20% = 18.77
Mean index value: 3.75

Teawares

Pattern	Decoration/ware	Vessel form	n	Index value
Landscape—Chinese	Blue CEP	Teabowl	1	3
Landscape—western	Printed	Saucer	1	2.25
Floral*	Soft paste	Teabowl	1	4.2*
		Coffee cup	2	4.2*
		Saucer	1	—
Total			6	

*1836 potters' list (Miller, 1991).
Sum index value: European Ceramics 14.85 − 28.8% = 10.57
      Chinese porcelain = 3
Sum index value: 13.57 + 20% = 16.28
Mean index value: 3.26

Table E–4b: Component 15

Tablewares

Pattern	Decoration/ware	Vessel form	n	Index value
Landscape—Chinese—Canton*	Blue CEP	Table plate	5	3
		Twiffler	2	3
		Platter	1	—
Landscape—Chinese—willow*	Printed	Table plate	3	2.67

(*continued*)

Table E–4b: Component 15 (*Continued*)

Tablewares (Continued)

Pattern	Decoration/ware	Vessel form	*n*	Index value
Landscape—western	Printed	Muffin (6″)	1	3.61
Floral	Flown	Table plate	1	4.17*
Total			13	

*Based on the relationship between flown and printed on the 1846 potters' price list (Miller, 1991).
Sum index value: European ceramics 15.79 − 28.8% = 11.24
                 Chinese porcelain = 21
Sum index value: 32.24 + 20% = 38.69
Mean index value: 3.22

Teawares

Pattern	Decoration/ware	Vessel form	*n*	Index value
Plain—molded	Soft paste	Teacup	1	4.2*
Landscape—Chinese—	Blue CEP	Teabowl	2	3
Nanking*		Saucer	1	—
Landscape—Chinese	Blue CEP	Saucer	1	3
Landscape—western	Printed	Saucer	1	3
Floral*	Painted	Saucer	1	1.5
		Slop bowl	1	—
Floral	Overglaze CEP	Teabowl	1	4.5
Floral	Hardpaste	Saucer	1	4.2*
Floral	Softpaste	Teacup	1	4.2*
Total			11	

*1836 potters' price list (Miller, 1991).
Sum index value: European ceramics 17.1 − 28.8 = 12.18
                 Chinese porcelain = 13.5
Sum index value: 25.68 + 20% = 30.82
Mean index value: 3.42

Table E–4c: Feature 9

Tablewares

Pattern	Decoration/ware	Vessel form	*n*	Index value
Plain*	cc	Soup	2	1
Shell-edged—blue*	Edged	Table plate	3	1.33
		Twiffler	1	1.28
		Platter	2	—

(*continued*)

Table E–4c: Feature 9 (*Continued*)

Tablewares (Continued)

Pattern	Decoration/ware	Vessel form	n	Index value
Shell-edged—embossed marly—blue	Edged	Muffin (6″)	1	—
Shell-edged—embossed marly—green*	Edged	Muffins (6″)	3	—
Landscape—Chinese— Canton*	Blue CEP	Table plate	2	3
		Twiffler	2	3
		Muffin (6″)	4	3
		Soup	3	3
		Boat	1	—
Landscape—Chinese— willow*	Printed	Table plate	9	2.67
		Unidentified plate	1	—
		Muffins (7″)	2	3
		Soup	1	2.67
		Tureen	1	—
Landscape—Chinese*	Blue CEP	Twiffler	2	3
Landscape—Chinese*	Blue CEP	Table plate	2	3
Landscape—Chinese*	Blue CEP	Muffin (7″)	3	3
Landscape—western*	Printed	Table plate	1	3.33
		Platter	1	—
Landscape—western	Printed	Table plate	1	3.33
Floral—Fitzhugh*	Blue CEP	Muffin (6″)	4	3
Other—landscape— Indian	Printed	Table plate	1	3.33
Total			53	

Sum index value: European ceramics 49.96 − 28.8% = 35.57
            Chinese porcelain = 66
Sum index value: 101.57 + 20% = 121.88
Mean index value: 2.83

Teawares

Pattern	Decoration/ware	Vessel form	n	Index value
Landscape—Chinese— Nanking*	Soft paste	Teacup	2	4.2*
		Saucer	1	—
Landscape—western*	Printed	Saucer	2	—
		Teacup	2	3.67
Landscape—western*	Printed	Teabowl, Irish	4	2.75
Landscape—western*	Overglaze CEP	Teacup	1	4.5
		Saucer	1	—
		Coffee cup	3	4.5
Landscape—western	Overglaze CEP	Teabowl	1	4.5
Landscape—western	Printed	Teabowl, Irish	1	2.75

(*continued*)

Table E–4c: Feature 9 (*Continued*)

Teawares (Continued)

Pattern	Decoration/ware	Vessel form	n	Index value
Landscape—western	Printed	Teacup	1	3.67
Landscape—western	Printed	Saucer	1	3
Landscape—western	Printed	Teabowl	1	3
Lafayette*		Saucer	1	—
Floral—Fitzhugh*	Blue CEP	Saucer	3	3
		Teapot	1	—
Floral*	Painted	Teabowl, Irish	3	—
		Saucer	5	1.38
Floral	Printed	Teabowl	1	3
		Saucer	1	—
Floral-geranium*	Printed	Teacup	3	3.67
		Saucer	3	—
Floral*	Painted	Saucer	3	1.5
Floral*	Printed	Saucer	4	3
Floral	Overglaze CEP	Teabowl	1	4.5
Floral	European hard paste	Teacup	1	4.2*
Floral	Soft paste	Teacup	1	4.2*
Floral	Caneware	Teapot	1	—
Total			53	

*1836 potters' price list (Miller, 1991).
Sum index value: European ceramics 84.97 − 28.8% = 60.5
                      Chinese porcelain = 36
Sum index value: 96.5 + 20% = 115.8
Mean index value: 2.97

[a] Unless otherwise noted, the prices used for computing the index values for the ceramics in the later group are those from the 1823 potters' price lists (Miller, 1980, 1991). The asterisks in the pattern column indicate that the pattern is represented by a "set," on more than one matching vessel, in the assemblage.

Like all samples, archaeological samples have certain inherent biases that are related to the nature of the artifacts that make up the sample. In their context of use, ceramics are unstable in that they are easily broken; once they are buried in the ground, however, their pieces, or sherds, are stable and do not decompose or disintegrate like many other kinds of materials. For breakable items like ceramics, the items that ultimately make up archaeological collections tend to be those that were used most often in the home; that is, the more often a breakable item is used, the more likely it is to be broken, to be discarded, and later to form part of the archaeological record. We therefore would expect to find fewer dishes from seldom-used ceramic sets, such as Sunday-best dishes or special dishes used for holidays or entertaining. In this study, this bias is not a problem because we are interested in studying the dishes that were used to present family meals that took place every day. These dishes were the ones that were most likely to be broken and thus to form part of the archaeological record.

In this part of the study, sample size is a relevant issue on two different levels: on the household level, where the dishes in each archaeological assemblage are used to represent all of those in use at family meals in a household, and on the level of the city, where the dishes from a mere 11 households are used to represent those in use in all of the middle-class and wealthy homes in the city over a 50-year period.

The number of dishes in the tableware and teaware assemblages varies greatly, from 5 (for the tablewares from Feature 51 in the early group; see Table E–2c) to 53 (for the teawares and tablewares from Feature 9 in the later group; see Table E–4c). However, even though the variability in the number of dishes in each of the samples could clearly be a problem in analyzing the data, the results of the analysis are so consistent for all of the assemblages for each of the chronological groups—regardless of sample size—that variability is not in fact an issue. This is evident in Chapter 6.

Naturally, the use of the dishes from 11 households over a 50-year period to represent cultural change in the middle-class and wealthy households in the city during that time presents another set of problems: It is difficult to know the extent to which these assemblages are representative of those in use. Naturally, we would have more confidence if we had samples from a larger number of households. However, this does not mean that the samples are too small to use. Instead, the analysis of small samples in this case is similar to analyzing the diary of one woman (such as Elizabeth Bleecker) to find out about the shopping patterns of middle-class and wealthy women in New York at the turn of the 19th century: We would prefer to have a larger sample made up of the diaries of many women, but we would certainly use our minute sample of one diary as a source of data to begin to answer the questions we are asking.

The tableware dishes that we are interested in analyzing for information on family meals are particularly striking in the extent to which the patterns used by the households in each chronological group are similar. All of the assemblages in each chronological group contain tableware dishes made of identical wares decorated with identical designs, and there is little variation in the detail of the decoration on even the hand-painted wares. All of the assemblages in the early group contain earthenware vessels decorated in the royal pattern; all those in the middle group contain earthenware dishes in blue or green shell-edged patterns; and all of those in the later group contain porcelain tablewares in the Canton pattern. It is this lack of variability in the tableware assemblages for each chronological period that suggests that, though small, these samples may in fact be representative of the tablewares that were used at family meals in New York during the period of study. The final answer to this question about the extent to which these samples are representative, however, will have to await the excavation of ceramic assemblages from many more of the city's households.

NOTES

1. The collection is at the William Duncan Strong Museum, Department of Anthropology, Columbia University. The features are all described in Appendix D in Wall (1987).
2. The collection is at the South Street Seaport Museum.
3. The collection is at the South Street Seaport Museum.
4. The collection is at the South Street Seaport Museum.
5. The collection is at the Institute for Archaeological Research, Drew University.
6. The collection is at the South Street Seaport Museum.
7. The collection is at the South Street Seaport Museum.
8. The collection is at the South Street Seaport Museum.
9. Reconstructed chains of occupation for all of the properties where the archaeological features were found are presented in Appendix D.2 in Wall (1987).
10. The prices used are from Miller (1991) and the discount and tariff rates are from Miller (personal communication, 1989).

References

Abbott, Carl
    1974   The Neighborhoods of New York, 1760–1775. *New York History* 55:35–54.

Albion, Robert Greenhalgh
    1939   *The Rise of New York Port (1815–1860)*, with the collaboration of Jennie Barnes Pope. Scribner's, New York.

Anonymous
    1804   Plan of the City of New York about 1804. Map Division, New York Public Library.

Arfwedson, Carl David
    1968   *The United States and Canada in 1832, 1833, and 1834*. Richard Bentley, London.

Askins, William
    1985   Material Culture and Expressions of Group Identity in Sandy Ground, New York. *American Archaeology* 5:209–218.

Austen, Jane
    1898   *Persuasion.* J. M. Dent, London. (Originally published 1818.)

Beecher, Catharine
    1842   *Letters to Persons Who Are Engaged in Domestic Service.* Leavitt & Trow, New York.

    1846   *Miss Beecher's Domestic Receipt-Book, Designed as a Supplement to Her Treatise on Domestic Economy.* Harper, New York.

    1855   *A Treatise on Domestic Economy, for the Use of Young Ladies at Home and at School.* Harper, New York.

Belden, Louise Conway
    1983   *The Festive Tradition: Table Decoration and Desserts in America, 1650–1900.* W. W. Norton, New York.

Bender, Thomas
    1978   *Community and Social Change in America.* Rutgers University Press, New Brunswick.

1982a   The American City: What Shaped Its Development. In *Cities: The Forces That Shape Them,* edited by Lisa Taylor, pp. 22, 77. Cooper-Hewitt Museum, New York.

1982b   Washington Square in a Growing City. In *Around the Square, 1830–1890: Essays on Life, Letters, and Architecture in Greenwich Village,* edited by Mindy Cantor, pp. 30–39. New York University Press, New York.

1988   *New York Intellect: A History of Intellectual Life in New York City, from 1750 to the Beginning of Our Own Time.* Johns Hopkins University Press, Baltimore.

Berger, Louis, and Associates
1987   Druggists, Craftsmen, and Merchants of Pearl and Water Streets, New York: The Barclays Bank Site. Submitted to London and Leeds Corporation. On file at the New York City Landmarks Preservation Commission.

Berry, Brian J. L.
1982   Geographic Factors in Urban Development: They Are determined by Social Values. In *Cities: The Forces that Shape Them,* edited by Lisa Taylor, p. 14. Cooper-Hewitt Museum, New York.

Bjork, Gordon C.
1967   Foreign Trade. In *The Growth of the Seaport Cities, 1790–1825,* edited by David T. Gilchrist, pp. 54–61. University Press of Virginia, Charlottesville.

Blackmar, Elizabeth
1979   Rewalking the "Walking City:" Housing and Property Relations in New York City, 1780–1840. *Radical History Review* 21:131–148.

1989   *Manhattan for Rent, 1785–1850.* Cornell University Press, Ithaca, N.Y.

Bleecker, Elizabeth
1799–1806   Diary Kept in New York City. Rare Books and Manuscripts Division, New York Public Library.

Blumin, Stuart
1976   *The Urban Threshold: Growth and Change in a Nineteenth-Century American Community.* University of Chicago Press, Chicago.

1989   *The Emergence of the Middle Class: Social Experience in the American City, 1760–1900.* Cambridge University Press, Cambridge, Great Britain.

Bodie, Debra C.
1992   The Construction of Community in Nineteenth Century New York: A Case Study Based on the Archaeological Investigation of the 25 Barrow Street Site. Unpublished M.A. thesis, Department of Anthropology, New York University.

Boydston, Jeanne
1986   To Earn Her Daily Bread. *Radical History Review* 35:7–25.

Braverman, Harry
1974   *Labor and Monopoly Capital: The Degradation of Work in the Twentieth Century.* Monthly Review Press, New York.

Bridges, Amy
    1984   *A City in the Republic: Antebellum New York and the Origins of Machine
            Politics.* Cambridge University Press, New York.
Broad Financial Center Collection, South Street Seaport Museum.
Burgess, Ernest W.
    1925   The Growth of the City: An Introduction to a Research Project. In *The
            City,* edited by Robert E. Park, Ernest W. Burgess, and Roderick D.
            McKenzie, pp. 47–62. University of Chicago Press, Chicago.
Burley, David V.
    1989   Function, Meaning and Context: Ambiguities in Ceramic Use by the
            Hivernant Metis of the Northwestern Plains. *Historical Archæology*
            23(1):97–106.
Carson, Barbara
    1990   *Ambitious Appetites: Dining, Behavior, and Patterns of Consumption in
            Federal Washington.* American Institute of Architects, Octagon Series,
            Washington, D.C.
Carter, Susannah
    1796, 1802   *The Frugal Housewife.* Matthew Carey, Philadelphia.
Chandler, Alfred, Jr.
    1977   *The Visible Hand: The Managerial Revolution in American Business.*
            Harvard University Press, Cambridge.
Chevalier, Michael
    1967   *Society, Manners, and Politics in the United States: Letters on North
            America.* Peter Smith, Gloucester, Mass. (Originally published 1836.)
Child, Lydia Maria
    1838   *The American Frugal Housewife, Dedicated to Those Who Are Not Ashamed
            of Economy.* Samuel S. & William Wood, New York.
City of Brooklyn
    1841   Tax Assessment Records, Brooklyn Historical Society. Brooklyn, New
            York.
City of New York, Common Council
    1917–1930   *Minutes of the Common Council of the City of New York, 1784–1831,*
            21 vols. City of New York.
City of New York, Tax Assessment Records
    1790, 1799, 1802   Tax Assessment Records. Historical Documents Collection,
            Queens College, New York.
    1809–1811, 1820, 1828–1830, 1839–1841   Tax Assessment Records. Municipal
            Archives, Department of Records and Information Services, City of New
            York.
Clark, Clifford Edward, Jr.
    1986   *The American Family Home, 1800–1960.* University of North Carolina
            Press, Chapel Hill.
    1987   The Vision of the Dining Room: Plan Book Dreams and Middle-Class
            Realities. In *Dining in America, 1850–1900,* edited by Kathryn Grover,
            pp. 142–172. University of Massachusetts Press, Amherst.

Coale, Ansley J., and Melvin Zelnik
  1963   *New Estimates of Fertility and Population in the United States.* Princeton
          University Press, Princeton, N.J.
Cochran, Thomas C.
  1972   *Business in American Life: A History.* McGraw-Hill, New York.
  1977   *200 Years of American Business.* Basic Books, New York.
Cochran, Thomas C., and William Miller
  1961   *The Age of Enterprise: A Social History of Industrial America.* Harper &
          Row, New York.
Commercial Advertiser
  1813   29 April. The New-York Historical Society.
Conkey, Margaret W.
  1978   Style and Information in Cultural Evolution: Toward a Predictive Model
          for the Paleolithic. In *Social Archaeology: Beyond Subsistence and Dating,*
          edited by Charles L. Redman, Mary Jane Berman, Edward V. Curtin,
          William T. Langhorn, Jr., Nina M. Versaggi, and Jeffery C. Wanser,
          pp. 61–85. Academic Press, New York.
  1982   Boundedness in Art and Society. In *Symbolic and Structural Archaeology,*
          edited by Ian Hodder, pp. 115–128. Cambridge University Press,
          Cambridge, Great Britain.
Coontz, Stephanie
  1988   *The Social Origins of Private Life: A History of American Families, 1600–
          1900.* Verso, London.
Cott, Nancy F.
  1977   *The Bonds of Womanhood: "Woman's Sphere" in New England, 1780–1835.*
          Yale University Press, New Haven.
Crowley, J. E.
  1974   *This Sheba, Self: The Conceptualization of Economic Life in Eighteenth
          Century America.* Johns Hopkins University Press, Baltimore.
Cummings, Richard Osborn
  1970   *The American and His Food.* Arno Press and the New York Times, New York.
Danforth, Brian J.
  1974   The Influence of Socioeconomic Factors Upon Political Behavior: A
          Quantitative Look at New York City Merchants, 1828–1844. Ph.D.
          dissertation, Department of History, New York University.
Davison, Robert A.
  1967   Comment—New York Foreign Trade. In *The Growth of the Seaport Cities,
          1790–1825,* edited by David T. Gilchrist, pp. 68–78. University Press of
          Virginia, Charlottesville.
Deagan, Kathleen
  1973   Mestizaje in Colonial St. Augustine. *Ethnohistory* 20(1):55–65.
  1983   *Spanish St. Augustine: The Archaeology of a Colonial Creole Community.*
          Academic Press, New York.
Deetz, James
  1977   *In Small Things Forgotten: The Archaeology of Early American Life.*
          Doubleday, Garden City, N.Y.

Degler, Carl N.
   1980   *At Odds: Women and the Family in America from the Revolution to the
           Present.* Oxford University Press, New York.
Demos, John
   1970   *A Little Commonwealth: Family Life in Plymouth Colony.* Oxford University
           Press, New York.
The Diary, or Evening Register
   1794   1 January, New York Public Library.
Dickens, Charles
   1957   *American Notes.* Oxford University Press, London. (Originally published
           1842.)
Dickinson, Nancy S.
   1985   The Iconography of the Dinner Table: Upper and Middling Customs,
           1760s to 1860s. Typescript in the possession of the author.
   n.d.   "Oᶠ Other Sorts of Wares, Too Tedious to Particularize": The
           Rhinelanders as Ceramics Merchants in Late Eighteenth Century New
           York City. Typescript on file, Colonial Williamsburg Foundation.
Douglas, Mary
   1975   Deciphering a Meal. In *Implicit Meanings: Essays in Anthropology,* by Mary
           Douglas, pp. 249–275. Routledge & Kegan Paul, London.
Douglas, Mary, and Baron Isherwood
   1979   *The World of Goods: Towards an Anthropology of Consumption.* W. W.
           Norton, New York.
Downing, Andrew Jackson
   1850   *The Architecture of Country Houses.* D. Appleton, New York.
Dreyfus, Hubert L., and Paul Rabinow
   1982   *Michel Foucault: Beyond Structuralism and Hermeneutics.* University of
           Chicago Press, Chicago.
Dudden, Faye E.
   1983   *Serving Women: Household Service in Nineteenth-Century America.*
           Wesleyan University Press, Middletown, Conn.
Duffy, John
   1968   *A History of Public Health in New York City, 1625–1866.* Russell Sage
           Foundation, New York.
Duncan, William
   1791–1795   *The New-York Directory, and Register.* William Duncan, New York.
Durkheim, Émile
   1933   *The Division of Labor in Society,* translated by George Simpson.
           Macmillan, New York. (Originally published 1893.)
Engels, Friederich
   1958   *The Condition of the Working Class in England in 1844,* translated and
           edited by W. O. Henderson and W. H. Chaloner. Basil Blackwell, Oxford.
           (Originally published 1845.)
Epstein, Barbara L.
   1981   *The Politics of Domesticity: Women, Evangelism and Temperance in*

Nineteenth-Century America. Wesleyan University Press, Middletown, Conn.

Ernst, Robert
  1949   *Immigrant Life in New York City, 1825–1863.* Kings Crown Press, Columbia University, New York.

Farber, Bernard
  1972   *Guardians of Virtue: Salem Families in 1800.* Basic Books, New York.

Fay, Theodore S.
  1831–1834   *Views in New-York and Its Environs, from Accurate, Characteristic and Picturesque Drawings.* Peabody, New York.

Folbre, Nancy
  1983   Of Patriarchy Born: The Political Economy of Fertility Decisions. *Feminist Studies* 9(2):261–284.

Foner, Eric
  1976   *Tom Paine and Revolutionary America.* Oxford University Press, New York.

Forster, Colin, and G. S. L. Turner
  1972   *Economic Opportunity and White American Ratios: 1800–1860,* with the assistance of Helen Bridges. Yale University, New Haven.

Franks, David C.
  1787   *The New-York Directory.* David C. Franks, New York.
  1851   *New-York Directory, 1786.* Republished by John Doggett, Jr., New York.

Geertz, Clifford
  1973   *The Interpretation of Cultures.* Basic Books, New York.

Geismar, Joan H.
  1983   The Archaeological Investigation of the 175 Water Street Block, New York City. Soil Systems, Inc. Report on file with the Landmarks Preservation Commission, New York.

Gilchrist, David C. (editor)
  1967   *The Growth of the Seaport Cities, 1790–1825.* University Press of Virginia, Charlottesville.

Gilje, Paul A.
  1987   *The Road to Mobocracy: Popular Disorder in New York City, 1763–1834.* University of North Carolina Press, Chapel Hill.

Gill, Harold B., Jr.
  1972   *The Apothecary of Colonial Virginia.* Colonial Williamsburg Foundation, University Press of Virginia, Charlottesville.

Glassie, Henry H.
  1975   *Folk Housing in Middle Virginia: A Structural Analysis of Historic Artifacts.* University of Tennessee Press, Knoxville.

Godden, Geoffrey A.
  1965   *An Illustrated Encyclopedia of British Pottery and Porcelain.* Bonanza Books, New York.

Gordon, David M.
  1978   Capitalist Development and the History of American Cities. In *Marxism and the Metropolis,* edited by W. Tabb and L. Sawers, pp. 25–63. Oxford University Press, New York.

Gottesman, Ruth Susswein
1941   New Delvings in Old Fields: The Partnerships of Van Voorhis. *Antiques* 39:314–315.
1954   The Arts and Crafts in New York, 1777–1799: Advertisements and News Items from New York City Newspapers. *Collections,* New-York Historical Society for 1948.

Grabill, Wilson H., Clyde V. Kiser, and Pascal K. Whelpton
1958   *The Fertility of American Women.* Wiley, New York.

Greene, Asa
1837   *A Glance at New York.* A. Greene, New York.

Greven, Phillip J., Jr.
1972   The Average Size of Families and Households in the Province of Massachusetts in 1764 and in the United States in 1790. In *Household and Family in Past Time,* edited by Peter Laslett, pp. 545–560. Cambridge University Press, London.

Griscom, John H.
1858   *A History, Chronological and Circumstantial, of the Visitations of Yellow Fever at New York.* Hall, Clayton, and Co., New York.

Grossman, Joel
1985   The Excavation of Augustine Heerman's Warehouse and Associated 17th Century Dutch West India Company Deposits. Greenhouse Consultants, Inc. Report on file with the Landmarks Preservation Commission, New York.

Grund, Francis T.
1968   *The Americans in Their Moral, Social, and Political Relations.* Johnson Reprint Company, New York. (Originally published 1837.)

Hall, Basil
1964   *Travels in North America,* 3 vols. Akademische Druck-U. Verlagsanstalt, Graz, Austria. (Originally published 1829.)

Halttunen, Karen
1982   *Confidence Men and Painted Women.* Yale University Press, New Haven.

Hamilton, Thomas
1834   *Men and Manners in America,* 2 vols. William Blackwood, Edinburgh, and T. Cadell, London.

Harrington, Virginia
1935   *The New York Merchant on the Eve of the Revolution.* Columbia University Press, New York.

Hartog, Hendrik
1983   *Public Property and Private Power: The Corporation of the City of New York in American Law, 1730–1870.* Cornell University Press, Ithaca.

Harvey, David
1973   *Social Justice and the City.* Johns Hopkins University Press, Baltimore.

Haswell, Charles H.
1896   *Reminiscences of an Octogenarian of the City of New York.* Harper & Brothers, New York.

Hayden, Dolores
  1982   *The Grand Domestic Revolution.* M.I.T. Press, Cambridge.
Hills, John
  1785   Map of New York. Surveyed in 1782 and drawn 1785. Map Division, New
          York Public Library.
Hodder, Ian
  1979   Economic and Social Stress and Material Culture Patterning. *American
          Antiquity* 44:446–454.
  1982   Theoretical Archaeology: A Reactionary View. In *Symbolic and Structural
          Archaeology,* edited by Ian Hodder, pp. 1–16. Cambridge University Press,
          Cambridge.
Hodge, Allen, and Campbell
  1789–1790   *The New-York Directory and Register.* Hodge, Allen & Campbell, New
          York.
Hodges, Graham Russell
  1986   *New York City Cartmen, 1667–1850.* New York University Press, New
          York.
Hooker, Richard J.
  1981   *Food and Drink in America: A History.* Bobbs-Merrill, Indianapolis.
Hooker, William
  1831   Map of the City of New-York. Peabody, New York. Map Division, New
          York Public Library.
Horlick, Allan Stanley
  1975   *Country Boys and Merchant Princes: The Social Control of Young Men in
          New York.* Associated University Presses, London.
Howard, David Sanctuary
  1984   *New York and the China Trade.* New-York Historical Society, New
          York.
Hull, Oliver
  1863   *Book of the Hulls: Being a Genealogy of the Hull Family: Containing Some
          Account of the Hulls of England, Massachusetts, Connecticut, and Rhode
          Island.* Peter Eckler, New York.
Jackson, Ronald Vern, and Gary Ronald Teeples (eds.)
  1976   *New York 1810 Census Index.* Accelerated Indexing Systems, Bountiful,
          Utah.
  1977   *New York 1830 Census Index.* Accelerated Indexing Systems, Bountiful,
          Utah.
  1978   *New York 1840 Census Index.* Accelerated Indexing Systems, Salt Lake
          City.
Jackson, Ronald Vern, Gary Ronald Teeples, and David Schaefermeyer (eds.)
  1977   *New York 1820 Census Index.* Accelerated Indexing Systems, Bountiful,
          Utah.
Johnson, Paul E.
  1978   *A Shopkeeper's Millennium: Society and Revivals in Rochester, New York,
          1815–1837.* Hill & Wang, New York.

Kerber, Linda K.
  1980   *Women of the Republic: Intellect and Ideology in Revolutionary America.*
            University of North Carolina Press, Chapel Hill.
Kouwenhoven, John A.
  1972   *The Columbia Historical Portrait of New York: An Essay in Graphic History.*
            Harper & Row, New York.
Laidlaw, Christine Wallace
  1986   The Silversmiths of Monmouth County, 1775–1850. Typescript in the
            possession of the author.
  1988   Silver by the Dozen: The Wholesale Business of Teunis D. DuBois.
            Winterthur Portfolio 23(1):25–50.
Landau, Sarah Bradford
  1982   Greek and Gothic Side by Side: Architecture Around the Square. In
            *Around the Square, 1830–1890: Essays on Life, Letters, and Architecture in
            Greenwich Village,* edited by Mindy Cantor, pp. 12–29. New York
            University Press, New York.
Laslett, Peter
  1972a   Introduction: The History of the Family. In *Household and Family in Past
            Time,* edited by Peter Laslett, pp. 1–89. Cambridge University Press,
            London.
  1972b   Mean Household Size in England Since the Sixteenth Century. In
            Household and Family in Past Time, edited by Peter Laslett, pp. 125–158.
            Cambridge University Press, London.
Lebsock, Suzanne
  1985   *The Free Women of Petersburg: Status and Culture in a Southern Town,
            1784–1860.* W. W. Norton, New York.
Leslie, Eliza
  1844   *The House Book, or, a Manual of Domestic Economy for Town and Country.*
            Carey & Hart, Philadelphia.
Lockwood, Charles
  1972   *Bricks and Brownstone: The New York Row House, 1783–1929: An
            Architectural and Social History.* McGraw-Hill, New York.
  1976   *Manhattan Moves Uptown: An Illustrated History.* Houghton Mifflin,
            Boston.
Lofland, Lyn H.
  1973   *A World of Strangers: Order and Action in Urban Public Space.* Basic
            Books, New York.
Longworth
  1797–1799 *Longworth's American Almanack, New-York Register, and City
              Directory.* Longworth, New York.
Longworth, D.
  1800–1803 *Longworth's American Almanac, New-York Register, and City Directory.*
              D. Longworth, New York.
Longworth, David
  1808   Plan of the City of New York, drawn and engraved for D. Longworth.

David Longworth, New York. Map Division, New York Public
Library.

1810   *Longworth's American Almanac, New-York Register, and City Directory*.
David Longworth, New York.

Longworth, Thomas

1820, 1830, 1840   *Longworth's American Almanac, New-York Register, and City Directory*. Thomas Longworth, New York.

Low, John

1796   *The New-York Directory and Register for the Year 1796*. John Low, New York.

Macfarlane, Alan

1977   *Reconstructing Historical Communities*. Cambridge University Press, Cambridge.

Maine, Henry Sumner

1906   *Ancient Law: Its Connections with the Early History of Society and Its Relation to Modern Ideas*. Henry Holt, New York.

Margolis, Maxine

1985   *Mothers and Such: Views of American Women and Why They Changed*. University of California Press, Berkeley.

Marsh, Margaret

1990   *Suburban Lives*. Rutgers University Press, New Brunswick.

Martin, Ann Smart

1989   The Role of Pewter as Missing Artifact. *Historical Archaeology* 23(2):1–27.

Marx, Karl

1976   *Capital: A Critique of Political Economy*, translated by Ben Fowkes. Vintage Books, New York. (Originally published 1867–1894.)

Matthai, Julie A.

1982   *An Economic History of Women in America: Women's Work, the Sexual Division of Labor, and the Development of Capitalism*. Schocken, New York.

Mayer, —

1844   Plan von New-York, 1844. Extracted from: Mayer's-Handatlas. Hildburghausen (etc.) Verlag des Bibliographischen Institute. Map Division, New York Public Library.

McDannell, Colleen

1986   *The Christian Home in Victorian America, 1840–1900*. Indiana University Press, Bloomington.

McMullin, Phillip (ed.)

1971   *New York in 1800: An Index to the Federal Census Schedules of the State of New York, with Other Aids to Research*. Gendex Corporation, Provo, Utah.

Medick, Hans

1976   The Proto-Industrial Family Economy: The Structural Function of Household and Family during the Transition from Peasant Society to Industrial Capitalism. *Social History* 3:291–315.

Miller, Douglas T.

1967   *Jacksonian Aristocracy: Class and Democracy in New York (1830–1860)*. Oxford University Press, New York.

Miller, George L.
  1980   Classification and Economic Scaling of 19th Century Ceramics. *Historical Archaeology* 14:1–40.
  1991   A revised set of cc index values for classification and economic scaling of English ceramics from 1787 to 1880. *Historical Archaeology* 25(1): 1–25.
Miller, George L., Ann Smart Martin, and Nancy S. Dickinson
  1989   Changing Consumption Patterns, English Ceramics and the American Market from 1770 to 1840. Fourth draft, to be published as part of the 29th Winterthur Conference.
Mills, C. Wright
  1951   *White Collar: The American Middle Class.* Oxford University Press, New York.
The Mirror
  1839   31 August.
Mohl, Raymond S.
  1971   *Poverty in New York, 1783–1825.* Oxford University Press, New York.
Moore, Sally F., and Barbara G. Myerhoff
  1977   Introduction: Secular Ritual: Forms and Meanings. In *Secular Ritual,* edited by Sally F. Moore and Barbara G. Myerhoff, pp. 3–24. Van Gorcum, Assen.
Mudge, Jean
  1981   *Chinese Export Porcelain for the American Trade, 1785–1835,* 2nd edition. University of Delaware Press, Newark.
Mumford, Lewis
  1961   *The City in History: Its Origins, Its Transformations, and Its Prospects.* Harcourt, Brace, Jovanovich, New York.
Nash, Gary
  1979   *The Urban Crucible: Social Change, Political Consciousness, and the Origins of the American Revolution.* Harvard University Press, Cambridge.
Nettels, Curtis
  1952   British Mercantilism and the Economic Development of the Thirteen Colonies. *Journal of Economic History* 12:105–114.
Nevins, Allan (ed.)
  1927   *The Diary of Philip Hone, 1828–1851.* Dodd, Mead, New York.
The New York Genealogical and Biographical Society
  1959, 1960   Records of Trinity Church Parish. *New York Genealogical and Biographical Society Record* 90, 91.
The New York Times
  1878   19 August.
Noel Hume, Ivor
  1968   *Historical Archaeology.* Knopf, New York.
  1969   *A Guide to Artifacts of Colonial America.* Knopf, New York.
O'Calaghan, E. B.
  1849   *The Documentary History of the State of New York.* Weed, Parsons, Albany. 175 Water Street Collection, South Street Seaport Museum.

Ortner, Sherry B.
  1984   Theory in Anthropology Since the Sixties. *Comparative Studies in Society and History* 26:126–166.
Ottensman, John R.
  1975   *The Changing Spatial Structure of American Cities.* Lexington Books, Lexington, Mass.
Perkins, Bradford (ed.)
  1960   Henry Unwin Addington's Residence in the United States of America, 1822–1825. *University of California, Publications in History,* 65. University of California, Berkeley and Los Angeles.
Pessen, Edward
  1973   *Riches, Class, and Power before the Civil War.* Heath, Lexington, Mass.
Plog, Stephen
  1983   Analysis of Style in Artifacts. *Annual Review of Anthropology* 12:125–142.
Polanyi, Karl
  1944   *The Great Transformation.* Rinehart, New York.
Pomerantz, Sidney I.
  1965   *New York, An American City, 1783–1803: A Study of Urban Life,* 2nd edition. J. Friedman, Port Washington, N.Y.
Pope-Hennessy, Una (ed.)
  1931   *The Aristocratic Journey, Being the Outspoken Letters of Mrs. Basil Hall, Written During a Fourteen Months' Sojourn in America, 1827–1828.* G. P. Putnam's Sons, New York.
Poppleton, Thomas H.
  1817   Plan of the City of New-York, the Greater Part from Actual Survey Made Expressly for the Purpose (the Rest from Authentic Documents). Prior & Dunning, New York. Map Division, New York Public Library.
Pred, Allan R.
  1966   *The Spatial Dynamics of U.S. Urban-Industrial Growth, 1800–1914: Interpretive and Theoretical Essays.* M.I.T. Press, Cambridge.
Rainwater, Dorothy
  1987   Victorian Dining Silver. In *Dining in America, 1850–1900,* edited by Kathryn Grover, pp. 173–204. University of Massachusetts Press, Amherst.
Roberts, Patricia Easterbrook
  1967   *Table Settings, Entertaining, and Etiquette: A History and Guide.* Thames & Hudson, London.
Roberts, Robert
  1827   *The House Servant's Directory.* Munroe & Francis, Boston.
Rock, Howard B.
  1979   *Artisans of the New Republic: The Tradesmen of New York City in the Age of Jefferson.* New York University Press, New York.
Rockman [Wall], Diana, Wendy Harris, and Jed Levin
  1983   The Archaeological Investigation of the Telco Block, South Street Seaport

Historic District, New York, New York. Soil Systems, Inc. Report on file with the National Register of Historic Places, Washington, D.C.

Root, Waverly, and Richard de Rochemont
1976   *Eating in Early America: A History.* Ecco Press, New York.

Rosebrock, Ellen Fletcher
1975   *Counting-House Days in South Street: New York's Early Brick Seaport Buildings.* South Street Seaport Museum, New York.

Rosenberg, Carroll Smith
1971   *Religion and the Rise of the American City: The New York City Mission Movement, 1812–1870.* Cornell University Press, Ithaca.

Rosenwaike, Ira
1972   *Population History of New York City.* Syracuse University Press, Syracuse, N.Y.

Rosner, David
1982   *A Once Charitable Enterprise: Hospitals and Health Care in Brooklyn and New York, 1885–1915.* Cambridge University Press, New York.

Roth, Rodris
1961   Tea Drinking in 18th-Century America: Its Etiquette and Equipage. *U.S. National Museum Bulletin 225, Contributions from the Museum of History and Technology* 14:61–91.

Rothschild, Nan A., and Arnold Pickman
1990   The Archaeological Excavations on the Seven Hanover Square Block. Report on file with the New York City Landmarks Preservation Commission.

Rundell, Maria Eliza
1823   *The Experienced American Housekeeper, or Domestic Cookery: Formed on Principles of Economy for the Use of Private Families.* Johnstone & Van Norden, New York.

Ryan, Mary P.
1979   The Power of Women's Networks: A Case Study of Female Moral Reform in Antebellum America. *Feminist Studies* 5:66–85.
1981   *Cradle of the Middle Class: The Family in Oneida County, New York, 1790–1865.* Cambridge University Press, New York.
1983   *Womanhood in America, from Colonial Times to the Present,* 3rd edition. Franklin Watts, New York.

Sahlins, Marshall
1981   *Historical Metaphor and Mythical Realities: Structure in the Early History of the Sandwich Islands Kingdom.* University of Michigan Press, Ann Arbor.
1985   *Islands of History.* The University of Chicago Press, Chicago.

Salwen, Bert, and Rebecca Yamin
1990   The Archaeology and History of Six Lots: Sullivan Street, Greenwich Village, New York City. Report on file with the New York City Landmarks Preservation Commission.

Sanderson, Warren C.
1979   Quantitative Aspects of Marriage, Fertility, and Family Limitation in

Nineteenth Century America: Another Application of the Coale
    Specifications. *Demography* 16:339–358.
Scott, Franklin D. (translator and editor)
  1952   *Baron Klinkowstroem's America, 1818–1820.* Northwestern University
          Press, Evanston, Ill.
Scott, Joan W.
  1986   Gender: A Useful Category of Historical Analysis. *The American Historical
          Review* 91(5):1053–1075.
Scoville, Joseph A.
  1885   *The Old Merchants of New York City.* Thomas R. Knox, New York.
Sedgwick, Catharine Maria
  1837   *Home.* James Munroe, Boston.
7 Hanover Square Collection, William Duncan Strong Museum, Department of
          Anthropology, Columbia University.
75 Wall Street Collection, South Street Seaport Museum.
Sherrill, Charles
  1971   *French Memories of Eighteenth-Century America.* Books for Libraries Press,
          Freeport, N.Y.
Siegel, Sidney
  1956   *Nonparametric Statistics for the Behavioral Sciences.* McGraw-Hill, New
          York.
Sjoberg, Gideon
  1960   *The Preindustrial City: Past and Present.* Free Press, Glencoe, Ill.
Sklar, Kathryn Kish
  1973   *Catharine Beecher: A Study in American Domesticity.* Yale University Press,
          New Haven.
Smith, Daniel Scott
  1973   The Demographic History of Colonial New England. In *The American
          Family in Social-Historical Perspective,* edited by Michael Gordon,
          pp. 397–415. St. Martin's Press, New York.
  1978   Parental Power and Marriage Patterns: An Analysis of Historical Trends in
          Hingham, Massachusetts. In *The American Family in Social-Historical
          Perspective,* edited by Michael Gordon, pp. 87–100. St. Martin's Press,
          New York.
  1979   Family Limitation, Sexual Control, and Domestic Feminism in Victorian
          America. In *A Heritage of Her Own,* edited by Nancy F. Cott and
          Elizabeth H. Pleck, pp. 222–245. Simon & Schuster, New York.
Smith, J. Calvin
  1839   New Map of the City of New-York, with Part of Brooklyn and
          Williamsburg. Tanner & Disturnell, New York.
Smith, Thomas E. V.
  1972   *The City of New York in the Year of Washington's Inauguration, 1789.*
          Chatham Press, Riverside, Conn.
South, Stanley
  1977   *Method and Theory in Historical Archeology.* Academic Press, New
          York.

Spooner, Alden
    1822–1825   *Spooner's Brooklyn Directory.* Alden Spooner, Brooklyn, N.Y.
Sproat, Nancy
    1822   *The School of Good Manners.* Samuel S. Wood, New York.
Stansell, Mary Christine
    1980   *Women of the Laboring Poor in New York City, 1820–1860.* Ph.D.
            dissertation, Yale University. University Microfilms, Ann Arbor.
    1983   The Origins of the Sweatshop: Women and Early Industrialization in
            New York City. In *Working-Class America,* edited by M. H. Frisch and D.
            Walkowitz, pp. 78–103. University of Illinois Press, Urbana.
    1986   *City of Women: Sex and Class in New York, 1789–1860.* Knopf, New York.
The Star, Brooklyn
    1824   17 June; Brooklyn Historical Society.
State of New York
    1827   *Laws of the State of New-York, Relating Particularly to the City of New-York,
            Published by the Authority of the Said City.* William A. Davis, New York.
    1855   Census of the State of New York, County of New York. Research
            Division, New York Public Library.
Still, Bayrd
    1956   *Mirror for Gotham: New York As Seen by Contemporaries, from Dutch Days
            to the Present.* New York University Press, New York.
Stokes, I. N. Phelps
    1915–1928   *The Iconography of Manhattan Island,* 6 vols. Robert H. Dodd, New
                York.
Strasser, Susan
    1982   *Never Done: A History of American Housework.* Pantheon, New York.
Strickland, William
    1971   *Journal of a Tour in the United States of America, 1794–1795,* edited by
            the Reverend J. E. Strickland. The New-York Historical Society, New
            York.
Sullivan Street Collection, South Street Seaport Museum.
Taylor, B., and J. Roberts
    1797   A New and Accurate Plan of the City of New York in the State of New
            York in North America. Map Division, New York Public Library.
Taylor, George Rogers
    1966   The Beginnings of Mass Transportation in Urban America, Part 1.
            Smithsonian Journal of History 1:35–50.
Telco Block Collection, Institute for Archaeological Research, Drew University,
            Madison, N.J.
Thompson, E. P.
    1971   The Moral Economy of the English Crowd in the Eighteenth Century.
            Past and Present 50:76–136.
Thorburn, Grant
    1834   *Forty Years' Residence in America: or the Doctrine of a Particular Providence
            Exemplified in the Life of Grant Thorburn, Seedsman, New York.* Russell,
            Odione, & Metcalf, Boston.

1845   *Fifty Years' Reminiscences of New-York; or Flowers from the Garden of Laurie Todd.* Daniel Fanshaw, New York.

Tilly, Louise A., and Joan W. Scott
1978   *Women, Work, and Family.* Holt, Rinehart and Winston, New York.

Tocqueville, Alexis de
1945   *Democracy in America,* edited by Phillips Bradley, 2 vols. Knopf, New York. (Originally published 1835.)

Tönnies, Ferdinand
1957   *Community and Society (Gemeinschaft und Gesellschaft),* translated and edited by Charles P. Loomis. Michigan State University Press, East Lansing. (Originally published 1887.)

Towner, Donald
1978   *Creamware.* Faber & Faber, London.

Trachtenberg, Alan
1982   *The Incorporation of America: Culture and Society in the Gilded Age.* Hill & Wang, New York.

Travis, John C. (ed.)
1927   *The Memoirs of Stephen Allen.* Typescript on file, The New-York Historical Society.

Trollope, Frances
1984   *Domestic Manners of the Americans.* Century Publishing, London. (Originally published 1839.)

U.S. Government, Bureau of the Census
1790   Population Schedules of the First Census of the United States, 1790. Research Division, New York Public Library.
1800   Population Schedules of the Second Census of the United States, 1800. Research Division, New York Public Library.
1810   Population Schedules of the Third Census of the United States, 1810. Research Division, New York Public Library.
1820   Population Schedules of the Fourth Census of the United States, 1820. Research Division, New York Public Library.
1830   Population Schedules of the Fifth Census of the United States, 1830. Research Division, New York Public Library.
1840   Population Schedules of the Sixth Census of the United States, 1840. Research Division, New York Public Library.
1908   *Heads of Families at the First Census of the United States, Taken in the Year 1790, New York.* U.S. Government Printing Office, Washington.
1975   *Historical Statistics of the United States: Colonial Times to 1970.* U.S. Government Printing Office, Washington.

Van Voorhees Association
1935   *Historical Handbook of the Van Voorhees Family in the Netherlands and America.* Van Voorhees Association, New Brunswick, N.J.

Van Voorhis, Elias W.
1888   *A Genealogy of the Van Voorhees Family in America.* G. P. Putnam's Sons, New York.

Walkowitz, Daniel J.
    1982   The Artisans and Builders of Nineteenth-Century New York: The Case of the 1834 Stonecutters' Riot. In *Around the Square, 1830–1890,* edited by Mindy Cantor, pp. 84–94. New York University, New York.

Wall, Diana diZerega
    1987   At Home in New York: The Redefinition of Gender Among the Middle Class and Elite, 1783–1840. Ph.D. dissertation, Department of Anthropology, New York University.
    1991   Sacred Dinners and Secular Teas: Constructing Domesticity in Mid-19th-Century New York. In *Gender in Historical Archaeology,* edited by Donna J. Seifert. *Historical Archaeology* 25(4):69–81.

Wallerstein, Immanuel
    1980   *The Modern World-System: Vol. 2. Mercantilism and the Consolidation of the European World-Economy.* Academic Press, New York.

Wansey, Henry
    1969   *The Journal of an Excursion to the United States of North America in the Summer of 1794.* Johnson Reprint Corp., New York. (Originally published 1796.)

Warner, Sam Bass
    1962   *Streetcar Suburbs: The Process of Growth in Boston, 1870–1900.* Harvard University Press, Cambridge.
    1968   *The Private City: Philadelphia in Three Periods of Its Growth.* University of Pennsylvania Press, Philadelphia.

Watson, Winslow C. (ed.)
    1856   *Men and Times of the Revolution; or Memoirs of Elkanah Watson, Including Journals of Travels in Europe and America, from 1777–1842.* Dana, New York.

Weiner, Annette B.
    1982   Sexuality Among the Anthropologists, Reproduction Among the Informants. *Social Analysis* 12:52–65.

Wells, Robert V.
    1975   Family History and Demographic Transition. *Journal of Social History* 9:1–19.

Welter, Barbara
    1968   The Cult of True Womanhood: 1820–1860. *American Quarterly* 18:151–174.

Wilentz, Sean
    1983   Artisan Republican Festivals and the Rise of Class Conflict in New York City, 1788–1837. In *Working-Class America,* edited by M. H. Hirsch and D. Walkowitz, pp. 37–77. University of Illinois Press, Urbana.
    1984   *Chants Democratic: New York City and the Rise of the American Working Class, 1788–1850.* Oxford University Press, New York.

Wilkenfeld, Bruce M.
    1976   New York City Neighborhoods, 1730. *New York History* 3:165–182.

1978   *The Social and Economic Structure of the City of New York, 1695–1796.*
Arno Press, New York.

Williams, Carl M.

1949   *Silversmiths of New Jersey, 1700–1825, with Some Notice of Clockmakers
Who Were Also Silversmiths.* George S. McManus, Philadelphia.

Williams, Phila A.

1844–1845   Diary. Manuscript Room, The New-York Historical Society.

Williams, Susan

1985   *Savory Suppers and Fashionable Feasts: Dining in Victorian America.*
Pantheon, New York.

1987   Introduction. In *Dining in America, 1850–1900,* edited by Kathryn
Grover, pp. 3–23. University of Massachusetts Press, Amherst.

Willis, Edmund Philip

1967   Social Origins of Political Leadership in New York City from the
Revolution to 1815. Ph.D. dissertation, Department of History, University
of California, Berkeley.

Wilson, Edith King (compiler)

1987   *Bowne Family of Flushing, Long Island.* Bowne and Co., New York.

Wobst, H. Martin

1977   Stylistic behavior and information exchange. In *For the Director: Research
Essays in Honor of James B. Griffin,* edited by Charles E. Cleland.
Michigan Anthropological Papers 61:317–342.

Wolf, Erik

1982   *Europe and the People Without History.* University of California Press,
Berkeley.

Wright, Gwendolyn

1981   *Building the Dream: A Social History of Housing in America.* Pantheon,
New York.

Wrigley, E. A. (ed.)

1973   *Identifying People in the Past.* Edward Arnold, London.

Yasuba, Yasukichi

1962   *Birth Rates of the White Population in the United States, 1800–1860.* Johns
Hopkins University Press, Baltimore.

Yentsch, Anne

1990   Minimum Vessel Lists as Evidence of Change in Folk and Courtly
Traditions of Food Use. *Historical Archaeology* 24(3):26–53.

1991a   Engendering Visible and Invisible Ceramic Artifacts, Especially Dairy
Vessels. In *Gender in Historical Archaeology,* edited by Donna Seifert.
Historical Archaeology 25(4):132–155.

1991b   The Symbolic Divisions of Pottery: Sex-related Attributes of English and
Anglo-American Household Pots. In *The Archaeology of Inequality,* edited
by Randall H. McGuire and Robert Paynter, pp. 192–230. Blackwell,
Oxford.

Zaretsky, Eli

1976   *Capitalism, the Family, and Personal Life.* Harper & Row, New York.

Tables and Figures

Tables

Figures

Index